GEORGE WASHINGTON'S MAP MAKER

George Washington's Map Maker

A BIOGRAPHY OF ROBERT ERSKINE

BY ALBERT H. HEUSSER

Edited with an Introduction by
Hubert G. Schmidt

RUTGERS UNIVERSITY PRESS
NEW BRUNSWICK, NEW JERSEY

28389

Contents

Introduction by Hubert G. Schmidt   vii

Author's Foreword   xvii

1 The Minister's Son   3

2 The Young Inventor   16

3 The Ringwood Mines   25

4 Ironmaster in the Making   43

5 The Long Voyage   67

6 In a Strange Land   78

7 Lord of Ringwood   96

8 The Approaching Storm   111

9 Erskine the Patriot   138

10 Geographer and Surveyor-General   160

11 The Hudson River Chains   175

12 Man in the Shadow   189

13 Last Days   204

14 What Happened Afterward   223

Appendix: List of Erskine's Military Maps   249

Index   257

Introduction

I T H A S been said on several occasions that biography is the real basis for the writing of history. Few professional historians would go so far, but none would cast doubt on its importance. In actuality, the biographer is in the same unique position of responsibility as other historians who are working in a limited field. His readers, perforce, are seldom in a position to examine and evaluate more than a small number of the sources from which he has garnered his story. The facts which he presents and, to a degree, his interpretation of them become the bases for the evaluation made by readers. Even more important, other historians, pleased that another area of darkness has been illuminated, lean heavily on the new work. Since a tale seldom loses in the telling, the virtues and faults of the biographer become magnified as its message is spread abroad in the land. A biographer, like any other recorder and interpreter of developments, must proceed with fear and trembling lest he warp and twist the story which will go down to the untold generations after him.

That a particular biography appears at all is the result of a number of circumstances. A man has lived a life, and at some later date some other person has become convinced that this life was of sufficient consequence to merit a biography, and that he is the proper person to write it. He delves and ferrets so far as his ability and drive permit, but always within the limitations prescribed by the evidence which comes to hand. He then attempts a word picture of those parts of this life which he considers significant or meaningful. The resulting document becomes to a greater or lesser degree the authority henceforth for the importance of the individual discussed. The adequacy of the treatment is thus a matter of some moment.

Any evaluation of the book produced as a result of this chain of circumstances must start with a scrutiny of the biographer himself, for at every turn his judgment is in question. Has he been right in believing that this particular life is worthy of more that the footnotes which hitherto have saved it from oblivion? Has he correctly assayed his own ability to reduce a life to capsule form, with just the right emphasis on its various parts? Do his training or intuition make it possible for him to judge the authencity, meaning, significance, and interrelationships of the items of evidence, and to make intelligent guesses where data are not to be found? Can he resist the temptation to think in black and white? Can he prevent his own enthusiasm for (or against) his defenseless hero from shading his story? Can he explain the man's actions and decisions without being partisan? Can he choose the significant from the trivial?

Let us say that the biographer has passed such tests with an acceptable score, realizing of course that too great strictness would rule out any writing of biography whatsoever. Shall we then ask that he paint the lily by so writing that his work will be read by others than his fellow scholars who wish to borrow from his findings? A biography as an exercise in the use of words is clearly one of considerable scope. If the author should show high literacy standards, it would be a most wonderful thing. In many cases, however, the reader will have to settle for something less. Be that as it may, some skill in organization there must be, some ability to categorize and point up, to maintain an even flow of prose, and to avoid the sin of repetition. Finally, and most difficult, the writer must exhibit an ability at character portrayal. Not only should he himself have rapport with the subject of his thesis, but he must bring him to life. If he can do this, the ultimate reader will be able to supply for himself in his mind's eye much of the trivia of existence, and will be able in the course of a few hours to traverse the whole life span of another person than himself.

Our solicitude is of course that the subject of the biography be neither dwarfed nor aggrandized in the process of putting his life to paper. He, poor man, now has no privacy except that which has been the result of chance. Had he guessed that someday he would be immortalized in a biography, he might have made some different disposition of his papers. He could well have attempted to bilk posterity by destroying part of the record and by preserving those parts which put him in the most favorable light. In any case, he might have co-operated with his biographer by systematically gathering and preserving written records. Seldom, however, has this been the case. Usually death caught him in the midst of living his life to the full. The documents which he left behind may be full or incomplete, and may or may not present a fair picture. In most cases they are already scattered at the time of his death. Even if there is a diary, the events of the years and decades are now mere caricatures. A significant happening which once loomed large in memory has perhaps been reduced to a halting phrase in a letter. Much that is needed to build the structure of the story and to explain the character of its chief actor may never have been put to paper at all, or may not have been preserved. Even should the biographer set to work the day after the funeral, there will be need for genius.

In some cases, the biographer does set to work at once. His nearness in time to his subject in such a case presents its own special problems. Available materials often are almost too plentiful and too diffuse. On the other hand, a part of the evidence may be suppressed by friends, relatives, or business associates of the deceased. Generally speaking, however, the advantage lies with promptness. Time does allow the dust to settle, but it also leads to the dispersal or destruction of documents. Usually the longer the time gap the greater the loss. Fortunate indeed is the biographer who finds that his raw material has been preserved for sentimental, antiquarian, or business reasons or, better yet, that they have acquired sanctuary in a library or other repository.

So often, chance, pure chance, has determined what the biographer can find. One of the greatest frustrations is to discover that a mine of promising evidence was at one time readily available but has now disappeared from sight. The researcher in such a case becomes a sleuth in search of the lost pearls, and with diligence and luck he may bring some of them to light. In many cases, however, the end of the trail is reached when he finds that an accidental fire or a diligent housekeeper has solved his problem once and for all. Even more often, the lost documents have vanished without a trace, and the biographer can only gnash his teeth because of his unrewarded efforts. Sometimes, with luck, something may still be retrieved if parts of the lost documents have been copied, paraphrased, or summarized by a local historian, a genealogist, or a family sentimentalist. Barring this, the researcher must resign himself to the loss. There are, therefore, many ways in which the writer of a biography may be thwarted. In any case, he will nearly always be handicapped by a paucity rather than a superabundance of evidence.

The biography of Robert Erskine by Albert H. Heusser, published in 1928 under the surprising title of *The Forgotten General*, illustrates and points up many of the problems involved in the writing of biography. The first question, and an inevitable and important one in this case, is whether he should have been the person to write the biography of Erskine. There was little in his own background to suggest such a development.

Born in Paterson in 1886, he was the only son of a Swiss immigrant and a native of Paterson who traced her ancestry back to a soldier of the Revolution. Though a high-school drop-out, he had early shown some facility in composition, and became a local reporter and writer of special articles at an early age. In 1911 and again in 1913, he traveled abroad for raw materials for his writing and for his illustrated lectures. After a time, with his widowed mother's help, he purchased a printing establishment, which he operated until his death in 1929. In 1916, he published a travel book on Palestine. In spare moments, he did hack writing on many subjects, including the silk industry, which had brought his father to Paterson. More and more he delved into local history.

It was a chance development in 1920 which interested him in Robert Erskine. Employed by the Hewitt family of Ringwood to trace the history of the "manor" and the iron forges at that place, he found at Ringwood a considerable correspondence of Robert Erskine. The immediate result of his work was a five-volume compilation of varied materials, which he tied together by his own running comment in typescript. Entitled *The Manor and Forges of Ringwood,* these tomes became a repository for all manuscripts and information which Heusser and the Hewitts were able to locate.

In 1921, Heusser published a book called *In the Footsteps of Washington.* In that same year, he helped organize a chapter of the Sons of the Revolution in Paterson. Two other books from his pen and press were one on the Indians in 1924 and one on the silk dyeing industry in 1927. But by now his real interest was in Ringwood, and particularly in Robert Erskine. He had done more work for the Hewitts in 1923 and 1924, and apparently Erskine Hewitt, himself something of a writer, encouraged him to utilize to the full the materials which they had gathered. In fact, it seems probable that Heusser had already begun to organize his materials and to write in 1925. The completed biography appeared in serial form in the magazine *Americana* in 1926, and Heusser received his pay in the form of two thousand reprints. He then tacked on an introduction and an index in his own shop, and had the volumes bound. It was a hard way to publish a book, but the already seriously

ailing man must have felt a sense of satisfaction in having it
completed. He died a few months later.

The quality of his various writings make it evident that
Mr. Heusser loved his country and its heroes but that he
lacked some of the attributes of the true historical craftsman.
However, one can only point out that no one else, then or now,
has shown interest in the task. On the credit side, it should be
said that here was available an author with a deep love of his
subject, a sincere desire to do a good job, and, above all, access to a wealth of documents. Heusser himself was not plagued
by soul searching or deterred by modesty. He enlisted financial
aid and set to work. Except for him, there would in all likelihood be no biography of Robert Erskine to this day.

Next comes the question of whether the task which Heusser
set for himself was a worth-while one. Robert Erskine was,
of course, not a general. But he was one of the foremost iron
masters in America, and, as a result of earlier training and
experience in Great Britain, he became the chief cartographer
for the American forces during much of the Revolution. Prior
to Heusser's biography, he was known to historians largely
because of his well-executed maps of many of the fought-over
areas. Here was a man whose abilities and virtues had been
incompletely understood and, of more importance, a man
whose influence had been underestimated. There can be no
doubt that Robert Erskine was worthy of a biography.

Heusser's approach to the life of Robert Erskine was one of
profound admiration. This personal liking is always apparent,
and undoubtedly there were times when it warped his historical
judgment, as is too often true for other biographers. In general,
Heusser never underestimated his man, and at times he over-
praised him extravagantly. On the whole, however, he valued
fairly well the plentiful source materials which he discovered.
His assiduity in searching for information merits the highest
praise, and his zeal in using it has to some extent made up for
his lack of formal historical training. His actual writing is
another matter. As long as he was recording the obvious, he did
a fairly competent job, though often his account becomes a

series of quotations. It is when he strayed into making what he himself called "suppositions" that one must be on his guard. Often his honesty is such that it is easy to forgive him. However, when he introduces an idea with the word "doubt-less" or "certainly," as if to persuade himself regarding a somewhat doubtful point, one must beware. There are times when one wishes fervently that Heusser had made even a slight study of historiography.

There is often a temptation to quibble as to Heusser's variegated side remarks. For instance, one may well doubt that fear of God and ardent patriotism necessarily go together, or that the Scots inherently have "thrift, determination, a respect for God, and a well developed mentality," and whether all Scotsmen are "canny and brave, and true to the core." We may doubt that Washington attended Erskine's funeral, or that he planted a tree at his grave. But since we permit other authors their pet ideas, why not Heusser also?

As editor of this new edition, I have accepted as my chief tasks the correction of errors of fact and interpretation, the airing of my doubts as to the wilder of Heusser's suppositions, and the pointing out of passages where evidence is inconclusive or lacking. I have been reluctant to "modernize" Mr. Heusser's text to any degree, lest I spoil its flavor. A few passages have been omitted because they are not pertinent, and a few others have been changed slightly where the style is simply too diffuse or heavy-handed. But such phrasing as "delightful expressions of Christian resignation and hope," "America's first character" (meaning George Washington), and "worthy Erskine," have been retained. As to punctuation, I have resisted the almost compulsive tendency of the editorial mind to make alterations, and for the most part successfully. Heusser's punctuation, like his style of writing, was already old-fashioned in 1928. But if either were changed, we would no longer have Heusser.

One of the characteristics of the book, perhaps meritorious in many cases, is the inclusion of numerous and often long quotations from many sources. Unfortunately, the author often felt it incumbent to change (or "correct") the spelling and punctuation. On occasion, he also changed the wording. Worse yet, he felt free to maintain original spelling and punctuation or to change it at will. As a single instance, "Hayman Levy" became "Hyman Levi" without so much as an apology. On occasion, he also changed the wording, even General Washington being so honored a number of times. Equally annoying was his habit regarding emphasis. In his quotations, "Ringwood," "Washington," and "Robert Erskine" were nearly always written in capitals or underlined. Italics were used at any time according to whim or impulse, but underlined portions in original documents are often given in roman type.

In the case of quotations, whenever possible I have located the original, though not always in the place assigned it by Heusser, and have quoted from it rather than from his altered varsion. Unfortunately, in the case of documents which have disappeared since 1928, the only course possible is to copy Heusser's quotations, with their added dashes and parentheses and their changed spelling. The footnotes of the original book which have been retained have sometimes been amended for accuracy and clarity. Those that have been added by the present editor bear his initials, "H. S."

Someday someone will write the definitive biography of Robert Erskine. Since I wish him well, it seems only fair to tell him what I have learned regarding the sources relating to Robert Erskine. After Erskine's rather sudden death, most of his voluminous papers remained at Ringwood, even after the moving away of his widow, who had remarried. As explained by Mr. Heusser, a large portion of them were given to the New Jersey Historical Society in Newark about 1859 by the Ryerson family, long-time owners of Ringwood. They constitute the "Erskine Papers" at that institution.

No one can say how it happened, but, a few years later, another part of the Erskine papers turned up in the possession of the Rev. Joseph F. Tuttle. Because these papers have entirely disappeared since that time, it is fortunate that a number of them were quoted verbatim in an article printed in the *Proceedings of the New Jersey Historical Society* in 1869. It is regrettable that Dr. Tuttle, a respected local historian, a native of Morris County, New Jersey, and President of Wabash College in Indiana, did not give the documents to the New Jersey Historical Society. The future biographer of Erskine may yet find them, but it seems unlikely, inasmuch as other manuscripts once used by Tuttle in his writings have also disappeared. As we have intimated previously, fire and housewifely zeal have often destroyed historical evidence. I suspect that something of the kind has happened in this instance.

A third and very important portion of the Erskine documents are those which Heusser put into the Hewitt compilation. How many of these documents had been preserved at Ringwood ever since Erskine's day is not clear, but probably most of them. Abram S. Hewitt, who made Ringwood his official residence from 1857 to 1874, became such an admirer of Robert Erskine as a result of reading his old letters, that he gave his youngest son the name of Erskine Hewitt. It was this son who added to the collection, under the guidance of Heusser, by purchasing every Erskine manuscript thrown on the market. It is clear that here, too, we owe Heusser gratitude. The Hewitt collection was once well known, and at least one researcher, John C. Fitzpatrick used it, when compiling his monumental *Writings of Washington*. It is presumed that all of the collection was put into Heusser's five volumes. When these were given to the State of New Jersey by Hewitt's nephew and heir, Norvin Hewitt Greene, in 1940, the documents which they contained were lost sight of by scholars. Fortunately, they eventually became accessible again in 1946, when they were placed in the State Library. The present writer confesses that he was thrown off the trail for some time by the rather unusual itinerary of the five volumes since 1929.

Besides the above collections, there are Erskine items scattered in some half-dozen libraries and museums, nearly all mentioned by Heusser, who photostated most of them for the Hewitt collection. The future biographer therefore has much of his leg work already done. Most of the Erskine maps are at the New-York Historical Society, which acquired them in 1845 by gift of Richard Varick DeWitt, son of Simeon DeWitt, Erskine's friend and successor as Surveyor-General of the Continental forces. A few others are in places indicated by Heusser. Unfortunately, quite a number are simply "missing." All in all, there can be no doubt that Heusser made a serious and extended search for all manuscript materials in any way connected with Erskine. A few letters, of no great importance, which he never saw are now at the musuem operated by the State at Ringwood. It may be possible to find others, in this country and in England, and it is hoped that this is the case. There are some regrettable gaps in our knowledge concerning Erskine, and another diligent search might discover the means of filling them.

I am grateful for the help which I have received at various libraries where Erskine materials are located. I wish also to extend my personal thanks to Messrs. Robert M. Lunny of the New Jersey Historical Library, Kenneth Richards of the New Jersey State Library, D. Stanton Hammond of the Passaic Historical Society, Alden T. Cottrell, now retired from the New Jersey State Department of Conservation and Economic Development, and Thomas W. Haigh, still a member of that Department. These gentlemen either aided me in locating materials or in marshaling the facts presented above, or both. Individual credit is given to various institutions from which came the illustrations in this volume.

HUBERT G. SCHMIDT

Rutgers, The State University, Newark, N.J.
June, 1966

Author's Foreword

WE have honored Lafayette, Pulaski and Von Steuben, but we have forgotten Erskine. No monument, other than a tree planted by Washington beside his gravestone at Ringwood, has ever been erected to the memory of the noble young Scotchman who did so much to bring the War of the Revolution to a successful issue.

Robert Erskine, F. R. S., the Surveyor-General of the Continental Army and the trusted friend of the Commander-in-chief, was the silent man behind the scenes, who mapped out the by-ways and the back-roads over the mountains, and—by his familiarity with the great "middle-ground" between the Hudson Highlands and the Delaware—provided Washington with that thorough knowledge of the topography of the country which enabled him repeatedly to outmaneuver the enemy.

It is a rare privilege to add a page to the recorded history of the American struggle for independence, and an added pleasure thereby to do justice to the name of one who, born a subject of George III, threw in his lot with the champions of American liberty. Although never participating in a battle, he was the means of winning many. He lost his life and his fortune for America; naught was his reward save a conscience void of offense, and the intimate friendship and confidence of great Washington. The story of Erskine, the master of the Ringwood iron mines, is worthy of the pen of a great novelist; but I am persuaded that, in this case, even prosaic history will be illumined by the light of that great love which inspires a man to give his all—himself—to the cause of freedom and justice for his fellow-men.

Robert Erskine was born at Dunfermline, Scotland, in 1735. Half-trained to the engineering profession, he engaged while very young in commercial pursuits and failed miserably. Escaping the debtor's gaol because of his high character and sincerity of purpose, he was given an extension of credit. Supplementing his education forthwith, and devoting himself wholeheartedly to the task of beginning life anew, he was soon on the road to advancement as a practical and efficient hydraulic engineer, gradually paying off his indebtedness, winning influential recognition in the London neighborhood, and being elected a fellow of the Royal Society. Then there came to him, in 1770, a call to journey to far-distant America to salvage the investments of prominent British capitalists who had sunk many thousands of pounds sterling in the "American Iron Co." After preparing himself for this commission by a personal survey of the major iron-mining and manufacturing operations of Great Britain, he emigrated to America in 1771, and took charge of the depleted resources of the syndicate at Ringwood, N. J. Scarcely had he begun to bring order out of chaos when the American struggle for independence interrupted operations. Realizing the justice of the patriot cause, Erskine threw in his lot with the struggling colonies, devoted the output of the English-owned mines to the Continental Congress and its poorly equipped armies, and soon thereafter placed at the disposal of General Washington his professional skill as a topographer and map-maker. Appointed by Congress in 1774 as Surveyor-General of the American armies, he not only continued to operate the Ringwood mines, but executed a series of over two hundred beautifully correct military maps of the "war-zone" in New York, New Jersey, Connecticut and Pennsylvania. He died in 1780, having contracted a fatal illness while prosecuting his surveys, and was buried on the beautiful estate at Ringwood.

GEORGE WASHINGTON'S MAP MAKER

The Minister's Son

BENEATH the ruined towers of Dryburgh Abbey, not far distant from the last resting place of Sir Walter Scott, is a tablet commemorating the Reverend Ralph Erskine, a Scottish divine,—eminent in his day— who passed from the affairs of earth November 6, 1752. Few tourists, wandering through the green aisles of this roofless sanctuary, whose ponderous arches and ivy-mantled walls are precious because of seven centuries of history and devotion, are aware that the name of Erskine is one most singularly connected with the history of our own country in that the son of him whose memory is here perpetuated was a trusted friend of Washington and an ardent participant in the struggle for American independence.

The tale to be related is a singular narrative, for the history of Robert Erskine reads like romance. It was a career in which Providence seems to have exercised a guiding hand—turning talents and misfortunes into character, and giving the result to the American colonies in the form of an eminently useful and God-fearing man. It affords an inspiring biographical study, replete with interest; and—after having enriched myself through a most minute and intimate digest of historic fragments gathered from many sources, and correspondence heretofore entirely unpublished—I should be guilty of injustice to the character of the man I have learned to love did I not submit the facts as an humble contribution to American history.

Robert Erskine, born at Dunfermline, sixteen miles from Edinburgh, on the 7th of September, 1735, was naturally endowed with those sturdy qualities which are inherent to the Scotch. Thrift, determination, a respect for God, and a well developed mentality came not by accident into Caledonian blood. One has but to consider the rugged land of Scotia, with its physical peculiarities, to understand the development of these characteristics in the sons of the Pentlands.

Scotland, but two hundred and fifty miles in length, and in some places not over thirty in width, has ever been the home of stalwart men. The rocky highlands and narrow valleys, the rigors of a far northern latitude, the long evenings of the summer and the whirling snows of winter —all have tended toward the making of men, canny and brave and true to the core. A Scotchman thus explained it to me: Thrifty the race became by reason of the natural poverty of the country; stubborn because of constant struggling with a stony soil; and studious through the improvement of the lengthened "spare hours" after the day's work was done, in the lingering radiance of departing day. This is logical and easily to be comprehended. The land and its people are distinctly co-related.

What visitor to the "land of heather," for example, can

forget the villages of the Trossachs? The first rays of dawn peeping over the mountains to the east, the last gleam of the setting sun reddening the summits of those in the west. Ever the craggy heights are present in a Scottish landscape, imparting a solemnity and dignity difficult to describe. Brought into cultivation only by earnest endeavor, the small land-holdings of the humble folk have made economy a tradition. Again, the uplands seem to suggest the nearness of God. Shut out the world, and you become instinctively spiritual and reverent.

Who better than "Ian Maclaren" (Rev. John Watson) has visualized the perils of a northland winter? Snow-covered trails, swollen torrents, tempestuous winds through narrow defiles, heroic collie dogs and helpless sheep—these are the ever-present elements calling for courage of a high order. And Burns, with his rollicking pictures (or melancholy, according to his mood) has done his part to help us understand. The cotters' homes, the taverns, the ancient bridges of the Dee—can we ever forget them? The groups around the chimney corner, the wealth of ingle-side wisdom, the black tobacco (and, perchance, a wee bit of something else to cheer the heart)— while tales are told of "Bonnie Prince Charlie" or the great theological discussions at Edinburgh or Glasgow— these things, too, give us an inkling into the temperament of the race. Of such stock came Robert Erskine.

No visitor to Dunfermline can forget its picturesque location on the brow of a slope which ascends from the Firth of Forth, nor the beautiful and extensive view from the tower of the Abbey Church where lie the remains of King Robert Bruce. It is so typically Scottish that were one permitted just one glimpse of Scotland he might ask to be taken to Dunfermline and be satisfied. A deep ravine intersects the town; undoubtedly little Robert Erskine played beside the stream which here still patiently wends its way toward the Forth. So, perhaps, did another lad, whose life was likewise destined to be linked with the iron industry in America; for Dunfermline was also the birthplace of Andrew Carnegie. Erskine, coming to our country in 1771, became the leading patriot iron-master of the Revolutionary period. Carnegie, following almost a century later, occupied a similar place in his day and age. He it was who, in 1877, presented to his native town the Carnegie Public Baths.

Industrially, Dunfermline is a place of considerable importance. First and foremost among the attractions of this quaint old town is its Abbey, in reality the community's center. During the winter of 1303 the Court of Edward I of England was held in this sanctuary, and besides the tomb of the Bruce, it contains the graves of seven other kings and two queens, while the burial place of Queen Margaret, the wife of Malcolm Canmore (to whom she was married in this church in 1070) lies immediately to the east of the session house.

Nor is the Reverend Ralph Erskine forgotten in Dunfermline. The town in which he proclaimed the gospel for over forty years still treasures his remains. He is buried in the Abbey churchyard, and—more appropriate than the memorial tablet at Dryburgh—a statue in the court of the Queen Anne Street United Presbyterian Church, which he founded, keeps alive an interest in his ancient ministry.

Rev. Dr. Chalmers, in his *History of Dunfermline*, says:

The inauguration of the statue on the 27th June, 1849, was celebrated by a procession of the Free Masons of the place, joined by a deputation of the Grand Lodge of Edinburgh, and the St. John's Lodge of Cupar, accompanied by the Dunfermline Instrumental Band, along with a numerous attendance of ministers and members of the Secession Church in Dunfermline and elsewhere. The principal shops in the town being shut during the ceremony, there was a great turn-out of the inhabitants, as well as of many persons from the neighborhood.

The Rev. Ralph Erskine was, in many respects, a remarkable man. The best account of his life and activities is contained in the meritorious volume edited by the Rev. Donald Fraser in 1834. It may not be amiss to quote at length from Fraser's work:

On the 15th of July, 1714, nearly three years after his ordination, he married Margaret, daughter of John Dewar, Esquire, of Lassoddie—an estate situated in the adjacent parish of Beath. Her mother's name was Elizabeth Ayton. From the Christian graces she displayed, as well as the sweetness of her natural temper, she proved an eminent blessing to her husband. After she had lived with him sixteen years, it pleased God to remove her by a sudden illness, in the thirty-third year of her age, on Sunday, the November 22, 1730. She had ten children, of whom five survived her, namely, Margaret, the eldest, and four sons, Henry, John, Ebenezer, and James. For some time after this afflicting bereavement, Anne Erskine, second daughter of his brother, Ebenezer, appears to have resided with the Reverend Ralph and taken care of his children. A second partner, however, was provided for him in Margaret Simson, a pious and respectable female, daughter of Daniel Simson, Esquire, Writer to the Signet, Edinburgh. This union, which took place on the 24th of February, 1732, was also felicitous, and supplied new cause of unfeigned gratitude to his heavenly Father. The second Mrs. Erskine treated the children of the former marriage with true maternal affection; and became herself the mother of four sons, only one of whom, however, reached maturity; and she survived her husband a few years. . . . Robert, the only member of the second family that reached maturity, was born Aug. 27 (Sept. 7, new style), 1735, and lived to the age of forty-five.

The birthplace of Robert Erskine—structurally much altered since the eighteenth century, is still to be seen at Dunfermline. It is the house in which his eminent father lived and died, and it was undoubtedly the home of Robert's youth. The ancient dwelling stands in one of the up-hill thoroughfares of the Scottish town . . . "down a close leading from the south side of the High Street to the junction of Maygate with Abbot Street. The house is an old one; the date 1607 is on the lintelstone of the door. The too-fall on the west side of this house is said to have been Rev. Ralph Erskine's library, and here it was that the Associate Brethren held their celebrated meeting with the Rev. George Whitefield."

The boyhood of Robert Erskine could not have been a time of luxurious indolence, to say the least. As a junior member of a frugal clergyman's somewhat extensive family, he must have learned early in life the saving quality of self-reliance which, in later years, was to make of him a man eminently worthy of his birthplace and of his forebears.

In all likelihood he received his elementary education at the Dunfermline Grammar School, which was at that time maintained by the Town Council.[1] The records of the University of Edinburgh show that he was a student at that institution in 1748 and again in 1752, but give no further data.[2] We are therefore in the dark as to his scholastic performances or the subjects in which he special-

---

[1] Statement of Andrew Shearer, Town Clerk of Dunfermline, in a letter to the author, 21st March, 1923.
[2] From letter to the author by Wm. A. Coutts, Asst. Sec., University of Edinburgh, dated 26th March, 1923.

ized. It may seem a matter of surprise that a boy in his fourteenth year should have advanced sufficiently in his studies to take up University work, but I am assured by those familiar with the habits of the period that Erskine's case is by no means unique. The circumstance demonstrates, nevertheless, that the youngster was no dullard and am further inclined to the belief that the four-year interval in his attendance at Edinburgh was an interruption made necessary because Erskine found it imperative to earn his own living and contribute to the support of the household after 1748. It was then that his father passed on to his reward, and the fact that the studies were resumed in that year lends color to the surmise that Robert invested a portion of his patrimony in rounding out his fragmentary education.

Laurence Hutton, in his *Literary Landmarks* of the *Scottish Universities*,[3] writes so entertainingly upon the very subject under consideration that I am constrained to copy several of his pleasingly worded paragraphs, which seem as though they were meant to form a part of Erskine's biography:

The students at the universities north of the Tweed were, as a rule, the sons of poor parents who realized exactly the expense of a college course, and who knew how well, or how ill, it could be afforded. And the lads went to Aberdeen, to Edinburgh, to Glasgow, or to St. Andrews with a fixed purpose of reaching the very best of results at the lowest possible money cost.

They selected, generally, the institution nearest to their own humble homes, in order to save charges of travel; they often walked to their destination, in order to avoid coach-hire; they had no one to look after them on their journey, or at their journey's end. They entered their own names on their college

[3] G. P. Putnam's Sons, N. Y. and London, 1904.

books; they found lodgings for themselves in some nearby street or alley; they not infrequently cooked their own food, which was brought with them or sent after them in the carts of local carriers; sometimes they made their own beds, and washed their own dishes and their own clothes; and they were rarely over fourteen years of age when their college careers began. They formed very few, but always economical, friendships; they shared their rooms and their meals and their thoughts with each other; they had their simple little clubs and societies for conversation or discussion; they read hard, they worked hard—hard was their life.

Mr. Hutton goes on to say that in point of discipline the Scottish universities stood high, but teaching was the weak point; that while the professors were learned men, there was little or no personal instruction. Opportunities were offered, it is true, but it was up to the students to turn them to account. He says that the yearly rental of chambers at Edinburgh in the middle of the eighteenth century was about four pounds, and quotes Alexander Carlyle as saying: "Living in Edinburgh continued still (1743) to be wonderfully cheap, as there were ordinaries for young gentlemen at fourpence a head, for a very good dinner of broth and beef, and a roast and potatoes, every day, with fish three or four times a week; and all the small-beer that was called for until the cloth was removed." Anent the strict discipline which the faculty endeavored bravely to enforce, it would seem that "vice and vageing" were frowned upon with equal severity. Mr. Hutton explains that "vageing" meant to gad about aimlessly—to loaf, to loiter. Quite evidently the worthy professors of the long ago knew full well the temptations which beset the idler. Then, too, stringent rules and penalties concerned profanity, gambling and fighting: of the latter there must have been enough and to spare, judging by the numerous enactments relative to the "suppression of tumults" for which the college then had a bad reputation.

What Mr. Hutton says of the students who attend the University of Edinburgh today is applicable to those of yester-year, and Erskine most of all:

A comparatively small percentage of these students obtain a degree, or attempt to be graduated. That is not what they go to the University for. They seek a certain amount of solid, valuable information on certain subjects and in certain lines; and, when they obtain this, they drop themselves quietly out.

Again, in the following words, Mr. Hutton seems to be referring to Erskine:

The list of the graduates of the University of Edinburgh is as long as the Moral Law which it has taught to its graduates, and which most of its graduates have taught, in some form or other, to the world at large. They have turned out songs, those Edinburgh men, and they have turned out sermons, innumerable; sermons predominating. But they have turned out very little that has not lived, or that is not worth living.

Robert Erskine, for one, was not minded to follow the example of some of his elder half-brothers by devoting his life to the exposition of theology; yet he possessed withal his full quota of staunch religious conviction (to which he firmly adhered throughout his life), and a steadfastness of purpose to deal justly with all men.

There is a gap of some six or seven years in the life-story of Erskine which it is difficult adequately to span. After his second period of tuition at Edinburgh, he seems to have set out to make his fortune, and eventually to have settled at London, where he secured employment to his liking and had opportunity to devote his leisure hours to study. There are, preserved in the valuable archives of the New Jersey Historical Society at Newark, two documents which throw a little light on this obscure period in his career.[4] One is a signed two-page thesis, written in an immature hand—unfortunately—without date, being "An Attempt to prove the force of Gun-Powder is chiefly Progressive from the place it is lighted at"; the other an interesting letter to Erskine from his mother. The first document [5] indicates that Erskine's mind was of a scientific turn, the second that he kept in touch with the home-folks.

Arthur Brisbane, in the *New York Journal*, once gave to the metropolitan public a masterly editorial upon the world's mothers. In substance, its purport was this: That our great men were the product of mothers' desires and mothers' prayers. Robert Erskine was, without doubt, blessed with a godly mother, and of this we have proof in the following communication. The date has been torn off, but it must have been written while Erskine was yet a very young man, probably about 1755. He seems to have been seeking a professorship at the University of Glasgow, although quite evidently engaged in earning his livelihood at London. I transcribe the letter literally:

---

[4] Repeated reference must necessarily be made in these pages to the Erskine Papers now treasured in the archives of the New Jersey Historical Society. In explanation let it be stated that these documents were presented to that body somewhere about 1859 by Peter M. Ryerson, son of Martin Ryerson, the iron-master who in 1807 moved into the original manor house at Ringwood, N. J., in which Erskine had resided during his career in America (1771–1780). Martin Ryerson found therein many of the effects of the former occupant.

[5] This document unfortunately is not among the Erskine Papers. However, there is a microfilm in Heusser's compilation, *The Manor and Forges of Ringwood* (5 Vol.), V, 11–12, now in the archives of the New Jersey State Library. The complete series of letters together constitute a noteworthy travel account. It is regrettable that Heusser's extracts do not include some of the first parts. H. S.

Dear Robie, I received your's this day I wrot to you this day eight days with a shipmasters recept for a box to you with some linnings which youl have got by this time. I shall be very glad that I am in a mistake about your being oblidged to be present as a candedat for yᵉ vacancy at Glesgow it was the openean of your Brother and many others that you should be present but if it is neadless it may be they may cause you yet for to be sure the professerss is not pleased with that Buchannan but it is like as yᵉ D of Argyl is hear he will oblidge them to take him fit or unfit if it serves his turn I think you have got a suffisceant swack of his Gress as I hope you will expect no favours from him it would be a great mercy if you could think of doing something hear for I am afrayd you will get some offers to go to Jeameky Gebrealter or some of the colonys abroad which would be very desagerable to me. You may be sure I would be very glad to see you hear for I almost desper of ever seeing you and if you go farther abroad it will certeanly be the case I hope you will take care not to medle with Lotry-tickets their being few gets anything that way Garvok give out 100 pounds ster for tickets and they came out all blanks. I will be glad to hear if you get anything that way and what you payed for your ticket. I hope it will be as you say that the people you stay with are religeuss sober folk but I thought it best to let you see my Brothers letter that you might be on your gaird—I hope the Lord himself will keep his hand about you and keep you out of evel company for to be sure their are many temtations in and about London and allmost in every place I am Dear Robie your loving and affecnat

Mother Margaret Erskine [6]

[6] The letter is not transcribed from the original, but as printed in an article by the Rev. Joseph F. Tuttle, "The Early History of Morris County, New Jersey," *Proceedings of the New Jersey Historical Society*, Second Series, Vol. II (1869), pp. 35–36. Unfortunately this letter is not in the Erskine Papers. However, there are a number of other letters to Robert Erskine from his mother, several bearing dates of 1756 and 1757. The last bears the date of March 22, 1758. There are also several from a sister, the one of August 16, 1758, mentioning the recent death of the mother. An interesting point which they mention is that Erskine tried at least twice to gain a university teaching position. H. S.

In 1759 Erskine formed a business partnership with one Swinton, which eventuated in a dismal failure. Erskine & Swinton dealt in hardware and agricultural implements; at least it would so seem from a bill to them which is preserved in the fruitful manuscript collection of the New Jersey Historical Society. Other old letters among the "Erskine Papers" in the same repository indicate that Erskine & Swinton attempted to do business in the American colonies, and that on some pretext or other, Swinton journeyed to the Carolinas with a goodly consignment of merchandise. Once upon this side of the broad Atlantic, he seems to have defaulted and disappeared, leaving Erskine bankrupt and disheartened, to shoulder the debts of the company and to face the clamorous claimants.

Just what happened to poor Erskine in the year 1761–62 is not quite clear. He made a proposition to the creditors of the defunct company, offering to devote to the liquidation of his and Swinton's indebtedness a certain percentage of the profits to be derived from the sales of his newly patented pump. Probably this came to naught, for the simple reason (as Erskine himself wrote) that an advance of some £600 was needed to put the invention in shape and place the finished product on the market. Truly "the destruction of the poor is their poverty" as the Scriptures put it.

That Erskine, although without funds, was nevertheless unbroken in spirit and striving to extricate himself from the quagmire of debt seems evident from the following:

Received of Mr. Robert Erskine a Bond for Two hundred & seventy seven pounds ten shillings on the following account viz. For Board to this day & Lodging to the Twenty-fifth

March next, Sixty-six pounds as pr. acct. delivered, & for four
notes of his and partners hand to me which I have indorsed
To the amount of Two hundred & eleven pounds ten Shillings;
the said notes to bear interest from the time they become due.

Philip Taylor, London, Febry 24th, 1762 [7]

Matters came to a crisis, however, on the 25th day of
June, 1762, when Erskine was "detained" by the order of
"J. Preston, Clerk of the Papers of the King's Bench" on
the application of some twenty creditors in the "Trinity
Term" of the London debtors' court. Although committed
"to the custody of the Marshall," he was shortly permitted to depart in peace on his own recognizance, possibly because his insolvency was hopeless beyond reclaim,
but more probably by reason of his assurances that, if
allowed time to recoup his fortunes, some settlements
might be effected. The commitment paper has either of
these significant notations written beside each claim:
"justified" or "to justify." [8]

[7] Erskine Papers, N. J. Historical Society.

In an "Address of Mr. Erskine to his and Erskine and Swinton's Creditors," Erskine accused Swinton, now safely in the Carolinas, of embezzling
or secreting about eight thousand pounds. The manuscript, undated, is in
the Erskine Papers. H. S.

[8] *Ibid.* Erskine, in his "last will and testament," tells something of the
kindly leniency of his creditors.

The Young Inventor

THROWN entirely upon his own resources, Erskine seems to have resorted to his natural mechanical talent, and to have turned to the engineering fields as a means of earning a livelihood, specializing in hydraulics.

By 1764, he appears to have "gotten on his feet," so to speak; his patent pump being the foundation upon which he proposed to build. On the 14th of May of this year, he gives permission to Thomas Stephens and John Wilkinson "to make each one Engine, for his own use, without claiming the privilege of my patent or any further demand," provided they will make one for him, which will "raise water seventeen or eighteen feet high." This agreement is executed at Hammersmith (London).[1]

Struggling as he was to make his own way, Robert Erskine did not ignore the pretentions nor belittle the ideas of others like-minded with himself. His letter of Nov. 19, 1764, to a fellow-inventor is an illuminating side light on his character:

[1] Erskine Papers, N. J. Historical Society.

I have considered further of your proposal, and before I see you next Thursday beg leave to communicate what at present occurs which I think equitable and doing as I would be done by, as it is quite contrary both to my inclination and principles to Curb genius and be of the least disservice to any one in rising in the world. Since, therefore, you think my machine will be of service to you when added to an invention of your own, and that with both together you could insure yourself £600 a year or upwards, for me who has so many ways of getting money by mine already, to prevent you from getting money too by your ingenuity, when by your own account it wont interfere with any of the purposes for which I intend mine I think would be inconsistent with a good heart.

I therefore propose to give you liberty to apply my machine to yours on the following conditions: (1) That for such liberty you give me such a sum down as we agree upon. The sum I propose is £300. (2) That as you design to get so much a year settled on you by those who are benefitted by your invention, I shall only ask £20 a year out of what you receive, for every machine of mine you use, and if you get £1000 a year for yourself, shall be so much better pleased. (3) You must agree not to apply my machine and yours to any of the purposes for which I intend mine, an account of which I gave you. The above proposal I think equitable both with respect to you and myself, but if you consider it in the light I do you will find that your proposing to give me £500 for the half of my invention is not at all so. I am very sure I can get more for a fourth, therefore, as there is no consideration you can urge for me to prefer your interest to my own, and in effect making you a present of so much money, you need not expect my treating with you on that footing. Further, as you have not proved your invention, as I would not willingly wrong any man, I will oblige myself to return the money I propose you should give me, with interest, if your invention should not succeed.[2]

2 *Ibid.*

Erskine evidently looked toward the Continent for an outlet for his genius, for among his papers we find the following, dated at London, Dec. 18, 1764:

I hereby acknowledge to have received of Mr. Robert Erskine, inventor of a New Machine for raising water, an account of the Principles on which the said machine is founded and by which it operates, to send to the Directors of the Salt Works in Westphalia, for them to judge which [whether] such a machine will be proper for their use.

(Signed) Bert'd Rappard

This and the previous correspondence refers to his "Continual Stream Pump" which was, in its operation, not unlike the red painted barnyard contrivance still in use throughout many rural sections of the United States. So, at least, is the inference derived from one of the printed circulars yet extant, which gives a wood-cut illustration of the invention and several comparative tables of dimensions and quantities. This is the only English commercial advertisement I have ever seen in which Erskine's name is displayed. In the Erskine Papers are several original drafts of letters addressed to "William Cole, Instrument Maker, at the Surrey end of Westminster Bridge, London" (who had been induced to manufacture the pumps), which indicate that the venture was neither so satisfactory nor profitable as the inventor had hoped. Although a number of pumps were turned out, and none failed to uphold the claims set forth, Erskine and Cole became involved in a protracted controversy in no wise uplifting, which seems to have discouraged the former from further attempts at being a party to the commercializing of his own inventions. Thereafter he kept aloof from participation in the selling end of the game, and his interest in a later development, the "centrifugal engine," was confined to royalties derived from patent rights. By nature Erskine was too visionary for the rigors and stringencies of mercantile pursuits; yet, as fate would have it, he seems never (even in his American career) to have been able entirely to free himself from business entanglements.

We know very little concerning Erskine's life while in London during this period. From the superscription of a letter addressed to him on the 3rd of January, 1765, by his cousin, Ralph Fisher, of Glasgow it appears that he was lodging at "Richard's Coffee House, Temple Bar," and was presumably a bachelor, although now in his thirtieth year. What Fisher writes is interesting and chatty, and gives a good idea of these days and doings. He says:

I am extremely glad to understand by yours to my Father that your machine has met with desired success, and that you'll retrieve all your losses with such advantage. Since I had the pleasure of seeing you last at Stirling, I have dropt my concern in the shop-keeping way here, with an intention of seeing more of the world. The place I always had in view was the East Indies, but was disappointed in a berth there. Lord Bruce of Kennet wrote to his brother in law, Sr. Laurence Dundass, a word from whom to any of the Directors would no doubt have procured me a place there; but he did not it seems, think it worth while to trouble himself about an affair of that nature, so that I am now turning my thoughts to the West Indies, viz Jamaica, for which place I will probably, in some weeks, set out. I shall write you from thence what Berth I get (as I go out upon venture) & how I agree with the Climate.

The inclosed is for a Nephew of Mr. Robert Donaldson's, who keeps a Ware Room at the Angel Inn, a very agreeable young lad. If you can be any how serviceable to him in his way, I should take it as a favour done myself. Please be so good as send the enclosed to him.[3]

[3] *Ibid.*

Long winter evenings in coffee houses or taverns afford wonderful opportunities—either for dissipation or self-improvement and study. Nothing which I have discovered among Erskine's papers conveys the impression that he was given to excesses, or fond of "Bohemian" frolics and revelry—although he used liquor in moderation, and mayhap the then-respected decanter provided inspiration for many a midnight hour. As a draughtsman he was exceedingly clever, as borne out by his drawings of his various inventions, preserved among the Erskine Papers. Whether or not the "Platometer" was practical in operation I cannot say. The original drawing is appended to a sheet of similar size giving detailed particulars as to construction, etc., whereupon Erskine says:

> The use of the PLATOMETER is to find the Latitude & variation of the needle at Sea any time of the day by two observations of the Sun & any time of the night by taking the altitude of two known fixed Stars at the same time.[4]

I am convinced that 1765 turned out to be the year of his marriage. To my readers, as to myself likewise, Robert Erskine's wife may only be known as "Elizabeth." All search as to her maiden surname has, thus far, been fruitless. And the only clue as to the date of the marriage is given by one of Erskine's own letters (dated London, June 10, 1768) to Mr. Fisher of Glasgow (an uncle, and the father of Ralph, above referred to), in which he gives an affecting account of his bereavement in the loss of an exceedingly sweet child, "almost two years old," who died of whooping-cough the 23rd of April preceding; and subjoins most delightful expressions of Christian resignation and hope.[5]

[4] *Ibid.*
[5] See Rev. Donald Fraser's *Life and Diary of Rev. Ralph Erskine.*

20

Of Mrs. Erskine herself, who appears to have been a
kind and good wife, many references will appear from
time to time as our story progresses, but of this first great
sorrow which came into the little family no mention is
ever thereafter made—save that, in an inventory of Erskine's effects, taken shortly after his death, this significant item appears: "One little bed for Sarah"! No
other children were granted by Providence to the Erskines, and it would seem that the tiny crib, brought with
them to America, was a constantly treasured memento of
the little lamb taken to the "upper fold."

The year 1765 meant much to Erskine professionally.
On May 14th, he records the results of experiments with
his Centrifugal Hydraulic Engine made at Woolwich
Dock (London) in which it was demonstrated that it was
far superior to the old chain pump turned by winches.[6]
On Jan. 18, 1766, he gave another demonstration at
Woolwich, aboard "his Majestys ship Princess Mary,"
before "a number of gentlemen and others," several of
whom signed a statement in proof of the fact that Erskine's engine was almost 30% more efficient than the
old-time pumps.[7]

The date of Feb. 27, 1766, is noted in these pages merely
as another milestone in Erskine's checkered career, because on that day he completed an elaborate specification
as to ways and means for increasing the fall in the River
Colme at "Hubbart's Mill." [8] This stream is one of the

---

[6] Erskine Papers. A letter of Nov. 12 of the same year states that Erskine
was also the inventor of a "horizontal" windmill. The same letter tells of
selling a "large Centrifugal Engine" to a salt works belonging to the King
of Prussia. H. S.

[7] *Ibid.*

[8] This document seems to have disappeared from the Erskine Papers.
There is a photostat in *The Manor and Forges of Ringwood*, V, 7. See the
introduction to this book. H. S.

picturesque waterways of the shire or county of Essex, some fifty miles to the northeast of London town. Whether Erskine's carefully worked-out scheme was put into execution in this instance is a matter of conjecture, but from the following letter, written at London, Sept. 16th, 1776, it is quite evident that his professional services were ere long availed of by persons of high estate.

To the Right Honble, the Earl of Litchfield, 8 Detchley, Ox-ford^{re}.

My Lord

I beg leave to lay before your Lordship the result of my Calculations, with respect to your Horse Engine, and a Machine for the Oxford Hospital.

The mean weight to be raised by the Horse, as the Engine is at present, is 264 pounds, exclusive of Friction:

The Quantity of water raised in one revolution of the great wheel is 4 Gallons and 3 Quarts; if the horse, then, makes one revolution, and an half in a minute, the Quantity thrown up in that time, supposing no waste at the Pistens, is 7 Galls. & a pint.

By the alteration I proposed of Cranks, instead of Rollers, &c., the Friction will not only be considerably diminished, but the mean weight reduced to 105 pounds, and the Quantity raised, at a moderate Calculation, will be about 10 Gallons in a minute.

The two Cisterns at the Oxford hospital, hold 16 Tons and 38 Gallons, or 8 Tons 19 Galls. each; the Machine to supply these, will stand, I think, most Conveniently, in a corner of one of the Rooms on the ground Floor, immediately under that Cistern next the Well; the water being conveyed to the Machine by a lead pipe laid under ground into the Well; and from it, by an other Pipe running right up the Corner, to the Cistern above; a Communication between the two Cisterns may be made, by carrying a pipe from one to the other, along the upper Corner of the long passage on the second Floor.

The machine I propose will raise three Tons an hour, or fill both Cisterns in Six; and as the Mechanical advantage gained by the Machinery reduces the resistance at the handle to 15 pounds, it may be easily worked by one man; and will cost about 40 Guineas, exclusive of Lead pipe, which can be done at Oxford.

I have given Mr. Cole orders about the Small Machine for the back Stairs, which shall be finished as soon as possible; and if your Lordship chooses the Particular Calculations on which the foregoing Conclusions are founded, I shall take pleasure in giving all the satisfaction in my power; tho I could not presume to trouble you farther at present by swelling this letter to an unnecessary length. I beg leave therefore to Subscribe myself

> With the Greatest Respect
> My Lord, Your Lordship's most obliged
> and Most Obedt. hum^le Servt.
>
> Robt Erskine [9]

Robert Erskine, as the natural result of his professional labors, soon began to interest himself in public affairs and civic improvements. Among his papers there are several voluminous "original drafts" of letters which he contrived to publish; most of which are—unfortunately—without date. The subject matter, in general, concerns rivers and tides, with arguments for their more efficient utilization and control. The Rev. Archibald Hall, in a letter to Mr. Fisher of Glasgow, dated London, July —, 1770, refers to one of these productions. He says:

[9] *Ibid.* Later correspondence in the Erskine Papers indicates that none of Erskine's inventions were very remunerative although one listing indicated sale of twenty-two items, apparently all "centrifugal engines" or pumps, including one to Germany and one to the West Indies. Erskine evidently turned to more remunerative pursuits. A letter from a cousin on July 28, 1768, is addressed to him as a "Land-Surveyor and Engineer," and mentions his success "in the Land-Surveying Ways." H. S.

Mr. Robert Erskine and Mrs. Erskine are very well. He has lately published an Essay upon the effect of bridges and abutments in rivers to cause shoals, dedicated to the late Lord Mayor, William Beckford, Esquire, which is thought by good judges to be a very ingenious performance. The City of London has the improvement of the river Thames in contemplation just now. It is hoped this seasonable discovery of the author's fine genius will recommend him to some useful place in forming and executing their schemes to that effect.[10]

The *London Chronicle* was one of the favored vehicles by means of which Erskine found an outlet for his effusions. While hydraulic engineering projects were uppermost in his mind, he seems likewise to have been keenly alive to anything and everything tending to better existing social conditions, or to ameliorate inconvenience and suffering—of which, Heaven knows, there was aplenty in the eighteenth century. One of his most interesting letters to the printer of the *Chronicle* concerns "a method of treating the Small Pox, which the voice of Humanity demands should be universally known." [11]

[10] Printed in Rev. Donald Fraser's *Life and Diary of Ralph Erskine.*

[11] Erskine Papers. A manuscript entitled "A Dissertation on Rivers and Tides" among the Erskine Papers, possibly overlooked by Heusser, shows the direction of Erskine's research at one period of his career. H. S.

3

The Ringwood Mines

I N 1763 an enterprise which was destined vitally to affect the industrial history of the American Colonies had its beginning in London. In that year there was formed a strange partnership under the name of Hasenclever, Seton and Crofts, with a joint capital of £21,000. Ostensibly these gentlemen were merchants, but Peter Hasenclever,[1] the leading spirit of the concern, aspired to be much more. In his fertile brain lay dreams, not of dusty

[1] A very interesting account of the life and work of Peter Hasenclever is given in a little brochure by Henry A. Homes, LL.D., being an address read by him in 1874 before the Albany Institute. There is a copy in the New York Public Library. Prof. Homes' original source of information was Hasenclever's own booklet of 97 pages, published at London in 1773, in which, under the title "The Remarkable Case of Peter Hasenclever," he tells his life story and defends his actions in America, appealing to the British Parliament for redress. Of this monograph one copy is in the archives of the N. Y. State Library at Albany. Peter Hasenclever was born in Remscheid in the Rhenish provinces of Germany, in 1716. In early life he had been a partner in a mercantile house at Cádiz, in Spain. On account of the climate, which was unfavorable to his wife's health, he went to London in the year 1763, where she had been living since 1757.

counting-houses, but of vast world-wide commercial monopolies. Accordingly he turned toward America as a profitable field for exploitation, and ere long induced such eminent and respectable persons as Major General Greene, Commodore Forest and George Jackson, Secretary of the Admiralty, each to agree to expend from £10,000 to £40,000 in the production of pig iron, hemp, potash, etc., in North America. This contract was made in January, 1764, and by June of that year Hasenclever had reached New York, eager to begin active operations. Already he had made arrangements with his agents in Germany for a supply of workmen who might shortly be expected to arrive, and he was naturally much concerned as to the matter of immediately finding or establishing an enterprise worthy of his talents. It is uncertain whether he knew, at the outset, just what he wanted; certainly he had not the least idea *where* he would inaugurate operations. Thus, at the very beginning of his career in America we see a rashness and want of calculation which it is difficult to understand. It is an axiom, however, that when one is determined upon spending money, some seemingly opportune way will easily be found. So it proved in the case of Hasenclever. For him and his confiding co-investors, the Ringwood iron mines lay awaiting. And again it is necessary to turn back the pages of history (in this instance to delve into some unfamiliar chronicles of the province of New Jersey).

The story of the Ringwood iron mines and furnaces is closely interwoven with that of the early workings for ore at Sterling, Long Pond, Charlotteburg, Hibernia and the numerous enterprises of similar character in Bergen and Morris Counties of New Jersey, and of Rockland County, New York. Credit for early exploitation of the mineral wealth of this region belongs to Cornelius Board, who somewhere about 1737, began operations at Ringwood.[2] The various early records, pieced together, result in a fairly complete narrative.

Copper had been discovered in the neighborhood of Belleville, prior to 1720. Members of the New Jersey branch of the Schuyler family were rapidly attaining affluence because of the rich yield of ore from their property on the ridge between the Hackensack and Passaic Rivers. Cornelius Board, a Welsh miner, came to America in 1730, as the representative of a rival interest seeking other deposits of copper at Bloomfield. When this expectation came to naught, he continued prospecting on his own account, but with a similar lack of success. He then went to the "Little Falls" of the Passaic, secured some land and put up a grist mill. After that, hearing from the Indians that there was iron ore in the Pompton Mountains, he and a companion, led through the wilderness by the redmen, went to the head of the Ringwood River (at the Sterling Pond) and erected a small furnace for the manufacture of iron. Doubtless this was the original iron furnace in the region. Board himself soon settled a few miles to the south of Sterling Lake at "Ringwood," being in all probability the founder of this industrial hamlet in the heart of the Jersey hills near the New York State line.[3] As to the origin of its name, there is much doubt. Certainly it is "ringed about" with heavily wooded mountains; but it is conjectured that one of the several "Ringwoods" in the British Isles (possibly well known to Board or his fellow pioneers) suggested the name.

In 1740,[4] Board disposed of his holdings at Ringwood to a

[2] *Proceedings of the New Jersey Historical Society*, Second Series, Vol. XI (1891), p. 126, letter of William Nelson.

[3] *Ibid.*, New Series, Vol. IV, p. 66. Most of this paragraph to this point has been taken, almost verbatim, from an article by the Rev. Garret E. Schenck, "Early Settlements and Settlers of Pompton, Pequannoc and Pompton Plains." H. S.

[4] The names of some of the worthies who constituted the "Ringwood Company" have come down to us. There were Colonel Josiah Ogden, John Ogden, Jr., David Ogden, Sr., David Ogden, Jr., and Uzal Ogden; as well as Nicholas and Samuel Gouverneur. Of these, Josiah Ogden (1679–1763) was the most famous, being one of the prominent and influential men of Newark, N. J. From 1716 to 1721 he represented his community in the General

syndicate of Newark and New York capitalists, who formed themselves into the first "Ringwood Company," securing additional land and greatly increasing the output of the mines and the product of the furnaces. They were both miners and makers of pig-metal. Many of the lesser iron-masters of these days confined themselves to mining only—in which case the ore was transported to the low country to be smelted—others engaged merely in making of pigs and ingots from the ore which they purchased from the mine owners. The laws of Great Britain did not encourage more than this in the colonies. The pigs of metal were supposed to be carried overseas to the old country for manufacture into commodities of commerce. For such finished utensils, of course, the American subjects of the Crown paid a fat price, when their own American iron came again to these shores as English merchandise.

The Ringwood Company continued operations for nearly a quarter of a century, but in 1764—possibly because of some dissatisfaction among the owners—the property was offered for sale. In these days purchasers of large enterprises were difficult to find—for Colonial "capitalists" were few and far between, and were, as a rule, ultra-conservative. So the Ringwood Company had recourse to advertising.

In *The New York Mercury* of March 5th, 1764, appeared the following notice, which undoubtedly referred to the Ringwood property:

To be sold, a new, well-built furnace, good iron mines near the same; two forges, one with 3 and the other with 2 fires—a saw-mill, several dwelling-houses and coal-houses, and several tracts of land adjoining; carts, waggons, utensils and tools proper for the works: The furnaces and forges are situated on

---

Assembly of the province. He was one of the pillars of the local Presbyterian Church, but later withdrew, to form—with the co-operation of some of his neighbors—the first Episcopal Church in Newark, now known as Trinity.

a good stream, 28 miles from Acquackanung landing [5] and 36 from Newark. Whoever inclines to purchase the same may apply to Nicholas Gouverneur in New-York, or to David Ogden, sen. Samuel Gouverneur, and David Ogden, jun. at Newark, who will agree for the same.[6]

In all probability it was this announcement which attracted the eye and attention of Peter Hasenclever, who was looking for exactly such a proposition. At any rate, Hasenclever soon possessed himself of the property and its equipment; for on the 5th of July, 1764, the Ringwood Company sold him for £5,000, all of the company's lands at Ringwood. In the same year Hasenclever obtained patents for 5,000 acres severally at Ringwood, Long Pond, and "Charlottenburg" (Charlotteburg)—in all 15,000 acres. This land gave promise of great mineral wealth, and was so abundantly wooded as to insure an inexhaustible supply of charcoal.

These purchases, and the consequent activities inaugurated by the ambitious adventurer from abroad, caused the London syndicate to denominate its new-found colonial investment "The American Iron Company," and thus it remained officially for upward of twenty years; although to the American public, and to everyone referring to it from that day to this, the title of "The London Company" has seemed all-sufficient.

Hasenclever now plunged heart and soul into a turmoil of business, not only giving his attention to Ringwood, but scattering his means and energies broadcast in a debauch of investment the like of which was never before known in America. By November of 1764, hundreds of his immigrants had arrived from the fatherland with their

---

[5] Usually written "Acquackanonck." This locality is now part of Passaic.
[6] This quotation may be found in *Archives of the State of New Jersey*, First Series, Vol. XXIV, pp. 328–29. H. S.

families—miners, farmers and mechanics aplenty; in
fact so numerous were they that Hasenclever was, for a
time, at his wit's end to know what provision to make for
their distribution and maintenance. Yet such was the
energy of this sanguine man that he was soon making
iron at Ringwood, having rehabilitated the decayed plant
with remarkable celerity. In August, 176 he purchased
a ship at New York, which he loaded for London with
iron, furs and timber—and potash to the amount of five
hogsheads. The iron and potash had been manufactured
by the company's workmen. So superior was his iron that
it was pronounced by his partners in London to be "the
best drawn which had ever made its appearance on the
London market from America."

Within a year from the time of his coming to America
Hasenclever had imported from Germany 535 persons,
including women and children, whom he had scattered
over the 50,000 acres of land which he had purchased in
the provinces of New York and New Jersey for the ful-
filment of the various schemes by which he hoped to en-
rich himself and his employers.

At the end of the next year, 1766, he had in operation
four furnaces and seven forges in New Jersey and New
York; besides a potash and pearl ash manufactory on the
Mohawk River; and had built stores, workshops and
dwelling houses to the number of 235, in addition to dams
for thirteen mill ponds, ten bridges, and many miles of
roads. He is said to have examined in all fifty-three mines,
of which however only seven proved sufficiently rich in
ore to be profitable. In the short space of two years Hasenclever spent, according to his own admission, £54,600 on
account of the company—being £14,000 more than the
amount for which his associates ever pledged themselves
to be responsible.

Hasenclever established his headquarters at Ringwood, where he lived in almost regal elegance. As "Baron Hasenclever" he remains one of the half-legendary characters of generations ago; and while the local histories of the communities where he lavished his money make little or no mention of him in their chronicles, his memory is perpetuated today by the Hasenclever Mountains in Herkimer County, N. Y.; in the title of the Hasenclever land patents; and in the "Hasenclever Iron Mines" in Rockland County, N. Y.

A gentleman spending money so lavishly as did Hasenclever most naturally acquired influential friends. Chief among Hasenclever's patrons was Sir William Johnson, the virtual lord of the Mohawk Valley. Through the cooperation of General Gage and Sir Henry Moore, the governor of New York province, Hasenclever was enabled to secure extensive rights from Johnson.[7] Hence we find record of his potash and pearl ash establishment at New Petersburg, near the German Flats, on the Mohawk— where he had built two frame houses and thirty-four log huts, and had begun a fine settlement for the cultivation of hemp, flax and madder. The "Hasenclever Patent," in Herkimer County, embraced some 18,000 acres. In connection with General Gage and Philip Schuyler of Albany, Hasenclever also acquired an interest in 11,500 acres of land on Lake Champlain, north of Crown Point,

---

[7] The *Johnson Manuscripts* at the N. Y. State Library at Albany include a series of letters written by Peter Hasenclever to Sir William Johnson, 1765 to 1770, with copies of two of the latter's replies to Hasenclever, and one letter written by Hasenclever to Gen. Thomas Gage. In the latter, the writer asks Gage (the Commander-in-chief of the British forces in America) to use his good offices with Johnson, in order to permit Hasenclever to obtain land grants and rights for establishing settlements in the Mohawk Valley and lands adjacent. Hasenclever's letters to Johnson are mostly concerning these schemes, although he discusses politics, history and industry with equal breadth of vision and flow of rhetoric.

presumably because of supposed mineral resources. Hasenclever was a frequent visitor at "Johnson Hall," so famous in colonial annals; and Sir William became an equal partner with him in the potash manufacturing scheme, although he had the good sense to demur when it came to a participation in other and more visionary projects of the erstwhile "London merchant."

Unluckily for Hasenclever, he was by no means his own master; nor was he able indefinitely to borrow funds without making some repayment. His promissory notes and bills became due, and his principals, alarmed at his extravagance, refused to countenance further outlays or to invest additional funds. Hence, the credit side of his accounts showing little in his favor, he came shortly to the end of his rope. Although his iron was good, very little had been sent over to England. Freshets carried away his dams (one of which was 860 feet long and twelve feet high), and roads and bridges had, consequently, to be rebuilt. Some of the ore which he had mined was too sulphurous; he quarreled with his potash manufacturer; his hemp seed failed to "spring up and bear fruit"—and troubles came thick and fast. In October, 1766, he learned that Seton, one of his original partners, had been declared a bankrupt, and forthwith journeyed to England. He succeeded, somehow or other, in making an arrangement with his solvent co-adventurers for the continued prosecution of mining in America, and came again to New York in 1768. But Hasenclever's difficulties increased and the output lessened, if such a thing was possible. Finally, all of his bills having been protested and his credit ruined, he once more proceeded (in 1769) to London, never again to return to American shores. In his own defense, Hasenclever stated that he had been unfairly treated, and— himself being declared a bankupt in 1770—attributed this crowning calamity to the clandestine machinations of the other members of the syndicate which he represented.[8]

The extent and character of the property belonging to the American Iron Company at the time of Hasenclever's recall may best be learned from the report submitted by the four appraisers who, in 1768, at the command of Governor William Franklin of New Jersey (acting upon Hasenclever's request—in order that he might be able to justify his proceedings before the English courts), made an exhaustive examination of the works at Ringwood, Long Pond and Charlotteburg, for the purpose of ascertaining how well and judiciously Hasenclever had fulfilled his stewardship. Their verdict was an unqualified "well done."

May I preface the same by saying that the spelling "Charlottenburg" is an error, a generally used corruption of "Charlotteburg"; this name, which had been bestowed upon the smallest of Hasenclever's New Jersey iron works, being an honor paid to Queen Charlotte, the royal partner of George II. The Ringwood forges were contiguous to the "residency" of the general manager on the Ringwood River; the Long Pond works were located on the present Wanaque River (the outlet of Greenwood Lake) near the modern hamlet of Hewitt; while the Charlotteburg establishment lay some ten miles to the southwest, beyond Federal Hill, on the Pequannock River.

Charlotteburg has long since become in very fact a "deserted village." Where once a thriving industrial community existed, wildest Nature has again come into her

---

[8] The subsequent career of Hasenclever is very interesting. He recouped his fortunes, became a successful merchant of Landeshut, and a highly respected friend of Frederick the Great. He died June 13, 1793. A biography was published by Professor Adolf Hasenclever of Halle University, a descendant of Peter Hasenclever, in 1922.

own. The turbulent rivulet plunges through the remains of a crumbling dam; weeds and rank vegetation fill the course of the ancient sluice-way, and copperheads bask undisturbed in the sunlight where, in the days of yore, the ponderous trip-hammer rose and fell with measured cadence. However, there has been preserved a very interesting relic of pre-Revolutionary days in the shape of a bar of pig iron, unearthed in the vicinity, bearing thereon the molded word "CHARLOTTEBURG."

The following is the report of the committee of investigation:

To His Excellency, the Honorable William Franklin:
Sir:—

In compliance with your Excellency's request, communicated to us by letter of the 27th of June last, we proceeded on Monday the 2nd inst. to view the iron-works erected by Peter Hasenclever, Esq.; within this province; and began with those of Charlottenburgh, on the west branch of the Pequanock River, which is the boundary between the counties of Morris and Bergen. We there found a very fine blast furnace, erected in 1767, and now nearly finished; this we think one of the best pieces of the kind we ever saw in America: The dams and water-ways, the casting-house, bellows-house, wheel-house, ton-house, coal-house, etc., are all well-contrived, and executed in a workman-like manner; here are also a number of dwelling-houses, store-houses, workshops, and stables, necessary and convenient to the works; also a good saw mill. This furnace when in blast is capable of making from twenty to twenty-five ton of pig-iron per week and can be worked at a small expense, as there is plenty of wood and ore at hand, and need never stop for want of water at any season of the year. On the same stream, about three miles lower, is a very fine forge and four fires, and two hammers for converting pig-iron into bar-iron, and is, according to the information we received from the overseer, and workmen, capable of making 250 tons of bar-iron yearly, single handed, and from 300 to 350 ton double handed. The dam here is upwards of twenty feet high, and is remarkably substantial and well secured: Here are also the necessary coal-houses, dwelling-houses, store-house, workshops, and stables. About a mile lower down the stream is another forge of the same dimensions and capability with the last, with all the necessary buildings: about half a mile lower down is another saw-mill, capable of sawing a thousand feet of plank per diem; all these works together are comprehended under the general name of Charlottenburg, and on the whole, consist of one furnace, two double forges, two saw-mills, three very large coal-houses, three blacksmiths shops, six large frame dwelling-houses, filled in with brick and clay, thirty-seven good and comfortable log-houses, besides a number of smaller houses in the woods for wood-cutters and colliers.

This work appears to us to have every natural convenience necessary to make them profitable, and these seem to have been improved with judgment, and to the best advantage; every part of them is well supplied with abundance of excellent wood for coaling; they are situated on a fine lively stream, which at most seasons is sufficient to keep all the works employed, and in times of very great droughts it is so contrived that the natural stream may have an addition of water from two large natural ponds of some miles in circumference, called the Makapin and Dunken ponds, in which the water is dammed up, and raised several feet above the natural surface, and have flood-gates to let off any quantity of water which at any time shall be thought necessary for carrying on the works; the roads which have been made here, we apprehend, have been very expensive. Places which before were inaccessible, even to horsemen, on account of the steepness of the rocks and mountains, are now good carriage roads, but this expense was absolutely necessary to enable them to carry off the iron to market, to have access to their woods and mines, and to a fine grain country from whence they are supplied with provisions, and to open a communication between the different works.

From Charlottenburg we proceeded about 13 miles to Ringwood, situate on a more northerly branch of Pequanock River, which is called Ringwood River, and is in Bergen County: here we were told were formerly the iron works belonging to a company from whom Mr. Hasenclever purchased, but very little of them remains now to be seen, the present works being entirely new; and here we found first, a blast furnace with nearly the same dimensions with that of Charlottenburg, and capable of making about the same quantity of pig-iron. This furnace is not at present in blast, but may soon be so, as there is nothing wanting but the finishing of a hearth, which was putting in; within fifty yards of this furnace stands a very good forge of three fires and two hammers, and a stamping-mill, for separating the iron from the cinder in the old cinder bank, which we were informed is a profitable work, and at about five hundred yards above the furnace stands another very fine forge, of four fires and two hammers, and also a very good saw mill. About half a mile below the furnace is another forge of two fires and one hammer, and a very good grist mill; and about two miles lower down the same stream is also another forge of two fires and one hammer; at each of these forges, and at the furnaces, are the necessary coal-houses and dwelling-houses for the workmen; and near the furnace is a large dwelling-house for the Manager, or Chief Clerk; also a new brick house for a store, &c. a large stone house and ovens, and, for various other uses; eight frame houses, four log-houses, four barracks, two blacksmiths shops, one powder magazine, one large horse stable and carpenter's shop, besides sixteen other log-houses in the woods, for wood cutters and colliers. The furnace at this place, as well as that at Charlottenburg, is capable of making from twenty to twenty five tons of pig-iron per week while in blast, which may with good management, be at least nine months in the year; the forges, like those at Charlottenburg, are capable of making yearly 250 ton of bar-iron single handed, or 300 to 350 ton double handed, at each four fires, of which there are in all eleven.

These works were formerly liable, in droughts, to be in want of water, so that it has sometimes happened that the works

were obliged to stand still for several weeks, at the best season
of the year for working; but this defect is now entirely
remedied, by an immense Reservoir in which the water is collected in rainy seasons in such proportions as is found necessary to supply the deficiency of the natural stream of the
Ringwood River. The Reservoir is a pond called Toxito Pond,[9]
about three miles long, and near one mile broad; it formerly
emptied itself into the Ramapough River, but by an immense
dam of 860 feet long and from 12 to 22 feet high, the natural
out let is stopped up, and the water raised to such a height as
to take its course with a head of ten feet high, into a long canal,
which conducts it into the Ringwood River.

When Mr. Hasenclever purchased the ruin of Ringwood
Works, there was to all appearances plenty of good iron ore, in
several places; within a mile or two of the furnace several
others have since been discovered; some of them have since
worked out; some proved coalshear, others have too much
abounded in sulphur or copper, or had qualities which rendered
the goodness of the iron dubious. But all doubt as to the quality
and quantity of iron ore is now removed by draining the water
off the Peter's mine, which was overflown, and by the discovery
of another mine which was first made in July 1767, on Wales
Mountain, about one mile and a half westward from the furnace, and since called the Good Hope mine; it has been opened
in five different places on the same course, and already shews
the extent of the vein for near a mile in length and in some
cases 14 feet in breadth; the quality of it we saw tried at the
Long Pond works, where it made a fine tough bar-iron. The
works at Ringwood can never fail for want of coal,[10] as there
are many thousand acres of wood-land in sight of them, within
a circle of two miles round. The woods, if cut regular and
clean, will grow faster than they can have occasion to use it.

The making of the Roads about Ringwood must have been
attended with great labour and expense, as they are very con-

---

[9] Tuxedo Lake.
[10] "Charcoal" is meant whenever reference is made to "coal."

siderable ones over rough rocky mountains to the oar beds and coal grounds, besides others for bringing provisions to the works of several miles in extent, which in some places, through swamps and over brooks, have considerable bridges of timber. From Ringwood we proceeded three miles south westward to the Long Pond works, which are situated on a stream, which issues out of the Long Pond, and falls into Ringwood River, about four miles below the furnace. The Long Pond [11] is about six miles in length, and near two miles in breadth; across the out let or mouth of it is a dam of 200 feet in length, and about 5 feet in height, by which the water is raised four feet above its natural level; and the pond is now a never failing resource of water for the supply of the works below, in the dryest season of the year. The Long Pond works are about two miles below the out let of the pond and consists of a blast furnace much like that at Charlottenburg; is now in blast, and is capable of making from twenty to twenty-five tons of pig-iron per week, and of a very fine forge of four fires, and two hammers; and is capable of making as much bar-iron as either of those at Charlottenburg or Ringwood. There is also a very good saw mill; the other buildings are two large coal-houses, three framed dwelling-houses, six logg-houses, one stone house, one horse stable and one blacksmith's shop, besides smaller houses in the woods for colliers, &c. The furnace here is now supplied with oar from the Peter's Mine and Good Hope mine, at three miles distance of which it makes excellent iron; there are other mines nearer to the works; but they cannot as yet, be depended upon.

The roads about the Long Pond works, like those at the other before-mentioned places, have been attended with much expense and labour, as there was a necessity of carrying them, in some places, along the sides of rocky mountains, and in others through deep swamps and gulleys, which could not be rendered passable by bridging them with timber.

We have now finished the survey of the works erected by

[11] Greenwood Lake.

Mr. Hasenclever, within this province, so far as they have been shewn to us. We shall subjoin a sketch of the situation of the works, in order that your Excellency may the better understand our description of them; and also a general table of particulars, by which the whole may be seen in one view; and we would here beg leave to remark that we think that Mr. Hasenclever has made several great improvements in the iron works under his direction; he is the first person that we know of who has so greatly improved the use of the great natural ponds of this country, as, by damming them, to secure reservoirs of water for the use of the iron works in dry seasons; without which the best streams are liable to fall in the great droughts we are subject to. He is also the first we know of, who has rendered the old cinder beds of the furnaces useful and profitable; for at Ringwood he has erected a stamping-mill to separate the waste iron from the cinders, by which means some hundred tons of small iron have and may be obtained; which is as good as the best pig iron; he has also made a great improvement in the construction of the furnaces, by building the inwalls of slate, which by the experience he has already had of it, will, in all probability, last many years; whereas the stones commonly made use of for that purpose, seldom stood longer than a year or two, and would often fail in the middle of a blast.

Another improvement worth attention, we think, is the building of the stack of the furnace under roof, so as to shelter them entirely from wind and water. The forges are also greatly improved, by the wheels being all made overshot, and the hammer wheel shafts being armed with strong cast iron rings, whose arms serve as cogs to lift the hammer handle; those are also new contrivances, at least they are new in America. Mr. Hasenclever has, in several places, cleared and made some extensive pieces of meadows, which, when in order, will yield at least 2 tons of hay yearly per acre; and must be of great use in supplying the working cattle belonging to the works with fodder, especially as there is little of the up-land near the works fit for raising corn, or any kind of water fodder.

On the whole, it is a matter of surprise to us, to see such a number of great works of various kinds, at different places, executed in so compleat and masterly a manner, under the direction of one person, in a new, uninhabited country, within the short space of time that has elapsed since Mr. Hasenclever first began them; and we must here observe, that the buildings of all kinds seem to us to be commodiously contrived, all of them useful, and none of them unnecessary. Mr. Homfray, the present manager, and the under-managers, on being asked of us whether they thought any of them superfluous, declared that they knew of none that could be spared. We are,

Your Excellency's most humble servants,

(Signed) Stirling,

James Grey,

Theunis Dey, and

John Schuyler

Newark, July 8th, 1769 [12]

After reading the foregoing, one is inclined to agree with Hasenclever's contentions and to credit him with the creative powers of a genius rather than to accuse him of extravagance, mismanagement and peculation. Coupled with his own assertions, this report of the Commissioners would seem to make a strong case in his favor. So indeed was the situation regarded by Lord Chancellor

---

[12] *New Jersey Archives*, First Series, Vol. XXVIII, 247 ff.

Of these Commissioners, the first signatory is of course "Lord" Stirling (William Alexander of Basking Ridge, N. J., claiming to be the titular Earl of Stirling). He was one of the owners of the Hibernia Iron Mines and, in later years, one of the patriot generals upon whom Washington most relied. Grey was an iron-master of Little Falls, on the upper Passaic River; he joined the British Army at the outbreak of the Revolution and was given a captain's commission, his real estate being confiscated and sold by the patriots. Colonel Theunis Dey, a resident of Lower Preakness, was destined to go down on the pages of history because Washington, in 1780, spent several months as his guest, occupying his spacious mansion as his "headquarters near the Passaic Falls." John Schuyler was one of the proprietors of the Belleville copper mines and a cousin of the Albany Schuylers.

Thurlow, who—after protracted litigation in the English courts—exonerated Hasenclever from any incriminating conduct. Yet a perusal of the letter which Erskine wrote to the *New York Mercury* some four years later, and which will hereafter appear, throws once again, and most strongly, the light of censure upon Hasenclever's régime, and we see the situation in another complexion entirely.

One may well ask, as did the puzzled Procurator of Judea, "What *is* truth"? In passing judgment upon this controversy between Hasenclever and the English proprietors—between agent and owner—we are forced, in a spirit of fairness, to look at both sides of the question. Having done this, we arrive at but one conclusion, viz., that Hasenclever attempted too much. Whereas he should have contented himself with a moderate degree of development and taken pains to build and plan within the means at his disposal, he made the stupendous error of starting more than he could possibly hope to finish. Had he kept within bounds, co-ordinated his resources, and devoted his talents toward making money for his employers, instead of spending what he had and asking for more, he might have won for himself a place unique in the annals of early American history—a place, by the way, which will always remain unfilled—that of an eighteenth century "captain of industry." Peter Hasenclever was the brightest exponent of "big business" known in America prior to the days of Stephen Girard, failing only because he knew not his limitations. Prof. Adolf Hasenclever, of Halle University, one of his 1922 descendants, in his biography of the famous schemer, clearly demonstrates that his life, despite its vicissitudes, was not without its triumphs and compensations. But insofar as our story of Ringwood is concerned, he now passes from the scene, leaving "Mr. Homfray" (about whom

little is known) working in conjunction with John Jacob
Faesch, another of his managers, in the effort to keep the
works moving; and awaiting further orders from England, where the stockholders were valiantly seeking a
solution to what was, for them, "the great American
question."

4

Iron-Master in the Making

THE utter ruin which now threatened the American investments of the London syndicate—that body of investors who had been lured into the placing of heavy stakes on a far-away venture because of the rosy pictures painted by Hasenclever—caused them to make heroic efforts to avert the pending catastrophe. While Faesch and other subordinates were struggling with the proposition in America and attempting as best they might to prop up the crumbling structure beneath which they found themselves, the capitalists at home held many an anxious conference, and forthwith began a nation-wide search for a man fitted for the emergency.

We are utterly in the dark as to the circumstances which led them into negotiations with Robert Erskine. It is quite probable, however, that his professional work in the neighborhood of London, his private commissions for various men of nobility, and his published communications to the newspapers regarding civic improvements, had brought him a sufficient measure of recognition to attract attention. During the winter of 1769–1770 he seems to have been approached upon the subject of taking the momentous step which was to result in changing his career from that of a British inventor, engineer, and scientist to that of an American patriot. With good reason he debated with himself for many months before making the fateful decision. His final choice, at which he arrived despite many misgivings, meant for him the relinquishment of a laboriously acquired foothold upon the rungs of the ladder of success, and a sinking of his life, his name and his fortune into the uncertainties of the new world— little dreaming that he was to have a most vital part in the evolution of the great American commonwealth of the future. Had Erskine remained in his native land, there is no doubt that he would have made a name for himself. As it transpired, the choice he made brought him little in the way of personal success save the consciousness of being a servant in a righteous cause. And for this reason, it should be the greater pleasure for you and for me to perpetuate his name among those of the patriot band who brought our republic into being and nurtured it into complete independence.

Having determined upon his course, Erskine found it expedient to fit himself for his new sphere of activity. Although a practical engineer, skilled especially in hydraulics, he was by no means a mineralogist nor did he consider himself sufficiently informed about mines and mining. Again, he knew only the general theoretical principles governing the manufacture of iron. Considering these things, it is more than ever apparent that he was chosen because of his character. As a businessman he had failed; as the head of a great industrial enterprise he was without experience. Certain it is, therefore, that he possessed some manifestly exceptional traits which appealed to those who sought to employ him.

It is not at all surprising, then, that one of Erskine's first moves, after deciding for the American adventure, was to arrange a two-months' tour of inspection through the mining regions of Great Britain. From early September to the end of October, 1770, he was continuously on the trail; beginning in the rich ore-bearing hills of the Welsh-English border near Monmouth and the estuary of the River Severn, and concluding his labors at Glasgow. We are enabled to trace his itinerary with great accuracy, because of the fortunate discovery of a packet of original letters,[1] covering this eventful period, written by him to Richard Atkinson, of Nicholas Lane, London—one of the principals of the London syndicate for whom he was soon to begin his work in America. I cannot do better than to quote freely from his copious source of information, because Erskine tells his story in an exceedingly interesting fashion. True, the letters were written for the acknowledged purpose of recording the necessary technical and mechanical details connected with the mines, forges and furnaces which he visited (and he seems to have had them returned to him, by pre-arrangement, before coming to America), but they abound in those observations upon men and affairs which always make letter-reading a pleasure. So it is, I suppose, that the collector of autographic material comes to a very close and intimate knowledge of his favorite characters, from whom he would otherwise be unavoidably separated by the gulf of years.

---

[1] These letters had been preserved by the Ryerson family, but were not given to the New Jersey Historical Society with the rest of the Erskine Papers. They are contained in Heusser's compilation, *The Manor and Forges of Ringwood*. H. S.

I copy the first of the series in its entirety, as it is typical of those which follow—from some of which I must necessarily limit myself to quotations:

Monmouth, Sepr. 15th, 1770

Dear Sir

I have seen some furnaces and forges of which I beg leave to give you an account, and that I may not omit particulars which hereafter may be useful, I hope you will excuse me, in this and all my future letters, for giving a detail of my observations, in the same order in which they occurred; by following this rule, tho I may mention some things trivial and of no avail, yet I shall run the less hazard of overlooking things of importance.

About 10 or 12 miles from Glocester the redish hue of the Rocks and stones seemed to indicate that the Country abounded with Iron, and at a village called Colford about six miles from this place, I observed a boy picking stones out of a Brook, as I supposed for the purpose of making Iron, because the banks and bed of the Channel had a very ochery appearance; the boy told me they were to be carried to the furnace at Red Brook, about two miles from this place, and which today I have been to inspect.

They had run off and moulded their metal about an hour and a half before I got there, the number of Pigs were about 50 and the weight two Tons and an half. The Furnace was in Blast again, and from time to time they supplied it with ore and Charcoal; but first let me describe the Bellows, which were two, worked alternately by an overshot Water Wheel about 30 feet Diam^r; they were upon the Common principle of Kitchin Bellows about 14 feet long, four feet at the Greatest end, and tapered to the nozel, they were expanded about 4 feet in order to be filld with air, by means of a Lever loaded at the opposite End, and four Coggs upon the axis of the Water Wheel pushed them down, alternately, to give the Blast, which was very strong. I have got sketches of the Machinery, etc.

The furnace was about 30 feet high, the widest part was about 10 feet from the bottom; there, it was 10 feet Diam^r. from thence to the Top it tapered to a Yard; at the bottom where the reservoir was for the melted Iron, it was two feet Diam^r. the reservoir being two feet wide and a foot deep. The nozzels of the bellows were upon a Level with the surface of the reservoir, and the air entered at a hole about 2½ Inches Diam^r.

The Scoria (which they send to Bristol to make Bottles) began to run off while I was there (about 12 at noon), but it would be three or four next morning before the reservoir would be full of Iron, to draw off.

There were several sorts of ores, which they put in at the same time together with the Charcoal: they knew when to supply the furnace, by an Iron road about 4½ feet long suspended to another in the manner of a flail; when the materials had sunk that depth, then they put in more. There were put in, first 4 baskets of Charcoal, which held, I suppose, 3 or 4 Bushels apiece, afterwards there was put in by *weight*, 5 large *scuttle fulls of oar* from the forest of Dean (this did not require roasting) nearly the same quantity of old cinders, from works which had formerly been wrought, and about two large *scuttle fulls of oar* from near Neath in Wales. Samples of the Different Ores I have sent to Dr. Fordyce [2] by his desire, a description of which I beg leave here to subjoin, because I have not time on acc^t of the post going off to write two letters

No. 1. Is Welsh Ore, some dug and some picked up on the sea shore

No. 2. The same Ore Roasted. N. B. it is roasted in a Reverberatory Furnace, and is 2 or 3 hours adoing

No. 3. Forrest of Dean Ore dug out of Mines there, small and very magnetical, does not require Roasting—(not *magnetical*)

[2] Evidently the American Iron Company's mineralogist. A subsequent letter conveys the impression that he was also an iron-master, operating works in Great Britain.

No. 4. Larger pieces of the same

No. 5. Some Curious pieces from the Forrest of Dean.

No. 6. A Flux which they do not use, as they say it is too hot, and there is flux enough in the Dean Ore to answer the purpose of lime, &c.

No. 7. Sample of Cast Iron from Red Brook furnace

No. 8. Do of Do at a forge which produces *Red shot* Iron.

No. 9. Do of Do at a forge which produces *Cold shot* Do.

No. 10. Cast Iron from America, (they could not tell the place.)

No. 11. Do from Red Brook; makes Good Bar Iron.

The samples of the American, Red shot and Cold shot Irons I had from a forge within a ¼ of a Mile of this, but as they were not today at work I shall not have an opportunity of seeing it till Monday, when they begin to Convert pig Iron into Bar. By Saturday next I shall be at Built Breeknock Shire.[3]

On the following day, still at Monmouth, he writes, among other things:

I omitted in my last of yesterday, to mention that the Welsh ore which was roasted in a Reverberatory Furnace was done by pit Coal, or as the Workmen called it, Stone Coal . . . The Workmen seemed to smile at the ignorance of the question when I asked them whether or not they could make Iron from one sort of Ore only, answering No Sire.

I found not the least difficulty of access, and the workmen were very communicative, and a few shillings was a very agreeable present to men who with families of 6 or 7 Children earned only 12 a week. [I]f more workmen were wanted, I suppose it would not be difficult to procure them. . . .

P. S. I have sent Dr Fordyce advice of the samples. They will be in town next Friday. The Monmouth Waggon puts up at the George on Snow hill.[4]

[3] *Ibid.*, I, 37. H. S.
[4] *Ibid.*, II, 4. H. S.

This postscript gives us an inkling as to the manner in which Erskine forwarded his collection of specimens to London. In lieu of a parcel post system, the express business must have been a profitable side-line for the stage and omnibus drivers whose lumbering passenger vehicles traversed the old highroads of Merry England in the eighteenth century, having fixed routes and stated halting places. They also carried the mails. From the postmarks on the Erskine letters, it is evident that three or four days were required for them to reach London from the places at which he wrote. In those days few envelopes were used. Usually the letters were folded square, and securely sealed with wax. The obverse bore the address and usually a note as to the number of written pages therein, upon which basis—and the distance traveled—the postage to be collected from the recipient was computed. The post-officials crudely hand-stamped the name of the sending office, while the day of the month was similarly imprinted at the town to which the epistle was delivered, with a hastily scribbled notation as to the fee. The "George, on Snow Hill" was evidently a London tavern.

Making Monmouth his headquarters, Erskine proceeded to find out everything possible to be learned as to the country round-about. He writes again from this place to Atkinson, under date of Sept. 19th:

I went Yesterday to Abbey Tinton (or Trintoon as it is on the map) about 10 miles south of this on the River Way.[5] [A]s four or five miles of the road was very bad, hilly, narrow and stoney, I went round by Chepstow to come here again; at Chepstow the tide commonly rises about 54 feet per. (?) sometimes above 60 feet.

They were repairing the Furnace at Abbey Tinton so that I

[5] The River *Wye* is meant.

could not see it at work. I saw however the Ore they Smelted, which was of three Kinds, viz, Forrest of Dean, Cinders, and Lancashire. I have sent a sample of the Lancashire (and to make up a package four sorts of Copper Ore) to Dr. Fordyce. The Ore at this furnace was not, as at Red Brook, put in by weight, but left to the judgment of the Workmen, who put it in by basket fulls, about equal quantities of Each. Between the Furnace and the Forge there were large Works for Wire drawing, the whole process of which I saw.

Erskine goes on to tell of his observations of the forge at work, turning the pigs into bar-iron, etc. He says, further:

I think I have got such an Idea of all the Machinery that I need not describe it for the sake of recollection; The Workmen work by the Ton, for which they have 10 Shillings [T]here are three to an hearth, and they can make about 3 tons a week.

The Furnace at Abbey Tinton was about 30 feet High, and about 11 feet at the Widest, which was about 8 or 10 feet from the bottom. . . . the Bellows and Water-Wheel were the same dimensions as those at Red Brook, and at a Forge about 5 miles from here I was informed that the Lancashire ore made the best Iron, and they had their pig Iron from Abbey Tinton on that account. They had likewise at this forge, which is called Newnair, American Pig Iron from near New York, on which was marked "Forest of Dean," [6] which they used to make a course iron, they called mill iron. This forge consisted of 4 hearths and two hammers, besides a Slitting mill, and making plates, &c, and they have the whole water of the River Way, which is larger than the Colne at Denham.

The Lancashire ore does not require roasting, therefore be-

[6] The only American locality known as the "Forest of Dean" was—according to the subsequently executed maps of Mr. Erskine—a region in the most southerly corner of Orange County, New York Province, about 3 miles to the west of the Hudson River and about this distance northwest of Bear Mountain.

fore I leave Wales I shall endeavour to see more of their Iron works, because the nature of what is here called Welsh Ore, comes nearer to that with which I am likely to have to do. I hear of so many different works in Wales that I cannot propose to see them all, the roads and accommodations being very bad. There are some Considerable Works near Cardiff, but, as that is upon the sea, they very possibly use Lancashire ore there. The works more inland are therefore likely to answer my purpose better. To-morrow God willing I set out for Brecon, and by the end of next week hope to have seen as much as necessary in Wales. This is my fourth letter, and I hope the preceding have come to hand.[7]

On the 21st of September, Erskine is at Brecknock, in the heart of the Welsh hills. He has seen and made mental appraisements of several additional forges, one of them consisting of six hearths. His conversation with the workmen at these establishments afforded him much information and food for reflection. From them he gathered valuable data regarding ore mixtures. Reverting to the matter of the American pig iron which he had seen at Monmouth, and which interested him greatly, he says that the workmen supposed it to have been imported at Bristol.

There were two letters upon it I think W. B.: This iron I was informed was so good that it might be beat from the first forging, as small as my Whip Cord, and was used for Gun Barrels. . . . I think I can know the same species again.

Speaking of the re-melting of the pigs preparatory to forging and hammering into malleable iron ("blooms"— so called) he says:

They push the pig which was melting out of the Blast, and keep stirring the metal till it unites in one mass, about the size

7 *Ibid.*, II, 5. H. S.

and shape of a Round half-peck loaf, it is then lifted by mere strength of hand, under the hammer, by one of the forgemen; the other in the meantime regulating the Stroke, which is at first slow and gradually increases to about two beats a second. Habit certainly increases there strength very much, as a lad much more slender than I can take a Pig about and hunder'd & a half, carry it with seeming ease, and throw it behind the Fire.

Singularly enough, the above paragraph gives the only known clue as to the personal appearance of Robert Erskine. Speaking as he does of comparative degrees of slenderness, we may presume that he was, himself, of average height and physique. Certainly his language would not justify the belief that he was a giant in stature, nor one inclined or used to unusually heavy manual labor.

As to the product of the forge,—which was in actuality a great anvil and trip hammer, he tells us:

At the first operation they beat the Iron into a mass of about 18 or 20 Inches long, and about 4 Inches thick, octangular: at the next they form it with great dexterity into what shape they please, such as Bars, Implements for Plows, Waggons, &c, . . .

That Erskine was a prudent man is easy to be appreciated from what he says about the mines:

I once thought of going to the mines in the Forrest of dean, but found the access difficult, they were in general very deep, and in some places it was necessary to creep through narrow passages upon hands and knees, I suppose as the Strata of the Ore lay . . . It would hardly have been prudent in a Stranger, without attendance, or being recommended to some of the Overseers, to trust himself above an hundred yards under ground, with miners of whom he knew nothing; especially as the passages must be intricate, and accessible only to those, who by habit had acquired the dexterity of a Rat.

The letter concludes in this characteristic fashion:

> It will be necessary to carry abroad with me some of each of the different samples I procure, in case some kinds of ore be overlooked in America, which may be better than that they use. . . . I hope, God willing, to be at Hereford on my way to Birmingham tomorrow night or sooner. it has rained almost incessantly all day, which, with bad Roads makes travelling disagreeable.[8]

Erskine's letter from Birmingham, Oct. 11th, 1770, is devoted largely to explaining the manner of converting iron into steel. This is a matter of no surprise, for was not Birmingham then, even as now, a great center of industry, with the manufacture of steel first and foremost? Among other things the visitor from London observes that:

> It is only Swedish Iron that they here convert into steel. Steel made of English Iron will not Weld, &c. To make Cast Steel, it must be twice Converted . . . There is a visible difference between the steel which has once or twice undergone the operation.

It is in this letter that the writer makes reference to certain details of furnace construction, as being similar to that of Dr. Fordyce's, lending support to the theory that the latter controlled certain iron works independently. Undoubtedly Dr. Fordyce was well qualified to pass judgment upon the many samples which his trusty messenger

8 *Ibid.*, I, 30. H. S.

ceased not to dispatch for his delectation. Erskine, on the
other hand, seems to realize that he has much more to
learn than he at first supposed:

The Science of knowing the different natures and properties
of iron, is not to be acquired in a day. I must Content my self
with knowing as much of it in general as I can, and the Chief
thing necessary seems to be, to know how to make good Malleable Iron, neither Red nor Cold Shot, and how to make the best
Pig Iron to produce this kind.

Without question, the largest iron establishment and
machine shop in all England at this period was that of
Matthew Boulton—the celebrated Soho Engineering
Works at Birmingham. The fact that Erskine visited this
superbly equipped plant and had access to its various departments causes one to wonder whether or not he was
acquainted with that other young inventor and fellow
countryman, James Watt, in whom Mr. Boulton had already taken more than passing interest, and with whose
great discoveries in the realm of science his name was
soon to be associated. Erskine is enthusiastic in his recorded comments:

At Mr. Boulton's Works, Mechanics are in perfection, both
inanimate and alive, but I must give the preference to the
Machinery, some engines being so Constructed that a man or
a boy will execute the work equally well, and in many cases, a
blind man could do as well as either, at some machines the
artist not only employs his feet, and his hands, but his elbows,
by pressing down of which a material movement is effected.
Among the numerous branches here executed none are more
striking than the Derbyshire Spar, which is made into vases,
urns, Branches, Candlesticks, and a variety of ornamental
pieces of furniture, highly decorated with Chased gilt orna-

ments; the spars of a variety of colours, shining through which, has a very pleasing effect. I saw several things of this kind which were executing for his Majesty and the Queen.[9]

Erskine, on the same day, supplements the foregoing communication to Mr. Atkinson with this delightful little "touch"; separately mailed:

Tho' I am in no immediate want of money, having a Bank note and some gold remaining, yet as I have received a letter from D[r]. Fordyce to go to Backbarrow before I go to your Brothers, in case I should run short, have drawn for Ten Guineas dated Oct[r] 10, at 7 days sight payable to D[r]. W[m]. Small or order.

I have given advice of this in a Separate letter, because had it been included in my long letter of this date, it might have been overlooked, as I cannot suppose you are at leizure to read such letters on their receipt.

P. S.—My Expenses Including Drinkmoney &c. has not exceeded 12/p[r] Day.[10]

The above reference to Dr. Small provides another link in the chain of circumstantial evidence. He it was who had introduced James Watt to Matthew Boulton; and from the foregoing letter it appears that Dr. Small was sufficiently well acquainted with Erskine to feel justified in cashing his draft on London for a considerable sum.

After Erskine's brief stay in Birmingham, he plunged again into the rugged fastnesses of the outlying districts where the iron was wrested from the rocks. Writing from Shrewsbury, England, October 15, 1770, at which point he re-emerged into civilization, he tells us of his visit to Bilstone:

[9] *Ibid.*, I, 39. H. S.
[10] *Ibid.*, I, 38. H. S.

I luckily met Mr. Wilkinson at Birmingham on his journey to London, who gave me an order to see his and several other works, had I missed him I should have been much at a loss. At his furnace near Bilstone, the Bellows is an Iron Cylinder about 6 feet diam^r., Worked by a fire Engine.

Then follows a detailed account of the mechanism of said bellows, which must surely convince every one unfamiliar with the progress of science, and the surprising attempts of this period to combine the powers of fire, water and air, that the world was on the very verge of the age of steam. Be it remembered, in this connection, that only a year previously (1769) James Watt had obtained his patent for the steam engine.

Erskine also relates the minutiae incident to "the casting of a wheel for a circular fire engine"—of which operation he was a keenly observant witness; as well as the making of cast-iron pipe, now beginning to replace the much-used lead of picturesque medieval days. A burning coal pit, another unusual spectacle, draws forth the following dissertation:

The Furnace I have now described is surrounded with Coal pits, the strata of the Coal is amazingly thick, being above ten yards. While I was there, one of the pits was on fire, which they said had kindled itself: and about an hundred yards to the Eastward of the Furnace the surface (and to a Considerable depth) of the ground was all on fire, and has been burning above ten years, the ground burnt may be about an acre. On viewing this Conflagration and the Effects of it, I could not help thinking, that some Centuries hence it may afford matter of speculation to a naturalist, who, instead of the Worlds having been drowned, may produce specimens to prove that it has been burnt, for here are Calcined stones beds of Clay converted into brick, and other phenomena in abundance, perhaps native iron, for bushes and shrubs fall down through the Cracks where they may soon be converted to Charcoal, and meet with Iron ore in plenty.

In this last facetious remark, Erskine calls to mind the fact that in all furnaces an admixture of charcoal is necessary to separate the pure iron from the baser minerals in the ore, which eventually constitute the dross. Of his adventures after leaving Bilstone, he says:

From Bilstone I went by Sturbridge to Brosely, Crossing the Severn at Bridgenorth which is the most curious romantic situation I ever beheld. Near Brosely there is a very large Iron work, which his been 5 years Idle, I had an opportunity however of Inspecting the furnaces and machinery which I dare say did not cost less than 10 or 15,000 £. . . .

From Brosely to Colebrook dale is about three miles, I crossed the Severn at an horse ferry, the Boat was Connected with a Rope about 200 y^{ds}. long one end of which was fastened to a Stake, and the other passed over a pulley at the Top of the mast, so that by means of the Rope and the Rudder, the Boat swung over by the assistance of the Current only.

The writer then describes certain nice castings which he saw at iron works in the vicinity of Colebrook dale (among them iron-pots "cast so thin as the 8th of an inch," from brass patterns); speculates as to the value of "Mr. Wood's patent" for making malleable iron from coke pig-iron; and closes with this informative statement: "In this country there are Waggon Ways for several miles together in which the tracks for the wheels, are all of Cast iron!" [11]

This arrangement was, without doubt, a fore-runner of the horse-car railways of picturesque memory. Another

[11] *Ibid.*, II, 7. H. S.

letter, begun at Lancaster on the 20th of October and concluded at Kendal on the 24th of that month, chiefly concerns the mode of casting cannon, and abounds in mechanical details. For example, Erskine describes the operation of rifling the guns in this wise:

The Boring machines are very simple, the Borer or drill is fixed in the axis of a water wheel, and for cannon or things of a Small diameter, performs an equal number of Revolutions with the Wheel: if the Cylinders are very large, the Borer is upon the axis of a Small Cog Wheel, turned by a larger, on the axis of the Water wheel, which gives the last a Mechanical advantage of about 4 to one. The thing to be Bored is fixed on a Carriage, where it is adjusted paralel to the Borer. The Carriage is upon four wheels, and is moved forwards or back, by a Rope or Chain, made fast to the fore part, then passing once around a Capstan, it goes under the Carriage and round another Capstan, when it is fastened to the back part of the Carriage. A man thus easily moves the greatest weight with an handspike, and gradually advances upon the borer . . . Kendal, 24th.

I have been at Backbarrow, than which, with respect to water, there cannot be a better situation for a Manufactory, in Europe; the River, which flows from a Lake called Winander Mere, is about the size of the Colne, and, on account of the great Capacity of its fountain, is never lyable to be flooded at any season of the Year . . . I met with a kind reception from the Gentleman to whom your brothers letter was addressed, who showed me a Charcoal furnace and forge. The furnace is blown with Leather Bellows the same In every respect as I have already described, at the Forge their Bellows are Cast Iron Cylinders. The Ore is the same with the Lancashire of which I have already sent a sample, it is dug out of Pits near Ulverstone, and is delivered on board Ship at Twelve shillings p^r Ton.

The writer then plunges into a very lengthy treatise upon ore mixtures, fuel for furnaces, additions of limestone in the charging process, and his proposed visit to other furnaces and forges in the vicinity:

> However, M^r. Dixon and I were on our way to see it when we met with a Brother of Mr. Wilkinsons, with whom I turned back and spent the evening, thinking I should reap more benefit by discoursing with him than by seeing the same thing repeated. He, like his Brother with whom he is connected, has been in the Iron way, all his days and has seen, I suppose, all the Iron works in England, Scotland and Wales, and lately was in Ireland & saw several furnaces and forges there; which he went on purpose to look at. Among other Works, he told me There are furnaces at Glamorgan shire very large, particularly one belonging to Anthony Bakon, Merc^t, worked with Coke, which is Sixty feet high. . . .
>
> Last year, at Back Barrow furnace, Mr. Wilkinson tried the Experiment for making Iron of coal made of Turf or peet, which succeeded very well and I believe they are now providing a quantity of Turf and going to build a furnace for working it somewhere in the neighborhood of this.[12]

On the 27th of October, Erskine is at Temple Sowerby, Cumberland County, in the far north of England, and we find him—this time in the role of surveyor—submitting to Mr. Atkinson a diagram of an upland region which he has carefully laid out for some unexplained reason. Inasmuch as it contains two or three witty and illuminating passages, the letter is given in its entirety.

> I yesterday measured the height, &c. of Cross Fell, from a meadow at the Bridge, the following are the Data [a sketch follows.]
>
> The above is not laid down to any Scale, because when I protracted the Triangle to the Summit, to a Scale of 32 chains to an Inch, it was near 16 Inches long.

[12] *Ibid.*, I, 32. H. S.

By Calculation the Distance to the Summit from the N. point of the base is 680.90, which is 6 miles and 90 Links, and its perpend^r. Height above the Instrument which was about 4 y^{ds}. higher than the Water is 3731 which wants only 269 of half a mile to the altitude however should be added the dip of the Earth which in 6 miles I believe is nearly 17 y^{ds}. We only had time to take the altitude of Cross fell by Hadleys Quadrant. the other altitudes are by the Theodolet, however as it agreed with Hadleys to three minutes in that of Cross fell, I fancy the whole may be looked upon as pritty accurate. When the Quicksilver was first poured out, there was such a Scum upon it that totally prevented the reflection, and we were obliged to strain it through an handkerchief which took some time, &c.

The old gentleman was so civil as to remain uncovered during the Whole of our operations, which was the more polite, as he had not been so long bare headed for many days before; he put his cap on however so soon as we were done, and there it now remains.

Your Brothers have been so kind as give me letters for introducing me to two Iron works between this and Carlisle. I have likewise Drawn for £30 and shall write agian to day to mention some things I have hitherto omitted with respect to the Iron works I have seen. The post now going away I am Dear Sir,

Your most obliged hum^l Ser^t,

Robt. Erskine

P. S. As I have been longer out than I expected should be much obliged to you to desire M^r. Dixon or any of the Clerks to call on Mrs Erskine to see if she wants money.[13]

The last of this series of letters is the most lengthy— possibly the comforts of good lodgings in a fine city like Glasgow, where he had many friends and was, without doubt, very much at home, furnished the inspiration for his five sheets of manuscript. He had been wandering

[13] *Ibid.*, II, 10. H. S.

about for eight weeks, and was now drawing his journey to a conclusion, with a visit to his relatives at Dunfermline, mayhap.

Last night I came here from Carron,[14] where I was from Wednesday afternoon, till yesterday morning. M^r. Gascoigne was gone for London, which however was far from being a disadvantage, for he might have engaged me in other pursuits, and had he accompanied me through the works, my view must have been more Cursory and superficial, nor could I in his hearing have taken the liberty to ask such questions of the workmen, as I did when by myself. The mentioning my name and acquaintance with him, I found a sufficient Introduction.

They have great plenty and variety of ores, all procured in the neighborhood or brought by sea from the Coast of fife. They had indeed a small proportion of Lancashire of which they used only one Basket in ten; but an ore every way similar to this, is now found a few miles north of Stirling, for which they have only to dig about 18 feet, and when this mine is worked, all the materials will be procured from within twenty or thirty miles of the Works, Chiefly by water carriage. Except the ore like Lancashire, the rest are either strata or nodule. The difference of the ores of the Strata kind, seemed to consist chiefly in their coming from different places, for in other respects they were very similar, and in general had much the appearance of the Ore used at Kitley near Shrewsbury, being very black. The Nodules came from the opposite Coast of fife, at a place called Lime Kilns and are found on the side of an hill, lying amongst sand or Clay. Besides these, there is another kind of Iron stone picked up within high water mark on the Coast of fife, opposite to Edinburgh. Samples of several kinds I have procured; and on my way here went to see a mine of Iron stone near Kilsyth, which they will have only to convey a mile by

[14] Dr. Roebuck, founder of the great iron works at Carron, Fifeshire, Scotland (near Falkirk), was another of the friends and financial supporters of James Watt.

land Carriage to the Canal, when that Communication is opened. This mine was found by the Strata Cropping out on the banks of a Rivulet. I entered the mine by a passage in the side of the hill; there were two strata, an upper and a lower, about 5 or 6 inches apart, the upper about 5 and the Lower about four inches thick, the substance between and above the Strata was a kind of Blackish stone, which when broke, has a gritty-dark-gray appearance. There were Ores from other places the strata of which was 8 or 10 inches thick, and one kind found below or above a Coal, from one to three or four inches Thick. The stones from the sea shore had a dark redish appearance, though it was with difficulty I could find one which had not been burnt in Calcining. All the ores are Calcined on the Ground with Raw pit coal, and in the Furnaces are smelted with Coke. The Charge at one furnace was 6 baskets Coke, about Two bushels each, Ten of ore and four of limestone. They said it was 40 hours of descending to the Blast, and if two Baskets of Lancashire had been put instead of one, it would make the Iron thick like Tar.

. . . . .

At Carron, I think I have almost finished my apprenticeship in Moulding. I had before seen moulds prepared for large Boilers and Vats for Soap Boilers &c., but did not see the manner of their being made; Give me leave therefore to describe the Construction of a mould for a Large Boiler, that from thence things of a similar kind may be conceived.

He thereupon goes into another long technical description. Writing as to the process of casting a large vessel, he says:

To cast this Vessel the metal runs in at the Center of the bottom being Cast the mouth downwards. The space which formed the thickness is filled with Common air, this air cannot well escape at the hole where the metal Runs. There are therefore three or four holes perforated in the outside cover, to let it get out; and that it may evacuate the faster, so soon as the metal begins to run, lighted straw is held over the air holes which immediately sets it on fire, these holes are filled up with metal which is easily broke off, and the surface is Chizeled smooth like the rest: but I should have mentioned that when the outside is replaced it is loaded with a great number of weights to prevent the liquid metal from buoying it up, which, if it did, the metal would Escape at the bottom, Run away among the sand and occasion Explosions both terrible and fatal to every one near it; such accidents have happened.

Erskine then proceeds to explain the casting of iron cannon, pots, pans and their covers, bath-stoves, rollers, smoothing irons, gates, box-irons (in four-piece moulds), etc., and tells, incidentally, that the scoria from the blast furnaces was, on occasion, used for ship-ballast, being ordered for that purpose. He tells us that the anvils at the Carron works, instead of being fixed in a large block of wood, "stand in a Mass of Cast Iron about a yard Diam^r. and near 4 feet thick. There was, likewise at the forge a water-wheel which turned a lathe and two grindstones the Construction of which is simple and easily Conceived."

Cannon here are Moulded Exactly as at M^r. Wilkinsons at Bersham (the iron rod for the cores is ground), but they are cast directly from the smelting furnace, which must require great care in the Charges, and I should be affraid the Metal of a Cannon would sometimes turn out to be of different kinds in the same piece. The Boreing too is very similar, only the Carriages do not run upon wheels: they have a separate Wheel for Cutting off the Mass at the mouth of the Cannon, at M^r. Wilkinson's the same Wheel & carriage serves both purposes.

I saw the manner of moulding variety of different things, such as pots with the frames of the Mould Cast Iron, pans & their covers, Bath stoves, Rollers, smoothing irons, gates, box irons—the mould of which is in four pieces, &c., &c., which it is needless particularly to describe; for from knowing the general principles of casting, the manner of executing any particular piece of work, may with a little thought and attention be easily conceived. The fire clay is found above a coal and ground between rollers. The moulding sand is mixed with charcoal dust; —a fine sort of sand, the grain very small, is procured from the new Canal. If holes are required in plates (such as the cheeks of bath stoves), pellets of dried sand are stuck in the mould.[15]

To this letter, moreover, is appended a list of fourteen samples of ore, &c., which Erskine states he has forwarded to "Mure Son & Atkinson." It may be conjectured that the first named partner was the "Muir" to whom reference will be made in later pages of this biography.

Some two months now elapse. Of the activities of Erskine during this interval we have no record. In the early days of 1771, however, occurred an incident which must have caused him to waver in his determination to go abroad, for there came to him, as bleak January was drawing to its close, the coveted distinction of fellowship in the Royal Society of London—indication enough that, by dint of continued application and effort, his future was assured in the homeland. The reason for the award of this fellowship, and its surrounding circumstances, had for months been a subject of much speculation on the part of the writer. From Erskine's papers it was evident that his "Centrifugal Engine for raising water" was exhibited before the Royal Society and that he had personally read a descriptive paper thereon, on which occasion "both engine and paper were universally approved." [16] For further enlightenment, however, an inquiry was addressed to the officers of that erudite body—ancient, honorable and

[15] *Ibid.*, II, 12, 14. H. S.
[16] Erskine Papers.

still very much alive—which elicited the following response, completely solving the question as to the why and wherefore of the "F.R.S." which Erskine was entitled to append to his name:

The Royal Society
Burlington House
London, W. 1,
May 24th, 1923.

Dear Sir,

In reply to your enquiry of the 7th instant, I have looked up the original certificate of Robert Erskine and find it recorded thereon as his qualification for election that he was "A Gentleman well versed in Mathematics and Practical Mechanics." He was elected a Fellow of the Royal Society on January 31st, 1771, at which date his residence was stated to be Scotland Yard, London. Among the signatories of his certificate were Sir John Pringle, Bart., President of the Society from 1772 to 1778, and Benjamin Franklin.

I am, Yours faithfully,
F. A. Towle
Assistant Secretary.[17]

A. H. Heusser Esq.,
140 East 25th St.
Paterson, N. J., U. S. A.

No one but an amateur biographer can understand the thrill which came with the reading of this reference to great Franklin, opening up an entirely new field for interesting speculation. Sir John Pringle (1707–1782) was a distinguished physician and author of books and lectures upon Hygiene. He spent many years of his life in Scotland, and was at one time a professor in the University of Edinburgh. Undoubtedly he was a friend and patron of Robert Erskine.

[17] *The Manor and Forges of Ringwood*, III, 24 B.

In 1753, the Royal Society of London had elected Benjamin Franklin to membership on the strength of his discovery that lightning and electricity were manifestations of the same natural force—this discovery being the result of the famous experiment of the key tied to a kite-string during a thunder storm. Franklin had been in London since 1764 representing the American Colonies (being their most distinguished spokesman), endeavoring to combat the short-sighted policy of the King and the British ministry. Not until 1775 did he return to America. In the interim, as may well be imagined, he moved in the most select and scientific circles; and it seems apparent that he and Erskine must somehow have met and formed a mutually-profitable acquaintance. As to the intimacy of these relations, we are not likely to know more than the inference to be drawn from the high compliment paid by the scholarly Franklin in his endorsement of Erskine as a desirable candidate for co-fellowship in the Royal Society. It is evident that Erskine had, by the exercise of his talents, made a place for himself among the chosen few of his day and age—the mental aristocrats who constitute the true "nobility." Having gained the confidence of such men as Pringle and Franklin (the latter already internationally honored and esteemed), it is plainly to be seen that Erskine was himself a man out of the ordinary, and one whose future would have been a brilliant success had he chosen to remain an Englishman.

5

The Long Voyage

TEMPTED though Erskine may have been to abrogate his engagements with the American Iron Company by reason of this highly-to-be-desired recognition, be it recorded to his credit that he considered himself firmly bound for better or for worse, and he hesitated not to fulfill his contract to the letter. With characteristic prudence and forethought he "set his face like a flint" and began careful and elaborate preparations for his long voyage. Be it remembered, moreover, that in those days the trans-Atlantic journey to America was no vacation jaunt: usually it meant years of separation or a permanent severing of all homeland ties. No thinking man can thus cut the cables and launch out into the unknown without many misgivings as to his own sufficiency. Thoughts of bidding farewell to life-long friends and associations lead one, involuntarily, to dependence upon that great and omniscient Providence beyond Whose love and care we cannot drift. It is therefore not at all surprising to read the words of Erskine, naturally devout, in a letter addressed to his widowed sister-in-law, Mrs. Henry Erskine, dated Jan. 23, 1771, in which—following an account of his prospects in America,—he says: "I hope we shall always recollect that here we are only passengers: that we may remember the better country, where many of our dear friends have gone before us." [1]

That those whom he was to leave behind regarded the American venture with equal concern is manifest by the words of Erskine's cousin, the Rev. James Fisher of Glasgow, in a letter of farewell addressed to him at London, in March, 1771. He hopes that the letter arrives "before you sail for America, as you propose about the End of this Month. Whether I shall ever have another Opportunity of meeting you again in this Life is known only to him who is the sole and sovereign disposer of all Events. . . ." [2]

Erskine made his arrangements and wound up his business affairs as though, by some intuitive premonition, he realized that he would never again see the heather-covered hillsides of his native Scotia, nor walk the busy streets of London. Original drafts of two letters written by him on the 1st of March, 1771, have come to light, together with a memorandum of points which he deemed it desirable to incorporate into his final agreement with the American Company. A careful perusal of these manuscripts gives the impression that Erskine was by no means certain as to the outcome of his venture, either for himself and her who was dependent upon him, or for the proprietors. The first of the letters, while addressed to Richard Atkinson personally, presents a frank statement of Erskine's hopes and fears for the consideration of his

[1] Printed in Rev. Donald Fraser's *Life and Diary of Rev. Ralph Erskine*.
[2] Erskine Papers.

prospective employers. The other communication is for
Atkinson's eye only, being an even more candid avowal
of his determination to deal fairly with all men, yet to
protect himself withal. Both of these epistles, presenting
as they do the "pros and cons" of the situation, with many
illuminating passages, deserve reproduction in full. This
is the formal letter:

As there is a great difference between acting for a Company,
and doing business for a private person, the first being lyable
both to a change of men and measures, whereas the latter has
a fixed opinion to pursue on which he cannot be control'd, I
have no doubt you will excuse the anxiety I show, to have every
part of both my duty and reward, expressed in as explicit and
certain terms as possible, for whatever my friends & the present
proprietors may kindly intend in my favour, their purposes
may afterwards be frustrated by a plurality of voices.

I am very far from desiring a reward I do not merit, and till
it is found by experience, that from my presence in America, a
general advantage has ensued, I do not even wish for the smallest adition to my salary, but if good effects follow, then and
not before let the agreement, now to be explicitly expressed,
commence.

From the passages which now ensue it will be apparent
that the writer was by no means unfamiliar with what
was transpiring in America; evidently he had been put
into possession of all the facts in so far as the proprietors
knew them:

M^r. Faesch the present manager has in some degree acquitted
himself to the satisfaction of the Company, a favourable circumstance for me, as it shows the undertaking is not desperate. Our
being upon the most amicable terms, as you recommended, will
certainly be for the Companies interest, I may profit by his ex-

perience of the works upon the spot, and he may reap advantage from the knowledge I have here acquired in Britain. I see no reason therefore, why, by a mutual interchange of sentiments, the Improvements at Charlottenburgh, may not keep pace with those of Ringwood, if it is in my power to make Such a method of proceeding, if must be of immediate advantage to the Company. This is the very point however, on which a difference of sentiments may arise if it is now left undecided; some, on finding that the general profits on the Iron, and stores are increased, may think I deserve 5 pct. on the net proceeds of the whole— the light in which I always understood it, whereas others may reckon me entitled only to so much on the works under my immediate Inspection, and alledge something is due M^r. Faesch. The allegation may, and I hope will be just, God forbid I could harbour a wish to deprive any man of his due, but then, I wish to go to America to act for the general good of the Company but not as a foil to whet anothers Industry, and raise a competition for the preference. From your own knowledge others have not only reapd the fruits of my Ingenuity, but even grudged me the honour of my inventions. if possible, I will avoid this for the future, and would therefore shun the risque. My Idea of going to America is as a General manager, and if general good results, and the Iron at the works immediately under my inspection and elsewhere, Improves in quality and quantity, I shall hope my claim in the general success will be allowed.

When I accepted of 200 G^s a year Salary, I the more readily acquiesced, as the share proposed was the object recommended to my attention, this I always viewed in a general light, and it cannot be thought unreasonable to fix that in such a manner now, that there may be no difference hereafter, especially if it be considered that I have given up all my prospects here, that I am going to devote the prime of life to the Companies service, and that I have declined all present business, as I did last week when the Dean and Chapter of Westminster wanted me to plan all their Estates, D^r. Blair having procured an order for that purpose, I having at times formerly been employed by them at the Rate of 5 G^s a week when I incurred no expense and they were satisfied both with my price and performance. . . .

If it is thought proper to continue two managers, I have not the least objection, the extent of the works seem to require it, the Burthen will be less, and it will be much for the Companies interest, in case of the death of one, but then the other may be rewarded as the Company think proper, if things flourish, they will afford it. As to myself, I would not willingly enter into a situation from whence uneasiness and jealousies might arise, which certainly would be the consequence of any kind of competition. This however may be totally avoided by making the Companies Interest and mine the same, and laying my recompense on the Whole of the Iron as proposed, for from various accidents such as a failure of charcoal and ore, the discovery of better ore, & many other such like occurrences One set of works may become abundantly more valuable than another.

From these considerations, I flatter myself that the Company will take what I say in its proper light, as my design is not to direct, but to give my sentiments of the manner in which I can serve them most faithfully, and their Intentions I have no doubt are to give me every proper encouragement.[3]

The companion note, in which Erskine opens his heart to Mr. Atkinson, comes as near to being autobiographical as anything else extant from his facile pen:

Dear Sir I have wrote the enclosed which if you think proper may be communicated to the Company, it being an act of justice and honesty in me to lay my sentiments Candidly before them. With respect to myself I cannot have forgot the abject state to which I was reduced some years ago, nor can I ever fail calling to mind your kindness in suffering me to be a burthen to you,

---

[3] *Ibid.*, I, 43. To get the above text, Heusser pieced together various parts of the rough draft of a letter, some of which had been crossed out by Erskine. The paragraphing is Heusser's. H. S.

and myself. At that time I would have cheerfully embraced the offer of going to America even with half my present appointment—not that I was less qualified to provide for myself then than now, but if a persons dependence is on a Commodity which nobody wants, he must of course starve, be it ever so valuable. I am thus free in acknowledging my sentiments & obligations to prevent the most distant suspicion of ingratitude, which were it to rise in the bosom of such a friend would hurt me as much as anything I ever met with. I have had such proof of your Benevolence, even with many, to a fault that I know only one, who, similarly situated, would have followed your footsteps.

I could heartily rejoice in such a knowledge of the rest of the Company as would induce me to place half the confidence on them as on you, but that is at present impossible to acquire. I am sure then you will not blame me for endeavouring to put every thing on as firm a footing as I can, for I have already suffered severely by fair professions, and since Providence has given me the opportunity (and the only plausible one I have yet met with) of being in a way to do justice to the world, living happily in it and providing for old age should I see that period I should fail in my duty to my friends, to the World, & to my self, if I did not pay it a proper attention.

While it pleases God to spare you, I have no doubt of justice being done me as far as your influence extends, but a true knowledge of mankind can only be acquired in the school of adversity. [I] beg to conclude by assuring you that in anything I have said I do not mean to dictate, but only to discover my sentiments for your approbation or amendment, and that in everything I shall be guided by your advice and Directions.[4]

A still existing sheet headed "Summary of the Instructions which Mr. Erskine expects to receive from the American Company" is a much interlineated and be-scribbled "original draft," wherein he has endeavored to set forth the terms of a hide-bound agreement by which

[4] *Ibid.*, I, 45. The paragraphing is Heusser's. H. S.

he shall not be the loser. It is a personal memorandum or brief, but it dove-tails nicely with other fragments of the documentary story of Ringwood and its Revolutionary iron-master:

1st That he will inform himself particularly and minutely of the state of the Iron Works as they are at present Carried on, and transmit the Account by the first opportunity, with his observations on their defects and the method he would propose to remedy what is amiss, and particularly annex his reasons for every proceeding or alteration he may propose.

2d That he shall order no material alteration till he has the Companies Consent transmitted from England, but in trivial matters, not exceeding the usual common expenses of the Company, he may proceed according to his own judgment by Common Expenses Mr. E. means Repairs of machinery, Securing Dams, making such regulations or alterations in the present mode of proceeding with the workmen, miners and Colliers as shall appear to be of advantage to the Company, improvements in the bellows. . . . [B]y material alterations, M^r. E. means Rebuilding furnaces or other Works Introducing new Manufactures such as Casting Vessels, &c.

3 That he shall minutely inspect the Ores now used, and send proper samples of Each kind, and also make tryals of any new earths or stones which he may judge to be ore, & which may have been overlooked, and send Samples, &c.

4 That he shall furnish the Company with such maps and drawings of all their land and property as shall, to the best of his ability, convey an adequate and Clear Idea of the whole of their Concerns in America.

5 That he shall punctually follow the instructions he may receive for the regulation of the Stores and the manner of keeping the Accounts, and likewise attend to the mode in which provisions of all kinds are furnished and make such regulations as appear beneficial to the Company.

6 That he shall as soon as possible transmit an Exact inven-

tory of the stores and everything belonging to the Company and punctually the instructions he may receive for the future regulations of the warehouse.

[7] That at all Convenient times he shall take the advice of the present agents in N. Y., and Communicate his intentions to them in any alterations he proposes; and should they happen to differ with him, he shall defer his proceedings till he receives orders from England.

[8] That as besides Iron the Comp^y had the growth of hemp & the manufacture of Potash in view, he shall after the Iron works are fully regulated attend to those objects, but not before; it being impossible to pay a proper regard to Many different objects at once

[9] That he shall freely and fully Communicate every circumstance which occurs to him or which may come to his knowledge for the Benefit & advantage of the Company and Their property. . . .

[10] In Consideration of M^r. E giving up his other business of Surveying and Engineering since the beginning of Augt last his salary shall Commence from that time

That his travelling expenses (his and Mrs. E.'s passage to America) be allowed, and in case of Mr. E.'s death within two years of his arrival in America, Mrs. E. shall have her passage paid, if she chooses to return, and £—— on her arrival in England.

M^r. E's salary shall be 200 Gs p^r an.,[5] and as a farther Encouragement he shall have a share 5 p^ct of the net proceeds after deducting all expenses on the Goods produced from the Companies lands & manufactories, sold in England or at any other markit.

That a Certificate, under the hand of any two of the Comp^y Mr E., shall appoint of the am^t of Profits shall be transmitted him for the specification of his share.

---

[5] According to entries in Erskine's American books of account and as shown also in the "Erskine Papers," his salary was eventually calculated as being the equal of £370 per annum.

That if the works are transferred to other hands, M^r. & M^rs. E's passage to England shall be allowed.

That the Salary and Allowance of 5 p^rc^t as above shall be in lieu of all Commission, Exchange, brokers Brokerages or other demands whatever for M^r. Es Transacting the Comp^ys business in America, except Extra Travelling Charges and occasional residence at New York.[6]

It is to be presumed that these stipulations formed the basis of the agreement finally consummated between Erskine and the proprietors of the Company, for there seems to have been no serious hitch in the proceedings at this juncture. The exact date of his departure for America is not known; that it was subsequent to the 9th of April, 1771, there can be no doubt, because of the testimony provided by a bill for tailoring, receipted upon that date by one William Graham of London, totalling £72.2.5. Hence we infer that Erskine was in the metropolis shortly before he set sail, outfitting himself for the long journey. If we are to judge by the following items from Grahame's invoice, our hero was by no means prejudiced against the wearing of fine raiment:

To Mak^g 6 prs. of Linnen Drawers	£1. 1.—
To 4 Superfine Stock^g. Pieces	1.16.—
Cleaning a Suit of Dark Colour	—. 2. 4
9 yds. Rich Blue Long Pild velvett	4.19.—[7]

We have no knowledge as to the port from which Erskine set forth on his fateful and epoch-making journey, although it was most likely London, because in those days the Thames was fully adequate to accommodate the

6 *Ibid.*, I, 47. H. S.
7 Erskine Papers.

meagre draught of the largest ocean-going vessels. That the name of the ship in which he took passage was the *Britannia*, and that she was commanded by Captain Miller, we learn from Erskine's surviving manuscripts and letters.

When a boy, I was impressed by the assertion that one could judge the status of a family by the contents of the van which moved their effects when they migrated from one apartment to another. If this be true, we have the means of taking the measure of "the Erskines" by the "List of Goods belonging to M^r. Robt. Erskine, Ship^t on Board the Britannia Miller for New York, marked R. E." I think it interesting enough to copy, because it shows how well equipped was he with the implements of his profession; besides having books to feed the mind, jellies to soothe the palate, soap wherewith to keep clean his person, and clothes aplenty to shield it from the cold. The last item refers, most likely, to the worldly possessions of a servant who probably accompanied the travelers. The figures represent a value in pounds sterling:

Case Tin Ware, value	4. 4.——
Cask Crucibles	1.18.——
[3 cases] Chemicals	——.——.——
4 D°	——.——.——
5 D°	——.——.——
6 D° Glass Retorts, &c.	——.——.——
D°	50.——.——
D° Linin	50.——.——
Bureau & contents	20.——.——
Round headed Trunk [instruments]	40.——.——
Old Chist, Books, &c.	15.——.——
D°—Sundries	10.——.——
Case Soap	2.——.——
D° Ores	5.——.——

D° Jellys	1.—.—
Three Hat Cases	6.—.—
Small p^t Mantua Trunk	10.—.—
Bag with Books	10.—.—
Close Trunk not matted	30.—.—
Tea Bd., Glasses & Pictures	1.—.—
Ins^ts Corded Together	11.—.—
Bedding	6.17.—
Rulers & Staves	2.10.—
Box, marked "J. MUSON"	5.—.—[8]

[8] *The Manor and Forges of Ringwood*, I, 34. B. H. S.

6

In a Strange Land

ERSKINE arrived in America on the 5th of June, 1771, New York being his port of entry. His impressions had best be recorded in his own words and from copies of his own letters. Fortunately some of them are preserved to-day; it was, in fact, the discovery of these letters by the author, while engaged in private research work, which furnished the inspiration for this biographical volume.[1]

It was Erskine's habit to keep the original copies of all his outgoing correspondence. In other words, he first wrote the epistle as the thoughts shaped themselves in his mind. Then he appears to have re-read and corrected, freely interlineating and revising. Finally he copied the letter in its revised entirety and dispatched it to its destination, retaining the first "rough draft" for his records. The specimens which have passed through my hands, and from which I now propose freely to quote, have been these

[1] See the introduction to this book. H. S.

self-same originals. The letters which passed over-seas will, most likely, never be recovered nor located. With commendable forethought, Erskine usually signed his record copies in full, and hence left for posterity a few of his exceedingly rare autographs.

The following communication is addressed to Richard Willis, Esq., of London (presumably a stock-holder of the American Iron Company and a personal friend of Erskine). It is dated at New York, July the 9th, 1771, and is—quite evidently—one of his earliest messages from America. I take the liberty of interrupting his narrative for the better understanding of the reader, but have not attempted to revise the text.

Sir

My last was a few lines of July 5th by the Packet, informing you of my return from the Works, the account of which I postponed till another opportunity, as she was just getting under Way when I arrived.

The country through which Mr Faesch & I travelled was pleasant and well peopled, and the Roads in general pretty good till within a few miles of the Works. We called at several places by the way, where we were kindly received, Mr Faesch having Cultivated a friendship with Most of the Gentlemen & justices of the province, which is of great service to the Iron Works, particularly the saving the Company a great deal of the Expense of Roads, for where it is the King's Highway, they are mended by the Country upon complaint being properly made.

The roads indeed not only want repair in many places, but a director to repair them properly, for several places are mended with Wood, where they might be done much more effectually with the stones upon the Spot; a few soldiers, who in this Country are lying Idle, would in one season make them many degrees better than at present, were they properly directed.

The mountainous and disagreeable situation of the Works, was worse in Idea than reality. I question if there is an Hill in view two hundred yards perpendicular, and tho' in some places the roads are stony and steep, yet I don't Imagine it would be difficult or very expensive to mend them, as there are plenty of materials everywhere.

The situation of Ringwood is tollerable, but has nothing about it enchanting, the Mansion house has been patched together at different times, which makes it a very acquard piece of architecture.[2] The furnace is in Blast, but the Bellows are old and not so good as at the other Works, which were built under Mr Faeschs direction; whereas Ringwood is a Work of thirty years standing. There the water wheel is exposed; but at Charlotteburg, &c., the wheel is under Cover, and by means of Stoves may be kept in motion when the frosts are pretty severe.

At Longpond the furnace seems better and more advantageously situated than at Ringwood, to be free from damps, &c. The great pond has been drained (to its natural Level) about 16 or 20 months ago: the country people complained much of it, and unless this had been done the workmen would have relinquished the spot, it rendered the place so unwholesome; there is however at present abundance of water without it, and perhaps some provision for a dry season may be found, not attended with such inconvenience.

Charlotteburg has the best supply of water in appearance, and tho at first view the situation is more confined than at Ringwood, yet the Rapid Current of a fine river between hills which rise sharply on each side, gives the Idea of its being a more healthy situation. It is a pity the Hibernia mine which supplies Charlotteburg is at such a distance from the furnace, not only because the ore is Carried 6 or 7 miles, but Mr Faesch likeways is obliged to pay Ld Stirling 3^s/ a Ton for it besides. [H]ere the bellows are superior to those at the other works, and the ore seems better too. Unluckily by mistake of the Waterman I

---

[2] From an advertisement which appeared in the *New York Herald*, Nov. 5, 1803, when the estate and its 6,200 acres were again offered for sale, I have it that the old Ringwood Manor House was a building in size about 30 feet deep by 62 feet front.

cannot forward some samples to Dr Fordyce by this opportunity.

The "Lord Stirling" of whom Erskine writes is, of course, William Alexander, titular Earl of Stirling, our own Revolutionary General, who owned the controlling interest in the Hibernia Iron Mines of Morris County. Apparently the London Syndicate had been purchasing a portion of the output of these ore beds.

At all the Works the Forge and Furnace men are under very good discipline. Their method of making Bar Iron is different from that of England, and seems to be attended with greater dispatch and saving of fewel.

Form the general view of the Country I think we may hope to find more ore and as the best ores in England are not at all Magnetical, I shall propose to Mr. Faesch to attempt some other ways of searching as well as by the needle, and as I find tho he certainly understands his business he is a person of Candour and not at all Conceited, I have not the least doubt he and I shall agree very well, and that any scheme which appears reasonable will be readily adopted by both of us—

It will be seen that, at this early stage of the game, Erskine expressed great confidence in John Jacob Faesch. This faith and trust, as we shall see, gradually gave place to suspicion and open hostility; yet both Erskine and Faesch were destined to prove true friends to the land of their adoption. But to proceed:

At Cortland there is enough of Water for a Furnace, but not for a forge; in other respects it is the only place for an Iron works, which Mr. Hasenclever in his hurry to provide a settlement for M^r. Faesch and his men, seems to have Chosen with judgment, for the Iron from Ringwood is Carried to Haverstraw 25 miles—from Longpond to Hackensack 27 miles,—from Charlotteburg to Acquackanonck 22 miles land carriage,—whereas the furnace at Cortland is within a mile of the great North River.

The "Cortland Furnace," of which Erskine here makes mention, was situated in Westchester County, New York Province, to the east of the Hudson River, not far from the outlet of Phillips Pond, between the modern villages of Crugers and Oscawanna. About it very little is known.

Quite informative, however, is the reference to the land transportation of ore and pig iron. From it we learn of three recognized outlets for the product of the American Iron Company's workings: i. e.,—to the Hudson River by way of Haverstraw; to the Hackensack River (probably at River Edge); and to the Passaic River at Acquackanonck Landing. By these three routes the refined mountain ore found its way to tidal streams and the open sea.

But I must beg leave to defer several particulars with respect to ores, mines, Cortland, &c till an other opportunity, and mention one great error which I perceive has hitherto taken place in Conducting the works by different managers, between whom there has subsisted a Constant Rivalship, which naturally arose from the works being under distinct heads. Instead of acting as if the works belonged to the same Company it was their business to strive to outdo each other to obtain your favour. At present, if any thing is to spare at one of the works it is freely lent to the other, &c. which was a new Circumstance, and far from the Case when the Works were separate.

If Erskine had lived in our day and age, he would have made an ideal "efficiency man" in some large industrial plant. In many of his English letters he harped upon his favorite strings,—co-operation in management and unity of effort, with the welfare of the whole enterprise as an incentive. Now, in America, we find his early opinions strongly confirmed. He aptly summarizes the situation in this wise:

There are many things which render it impossible for the different works to be either now or hereafter upon the same footing in every respect. At some the ore is farther to Carry than at an an other, the ore, too, may and does unavoidably differ in quality, Charcoal made of young wood is better than that of old; the Roads more Convenient and the distances different, wood may fail in one place and grow up in another, ores may fail and be found which would entirely alter the face of things. Could good ore be found for Cortland, it would have great advantages over the other furnaces by its proximity to the River, from these and many other Circumstances your managers in future should I think act in Concert for the good of the whole, without having separate Interests, and the property of the same Company dismembered again, and as all the works can be visited in a few days; the place of residence of a manager is very immaterial, tho' indeed if they agree in their plan of operations before hand, they certainly may diminish each others care greatly, for from what I have already seen— it seems too much for one to attend to the whole.[3]

The first summer in America was an exceedingly busy one for Erskine; during which time he became acclimated not only to the antics of the thermometer and the elements, but to the eccentricities of Faesch and his polyglot employees. It is evident that he was regarded as an interloper; one sent out from London to maintain an unwelcome check upon the operations of Faesch, which— quite naturally—was not to the liking of the latter. The

[3] *The Manor and Forges of Ringwood*, II, 15, 16. H. S.

situation was, indeed, very much like that recorded in the Scriptural parable wherein the "Lord of the vineyard" sent a trusty messenger to ascertain just what the supposedly "unfaithful husbandmen" were doing in the far country. I doubt not that Faesch and his henchmen (to whom Erskine refers in the next communication to Mr. Willis of London—which I copy in part) would have been exceedingly gratified had he speedily come to grief, or fallen into instant disfavor and been summarily recalled. Again, in quoting Erskine's own words, I avail of the privilege of editorial comment:

Ringwood October 31st, 1771

Sir

My last was of Sept. 16th from New York by the packet of which I likewise left a duplicate to be sent by the first ship, since which I have received to Companies favour of Augt 7th. [I]t gives me great satisfaction to find that my conduct has met with their approbation, only I am sorry to observe that the alarm of the works being in danger has reached across the Atlantic. I have wrote very fully already in my several letters which must long before this be come to hand, and as in the I continued to follow my original plan of representing things as they appear at the time, and in which I shall persevere, I have no doubt that ere now you are convinced the alarm of either Mr Faesch or the workmens quitting the Works was a false one, with respect to the latter I am now satisfied, that if there was any alarm in the Case among them, it was the fear of being turned away for this good reason, that there are no Iron works in America where they can get better wages or even as good as here nor anywhere else are they so sure of their money, nay some who were represented as the most ticklish have been making their Court to me in case of accidents.

As to the former, I very much doubt that he had any determined intention of qutting your employ either. I now think the whole treatment received was only a Concerted scheme between Mess^re. Yates Kemp and Faesch to puzzle and alarm me, because M^r. Faesch has acknowledged he was apprised of my Coming six weeks before I arrived, and therefore my appearance could not have been so abrupt as they pretended to give out, they had sufficient time to lay the plan for my reception, but as to the reasons for their behavior it is a mystery which perhaps may best be explained on your side the water for my own part, I have not yet got to the Bottom of it. Perhaps, from the character Capt. Miller might give, of my quiet and easy & possibly silly disposition, they expected I would return again immediately with him, for I must say that—till they had the perusal of my letter to M^r. Jackson, the treated me more like a fool than a man of sense. However tho my puzzles and alarms have been long over, I believe theirs still continue. M^r. Faesch is now at York,[4] where he had been once or twice before since the last packet, and I shall be neither alarmed or surprised at any new project which may be set on foot to get rid of such a disagreeable visitor.

Here Erskine acknowledges the fact that his presence among his colleagues is not at all a pleasure from their point of view. Yates and Kemp seem to have been the New York City factors of the London Syndicate. In concert with Faesch they appear to have feigned surprise at Erskine's appearance upon the scene; which farce, however, he soon penetrated. Captain Miller, already referred to, was the sailing master of the vessel which brought him from England; the identity of "Mr. Jackson" I do not know, although he may have been one of the iron-masters of Morris County, N. J., of whom several bore that name during the days of the Revolution. It is certain that,— notwithstanding the obstacles placed in his way,—Erskine employed his first four months in America to good advantage:

[4] New York City.

Perhaps I am to be threatened with M[r]. Faeschs going to Andover Works in Pennsylvania, as I have heard a flying report that he had taken them, but any scheme to prevent my answering the purposes for which I came will not take effect, now that I know something of the country and of which their bad success at the beginning I think might convince them. I hope however the next instructions I receive, which I expect to be the establishing M[r]. Faesch and I as joint managers over the whole will put an end to all further embarrassments, and then we shall go on Cooly & quietly for your advantage; in which I flatter myself there are some prospects of success, for tho I have as yet discovered no new mines myself yet two have made their appearance since I came here, one on your land at Charlotteburg, where they have not got to the right vain yet and an other within a mile of long pond furnace, which has been tried in the furnace and forge, and makes exceedingly good, tough Iron.

M[r]. Faesch denies positively his ever insinuating that the mines were likely to fail; therefore as you must know the quarter from whence that intelligence came you will be enabled to judge properly of the person who sent it. The long pond mine is only begun to be worked now; it has been acknowledged by one of the overseer's wives to M[rs]. Erskine that they had some *suspicions* of such a thing two years ago. I am preparing large samples of all the ores for D[r]. Fordyce and getting the boundaries of your Lands marked out by the surveyor who laid them out at first previous to my survey; which now the Woods begin to be a little clear, I shall soon begin upon.

Erskine's experience in Great Britain as an hydraulic engineer had made him keenly alive to the possibilities of applying his inventive genius to the improvement and greater efficiency of the water power at the Ringwood forge. He realized, as had Hasenclever before him, that the Ringwood River was at best a little stream; but, far from emulating the former's costly experiments with aqueducts to convey water from the far distant Tuxedo

Pond, we see him attempting conservation in his own dooryard:

On the Stream from the Forge which passes by our door, I have made a flood gate which draws and shuts of itself, as the forge hammer is or is not at work; the more water comes down, the higher the gate rises, and the Contrivance is very much liked, as a simple and easy expedient to prevent accidents in all dams whatsoever. There are two buoys in two buoy boxes on either side the gate with which they are Connected. The Boxes are the whole height of the Dam and have a small apperture to let the water run out of them but not so quick as it can run in if the water rises an inch, and when the gate is shut the buoys are within an inch of the bottom, whenever the water rises so high as to run into the buoy boxes, the buoys float, and consequently draw the gate. If the water comes in such quantities as to fill the boxes, the gate is drawn almost the whole height of the dam; when the water subsides and no longer runs into the boxes, the water in them runs out, and the weight of the gate and the buoys sink and shut of themselves. The gate runs upon rollers and moves with the greatest ease.[5]

There is much more mechanical detail in this letter, but I believe I have given enough to show Erskine's method of procedure, in contrast to that of his predecessors. To-day, although all traces of these ancient contrivances have disappeared, I cannot contemplate the turbulent Ringwood brook (which has once more reverted to its original ways) without thinking of Robert Erskine and the thrift which prompted him in his praiseworthy efforts to turn even these meagre waters to good account, and to harness them into service.

[5] *The Manor and Forges of Ringwood,* II, 19. This is a rough first draft, the parts of which were crossed out as Erskine wrote his finished letter. The paragraphing is Heusser's. H. S.

In view of the fact that circumstances beyond his control made it imperative for Robert Erskine to have almost
daily intercourse with Mr. Faesch,—whom he seems
never fully to have understood because of differences in
training and temperament,—it might not be amiss, at
this juncture, to set down a few facts as to the latter's
career. It is much easier for us to appraise his worth than
it was for Erskine, who knew only Faesch's record of past
and present performances, whereas we have at our disposal the more satisfactory chronicles of his latter years.

John Jacob Faesch was probably a Swiss, although by
some authorities it is claimed that he was a native of
Hesse Cassel.[6] He was brought to America by Hasenclever
in 1765 because of his fitness for the particular character
of the work to be done in connection with the manufacture of iron, and very soon came to be regarded as his
chief lieutenant. Faesch was, however, kept somewhat in
the background by Hasenclever, and of his brief tenure of
individual management at Ringwood after the latter's recall but little is known. It is said that he was able to urge
on his German workmen to the maximum of productivity
because of his ability to upbraid them in their native
tongue. With the coming of Erskine, Faesch (who had
been engaged under a seven year contract with the London proprietors) seems at once to have regarded the inter-
ference with his conduct of the works as being tanta-
mount to a challenge. Although they labored jointly for
some months, the barrier of competition which existed
between them prevented anything like true cordiality in
their relations.

Yet, notwithstanding all this, Faesch became locally
known as "the smart little Dutchman"; and when, hav-

[6] See article by Rev. Joseph Tuttle, in the *Proceedings of the New Jersey
Historical Society*, Second Series, Vol. II (1870–1872).

ing withdrawn from a participation in the management
of Ringwood, he established himself at the Mount Hope
Iron Works (Feb. 1, 1773), he became—like Erskine—a
friend and citizen of struggling America, and placed himself on record as being well worthy the land of his adoption. At Mount Hope he occupied a position akin to that
of the master of Ringwood. Both he and Erskine served
the infant American nation most acceptably, and each of
them merits the respect of posterity.

Faesch's house at Mount Hope, on one occasion, was
visited by Washington, and, as a result of the conference,
he was given permission to employ a considerable number of Hessian prisoners at his iron works, which were
devoted largely to the manufacture of pots and utensils
for the use of the patriot army. After the war, most of
these Germans remained in this region, taking wives
from among the inhabitants of Morris and Bergen Counties. Their descendants are to-day among our most respected citizens.

In the *New Jersey Journal* of Oct. 24, 1781, appears an
advertisement which conveys an adequate idea of the
character of his establishment:

To be sold, or exchanged for country produce and other
articles necessary to carry on iron works, &c.: All sorts of cast
iron kettles, pots, large and small tea kettles, pie pans, large
and small skillets, small mortars, griddles with and without
legs, wagon, chair and cart boxes, close stoves, six and ten
plate stoves, open fire places, commonly called 'Franklin
Stoves' etc. etc. etc.—wholesale and retail by the subscriber at
Morris Co. Furnace.—*John Jacob Faesch.*

Faesch, in the latter years of his life, was not only a
local magistrate but served as a member of the New Jersey Assembly. He has left many of his queer-looking sig-

natures attached to old Morris County documents and conveyances. Whereas Hasenclever wrote his name beautifully (like a true Spencerian devotee of the present day), with several fine flourishes fore and aft,—in keeping with his fabled luxuriousness of character,—Faesch's scrawl was fearful and wonderful; the name being followed by a laboriously-executed cryptogram which was intended to represent a pipe! At Mount Hope he doubtless emulated some of the expensive niceties of Hasenclever; and the town of Rockaway, N. J., still cherishes many "great-grandmother stories" of his ponderous coach rolling through the main street, with invariable stops of long duration at the village tavern. He died at Boonton, May 26, 1799, aged 70 years, and was buried at Morristown.

And now, after the above digression, we revert again to our own biographical subject, for whom the coming of 1772 brought welcome relief in that it saw the rounding out of Mr. Faesch's contract with the London Syndicate and his withdrawal from their employ to venture into business for himself. As illustrating this period of transition, let Erskine tell the story:

Ringwood, March 27th, 1772

Richard Willis Esq., and the
Rest of the American Company

Gentlemen: My last was from New York of February 28th, of which you have likewise a duplicate.

Mr. Faesch is at present here, where we are engaged in making up last year's accounts and closing the books to ascertain exactly the cost of Bar Iron, abstracts of which, at least, I hope to furnish you with by next packet.

Mr. Faesch and I have had some conversation on your affairs and his own, from which I find that, on mature deliberation, he is very willing to acquiesce, in general, with your instructions and the plan I laid down in January last. However, if no un-looked-for obstacle intervenes, he seems still resolved to build a furnace at a place about nine miles from Charlotteburg, which I am told is well situated for the purpose. In this province there are a great many forges where they make bar iron directly from the ore, which occasions a much greater consumption of coal than by pigs. Where that process is used they go by the name of Bloomeries; therefore as there are not a proportional quantity of furnaces to supply pig metal, Mr. Faesch supposes he may get a ready sale for his pigs in the country, which he thinks will turn to good account. He declares positively his resolutions to have no forges of his own, nor any other connections with those he may deal with than perhaps sometimes the taking payment in bar iron, if he should find it difficult to procure the value in cash, and further supposes that were he settled and resided at his proposed furnace, he would have at least half his time to spare.

This evidently refers to Faesch's proposed venture at Mount Hope. The following paragraph has been deleted from this letter by Erskine, for some reason or other:

These then are his views. His undertaking, he thinks, if carried into execution, can very little interfere with the Company's interests, unless they were to sell pig metal, which at present is hardly ever done, except sometimes hammers and anvils, upon which there is good profit, and which our neighbors take as a favour.

These views are expressed in somewhat similar words on the second page of the letter, and Erskine proceeds:

Since these, then, are his views, the footing upon which he thinks it would be agreeable both to the Company and him to continue in their employ, is, first, that he shall leave the cash transactions entirely to me, at all the works; because, if he has works of his own, he says it might be supposed he would apply some part of the Company's money to his own use, at least, people would imagine that though he might not embezzle their property, he might now and then make free with a few hundreds for a month or two and replace it. He next offers to consult with me upon the Company's affairs, and that we shall concert the proper plan for proceeding at all the works, at any of which he is willing, by his presence, to give me his best advice and assistance when I think it necessary. And, when residing at his own place, as he will have so much time to spare, he would be willing to continue in the Company's employ in the same manner, only in that case he does not expect or desire so much salary as at present.

Such now are Mr. Faesch's sentiments and proposals, which I told him I was very sorry he had not determined upon sooner, because had they come to hand before my last letter, I had very little doubt of the Company's refusing to acquiesce. . . . I suppose would have agreed to them without reluctance, though beyond a doubt they must be greatly offended on the receipt of my last letter . . . and I suppose their next would be ordering me to take Charlotteburg off his hands immediately.[7]

However, since I had done ample justice to his merits both here and at home and in my former letters had given the Company great hopes that he and I would proceed in the same sociable manner for their interests which he now proposes to do, their was only one thing I said which might obstruct his views, that was the Company's engaging another manager, which probably they might do, before this came to hand. If they had not taken this step, I flattered myself they might still agree to his proposals, but then it would be necessary for him to propose—as an inducement—entering into obligations to give them proper assurances that his works should not interfere with theirs, so far as to deprive the Company of any of their forgemen or other useful hands whose absence would incomode their works.

[7] Erskine's letter is somewhat blurred and obscure at this point, and the text has been deciphered with difficulty.

For my own part, I told Mr. Faesch, it would be more agreeable to me to have him for a fellow manager than a stranger, as we now were acquainted with each other's disposition, whereas, if the latter should prove hot and obstinate, I could not agree with such a temper a month; that I had no objection to the care of the cash, which I would accept whenever he thought proper (which he designs I should do in about two months), because keeping the whole cash account for all the works cannot take up above a day in a week.

Though I told Mr. Faesch at Charlotteburg, when I was a little warm on account of the value in which he seemed to hold his knowledge, that I would never trouble him with a single question relating to Iron, (to which I should have religiously adhered had things continued as at that time) yet, since circumstances are altered, Mr. Faesch won't find me backward either to convey or receive knowledge, in both of which I take pleasure. Wherever he is present, I should choose him to exert his usual authority over the Germans, which he may do with a good grace when they know we have agreed to act in concert. Though I perceive they will be tractable enough for me with proper looking-after, yet the other day I regretted my want of ability to scold some of the forgemen most heartily in their own language, who, through mere carelessness and hurry to get a quantity of iron worked off, had drawn a good many bars unfit for market. However, they will be more careful in future, as I have threatened to stop payment for this, and shall certainly do it for any such iron in future.

Therefore, as Mr. Faesch and I understand each other, and neither will do a rash or precipitate thing, or give any essential orders without consultation (without the hazard of one contradicting what the other has enjoined), we can freely leave common matters to each other's discretion: when we are separate, each may act as if there was no other manager, when together I shall choose Mr. Faesch to command the forgemen and founders, and when he is absent I shall endeavor to keep up the idea of his being their master, and then I have no doubt they will obey me still more readily.

My last was chiefly filled up with the subject furnished me by Mr. Yates, and I thought to write in a very different strain from the above had Mr. Faesch continued in his primary resolves; however, as your business is likely now to proceed in the agreeable manner I, from the first, expected, I have no doubt the Company will make proper allowance for the unavoidable interruptions which have occurred to interrupt my train of thoughts illustrating the nature of their business situation.[8]

From this letter, in its entirety, we conclude that Erskine had not come to America with the idea that he was entirely to supersede Faesch nor to supplant him. At the time of the writing of the above, Erskine seems to have come to hold Faesch in somewhat higher regard, although rather nettled by the latter's self-esteem. If we are to judge by letters written by Erskine a few months later, he was soon due for another change of opinion as to Mr. Faesch's motives. At this time, however, he exhibits a remarkable degree of forbearance and unselfishness, with a surprising frankness as to his own impulsive disposition.

That Mr. Faesch continued to function in an executive capacity so late as July, 1772, seems demonstrated by the following advertisement to be found in the *New York Gazette* of November 23, 1772:

Lost at Charlotteburgh Iron Works, about the 15th of July last, two Orders, drawn by Mr. John Jacob Faesch, on Messrs. Reade and Yates, Merchants in New-York; one in Favour of Conrod Frank, dated the sixth of April, for 130 l. York Money, payable three Months after Sight; and the other in Favour of

[8] Unfortunately, the original manuscript, evidently a rough first draft of a letter, has disappeared from its place in *The Manor and Forges of Ringwood*, I, 49. It has been given here as Heusser copied it in 1920, except for the small passage which Erskine "deleted." The punctuation, etc., is therefore Heusser's, not Erskine's. H. S.

Peter Westerman, dated the 14th of April, for Fifty Pounds like Money; also payable in Three Months after Sight and both Orders were accepted the 20th of April. Therefore, notice is hereby given that the Payment of said Orders is stoped, consequently they can be no Service to any other Person but the Owners, who have given the Printers Directions to Pay Three Pounds Reward to any Person that should deliver said Orders to him, no further Questions shall be asked.[9]

[9] *New Jersey Archives*, First Series, Vol. 28, p. 339. H. S.

7

Lord of Ringwood

TROUBLED though Erskine may have been with countless details of business management, and impatient for the time to arrive when he could show tangible results of his stewardship by the return of some adequate interest upon the tangled investments of the English proprietors, the fact remains that, at Ringwood, he found himself not only comfortably but luxuriously quartered. Had he been less conscientious, he might have enjoyed his lordly position the more. Although, in one of his early letters to his employers, he describes the situation at Ringwood as "tolerable," it was and is a region of exceptional beauty—a little world apart—a peaceful and well-cultivated valley between gently rising hills abounding in mineral wealth.

Here, at Ringwood, Erskine and his good wife occupied the old manor-house, which stood somewhat to the south of the present mansion erected by the Ryersons over a century ago and subsequently enlarged by the Hewitts. No known pictures of the old residency exist, but it must have been a commodious and comfortable dwelling despite Erskine's implication that it was architecturally ungainly. As the successor to Hasenclever and Faesch, Robert Erskine fell virtual heir to an American earldom, and —being the only exceptional person in a sparsely settled region—seems soon to have gained not only the respect but the greatest confidence of the tenantry, most of whom were humble workmen of foreign extraction, although as near neighbors he had the Wards, the Erwins, and the second generation of the Board family; while to the northward were the Sloats, the Nobles and the Townsends,— all these being of ancient stock. As business rivals were the Jacksons of Rockaway, and the Fords of Morristown; as well as the Hoffs and the Brinkerhoffs; and Lord Stirling (William Alexander of Basking Ridge) who controlled the mines at Hibernia.

Very few "social items" as to these long ago days have come down to us. Therefore the following brief note, which shows Reade & Yates of New York in something more than the role of hardhearted business agents, is interesting:

New-York 7 April 1772

Robert Erskine Esqr.

Dear Sir

We are indebted for yours of the 30th ultimo, agreable to your desire, we have sent up every thing you ordered by Stoe's Boat, except the barrell of Lamp Oyl and the Artichoak Success, the latter is not to be gott in this Town.—The letters for the Company are forwarded by Packett—we hope they may arrive in time to prevent any New Manager being appointed. We are very truly

Dr. Sr.,

Your most humble Servts.

Reade & Yates

Mr. & Mrs. Yates Compliments to your good lady, and desire Mrs. Erskine to accept of a few Yams which are sent by Stoe's Boat; the Garden seed Mr. Titt's takes up with him [1]

The isolated situation of Ringwood would have made it a rather unsafe place of residence, had not the presence of the miners and tenants of the estate been equivalent to a small-sized army of retainers. Nevertheless Erskine was not immune from the petty thievery which has ever been the bane of those who possess anything worth stealing, whether they live in the city or in the country. The following interesting item, from one of New York's ancient weeklies, bears witness to the circumstance that the new master of Ringwood had occasional troubles with the prowling rascals who infested the mountain regions:

Ringwood Iron Works, Nov. 16, 1772
Stolen out of Ringwood Stables about three Weeks ago, an Iron Roan Horse, about nine or ten Years old, a natural Pacer, fifteen Hands and a half high, has a large Head, and carries it much out from his Chest, his Brands or Marks, if he has any, are not known, but as he has been work'd in the Waggon all Summer, the Marks of the Gears are visible. Whoever secures the Thief, shall be paid all Charges of Commitment and Prosecution, together with Ten Dollars Reward, and all reasonable Charges for the Horse, by   Robert Erskine [2]

Thievery, however, was not confined to horses. Robert Erskine, being an accountant of no mean ability (for his precision is well attested by the condition of his books) was continually unearthing much evidence of petty connivance and double-dealing on the part of those who, be-

[1] Erskine Papers. The name Titts appears in the Bellgrove Store Accounts in the Erskine Papers as "John Titts alias Dietz." H. S.
[2] *The New York Gazette and the Weekly Mercury*, Nov. 23, 1772, reported in *New York Archives*, First Series, Vol. 28, p. 339.

ing indebted to the Company, were endeavoring to evade their obligations and to profit by reason of his own presumed unfamiliarity with the loose system of his predecessors.

The following advertisement, which appeared in the *New York Gazette* and the *Weekly Mercury* under date of March 22nd, 1773, throws further light upon his tribulations and his valiant efforts to round up the delinquents:

> Notice is hereby given, to all those indebted to the American Company, by bond, note, book, debt, or otherwise, at Ringwood, Long-Pond, and Charlotteburg works, or elsewhere, that Robert Erskine, the present manager, the company's agents in New-York, or such person or persons as he or they shall appoint, are alone authorized to receive debts due to the company and to give proper discharges for the same. Whoever therefore shall pay any debts or ballances to any other persons, will, undoubtedly, be sued for the same again by
>
> Robert Erskine [3]

That Robert Erskine, despite his own perplexities, was intensely alive to the social and domestic needs of his neighbors and the welfare of the community cannot be doubted. As he had, in his native land, taken a keen interest in current affairs, civic development and regional improvement, so, in America, we find him entering with hearty good will into the activities of upper Jersey. Within two years of his coming to Ringwood we have record of his appointment as a local magistrate.

Prior to the adoption of the provisional State Constitution of 1776, justices of the peace for the Province of New Jersey were appointed by the governor. They acted, on occasion, as County Judges, a special commission being

[3] *Ibid.*, March 22, 1773, reprinted in *New Jersey Archives*, First Series, Vol. 28, p. 482.

issued to them (or some of them) from time to time, to hold courts of oyer and terminer. They held office during life or until superseded. The commission issued March 24th, 1773,[4] included Robert Erskine of Ringwood; John Jacob Faesch (who, as we recollect, was at this time operating mines of his own in Morris County); and Henry Mandeville, of Pompton Plains.

There is every reason to believe that Erskine continued to exercise his judicial prerogatives until his death. As the virtual master of Ringwood Manor, it was fitting that he should thus be vested with recognized authority, and equally natural that not only the tenantry of the estate, but also the lesser land-owners and dwellers in the mountains, should regard him as sage, peacemaker, and adjudicator of honest differences and annoying squabbles. We know that Erskine kept a set of books recording the details of his work as magistrate, but these have not been found.

It is indeed true that, in 1773, Erskine occupied a singular position. To the people of this mountain region he was employer, friend and law-maker. To his competitors in the iron business, to himself, and even to his employers, he was still an unsatisfactory and "unknown quantity." To explain this last assertion, it is necessary again to recapitulate.

Like many another speculative enterprise of great magnitude, the American investment of the London syndicate had become almost a forlorn hope before it reached a productive stage. Under Hasenclever, development had meant more than dividends; and it is exceedingly doubtful whether the few consignments of iron, potash and the like which had been sent overseas to England produced enough to provide for his own salary, let alone other ex-

[4] See *The History of Morris County, N. J.* W. W. Munsell & Co., N. Y., 1882.

penditures or any percentage of interest upon the capital invested. During the interval between Hasenclever's recall and Erskine's coming, the managers of the works had been chiefly concerned with making the establishment yield enough to keep itself in motion and to provide a livelihood for themselves. Erskine had been sent to America to turn the tide, if possible. Whatever may have been his sanguine dreams at the outset, he, too, soon came to realize the seriousness of the situation. Under the most favorable circumstances, a good ten years ought to have been allowed for rehabilitation and production before anything in the way of financial return was expected of him. Had further working capital been forthcoming from England, this period might have been materially reduced; but there was—quite naturally—no disposition on the part of "my lords and gentlemen" to throw good money after bad. Summing up the situation then, after two years of Erskine's best endeavor (hindered as he was at every turn by lack of support, open antagonism and shortage of funds) and with only his own strategic ability to wriggle out of tight places as a means of escape from pressing demands,—we find the works gradually increasing in efficiency and output, but with no resulting profit for the pockets of the investors.

One would infer, from the following advertisement, (printed in the *New-York Gazette* of September 21, 1772), that both Erskine and the English stockholders had become discouraged, and had, by agreement, decided to make an attempt to sell out everything, and save a trifle from the apparent wreck:

American Company Iron Works.   New Jersey.
Notice is hereby given that Reade and Yates in New-York, or Robert Erskine Esq. on the premises, are impowered to receive

Proposals either for the Sale or Lease of the Well Known Works of Charlottenburg, Long-Pond, and Ringwood; Whoever therefore is inclined to treat for the Sale or Lease, either of Part or Whole, are desired to apply as above. Subjoined is a Description of the Works, taken by the desire of His Excellency Governor Franklin in the Year 1768.[5]

Then follows a detailed description of the various items of real estate and equipment, as found on preceding pages of this work.[6]

No purchaser was forthcoming, however, and Erskine was fated to plod along as best he might. In the end, of course, this was fortunate for the destinies of America. "Man proposes," indeed, but the God of men and nations "disposes,"—and those who come after, if not we ourselves, see the wisdom of Providence.

What is by far the most important collection of facts concerning Ringwood under the management of Peter Hasenclever, is the communication forwarded by Erskine to the proprietor of the New-York *Gazette*. Hasenclever, having returned to Europe to stay, had issued the booklet (already referred to) entitled "The Remarkable Case of Peter Hasenclever," in which he criticized his former employers and stoutly defended his course and system of management while in America. Erskine's letter is in rebuttal; and abounds in caustic comment and wit, besides supplying interesting data for our enlightenment:

New-York, July 10, 1773

To the Printer of the New-York Gazette:

Give me leave, Sir, to lay before the public a few remarks, upon a certain pamphlet which has been industriously circu-

---

[5] *Ibid.*, Sept. 21, 1772, reprinted in *New Jersey Archives*, First Series, Vol. 28, 246.

[6] The report to Governor William Franklin. H. S.

lated here, on purpose to throw an odium on the characters of a set of Gentlemen to whom these colonies are under inexpressible obligations, not only on account of the money they have expended, but for the sums they still continue to circulate in America, which (even at present) is above twenty thousand pounds a year.

The confidence reposed in me, by the proprietors of Hasenclever's iron works, I have no doubt, must sufficiently apologize for my endeavours to do them justice, by publishing my observations and sentiments: but before I begin to point out some of the many glaring absurdities in Mr. *Hasenclever's case,* I beg leave just to mention, that I never saw that gentleman, that I came to this country totally unacquainted with the proceedings of my predecessors, except in general, that they had spent immense sums of money, and that so far from my knowing any material circumstance relative to the works, or the situation of their affairs, the proprietors expected an account of their condition from me, as they should appear from inspection and observation.

To Mr. *Hasenclever* himself then we are indebted for the history of the rise, the progress, and the fate of an undertaking, projected, commenced and carried on with all the rapidity, the imprudence, and the profusion that the most sanguine schemer could suggest. He tells us in his pamphlet, that he arrived in London, in summer 1763, with an *easy fortune,* which however he is evidently anxious to encrease by a scheme which he communicated to the Lords of trade, a few months after his arrival. In April 1764, he sets out on his expedition to America, where we find him landed the beginning of the following June. Twelve months, therefore, had scarcely elapsed his commencing merchant in London, to his commencing—I know not what to call him—a meteor, a projector, a dupe, are equally applicable, the reader may therefore take which he will, or all three to do him justice.

His only view in establishing a house in London, seems to be for the purpose of carrying his wild projects into execution, to effect which it was necessary to procure from 10 to 40,000l.

of the easy fortunes, of easily imposed on Englishmen, over and above his own easy fortune, and that of his partners; he appears so industriously assiduous to engage such sums, even in a few weeks (20 or 30 at most) after the commencement of his partnership, that one is almost tempted to suspect, it is as probable his 8000l. share was thrown into the house by means of a foreign circulation; as th[at] his partner Mr. *Andrew Seton's* 8000l. was supported by a domestic. For, would any man with real, solid, and permanent funds have proceeded with his celerity and want of caution? Granting that America had all the advantages for the manufacture of iron, of potash, of *salt petre*, of *reducing flax to silk*, and of every article the most fertile brain could suppose, would not any man of prudence, who was going to risque his own money in such schemes, and who was not under the necessity to strike a bold stroke at once—would not any sensible man, I say, have taken a view of the proper places for establishing his works, and agreed for the purchase previous to his being at a prodigious expence of transporting workmen from Germany, to—where? but let us suppose him to speak for himself—"Indeed I cannot tell, gentlemen, the place is not yet fixed on, the workmen are ready, though the works are not; here I am in *New York*, and they are all arrived at *Philadelphia*, and must be supported in idleness at another prodigious expence, because the truth of the matter is, I could not possibly get to *America* above six or eight weeks before them."—A comfortable length of time to explore a continent and to fix upon the most proper places for establishing works of such importance!—"The workmen are eating, when likewise they ought to be at work; a place must be had, and such is the urgency of the case that I bought—any place rather than none,—I bought a decayed iron work!!!" Mercy upon those who had mercy upon his pocket; but necessity has no law—money had been obtained, and it was necessary to make a shew.

The workmen were refractory—most undoubtedly true—they made bad work—a certain fact, they do so still when they can, he complained, he reprimanded them; but yet, most strange! he had the satisfaction in the next page of hearing from England, that his iron was of an excellent quality, and the *best drawn* of any that appeared from *America.*—It was practicable then to send a *sample* of good iron from New-York, though they made bad work at Ringwood—O poor John Bull, your pocket pays for all!

Shall I follow this schemer, to say no more, farther—you would justify the phrase were you to see the instructions he left on his going to England, what orders, what contracts, what purchases were there not to be carried into effect; had they been all complied with, as indeed too many of them were, the 54,600l. already expended, would have been doubled in a twinkling.

We next find Mr. *Hasenclever* in England, where he made over the dear bought property to the real owners; He then returned to America a partner in the iron-works, with emoluments in his own imagination, to the amount of 12 or 1400l. ster. a year. Mean time the works had been conducted in the absence by a set of—negligents, to *say* no worse as the pamphlet expresses it, whom he justly accuses—he sets about repairing the faults which had been committed, and laid a plan of the strictest oeconomy—pity this plan came to last!—In his operations however, he was unfortunately interrupted by the coming of Mr. Homfray, whose arrival, among other misfortunes, not only deprived him of his 1400l. a year; but prevented the carrying many oeconomical plans into execution, particularly that of floating of coal wood from eight to ten miles distance by lakes, by rivers, and by canals, to save land carriage—pray observe—this oeconomical plan of navigation was to be effected in a country where the rivers have from 50 to an 100 feet fall in a mile; where they struggle through a channel of rocks, and are verged with stony mountains and precipices.—what a pity this most elevating and surprizing plan was interrupted, since it might have been carried into execution at the trifling expense of four or five millions sterling —with great reason then he refused to pay his calls, because Mr. Homfray was sinking 10,000l. a year; but to be serious,

Mr. Homfray was a gentleman to whom the works are even now highly obliged, the good effects of many of his regulations are still felt; being dead, as Mr. *Hasenclever* must have known, he cannot speak for himself, this tribute then is due to the memory of an honest man, who was combined against, misrepresented and artfully supplanted, which must be the more easily credited, since it can be proved that the greatest art and chicane has since been made use of, to retain the sole management in the same hands who supplanted him, but without effect.

The gentlemen at home, who are vilified in this pamphlet, as they are very able, so no doubt they will fully confute the aspersions thrown out against their characters. I beg leave in general to observe, it was not at all surprising that gentlemen who found their substance in such hands, should endeavour to rescue as much of their property from destruction as possible; the means they took were laudable, nor could they apologize to themselves or to the world, for their former imprudence in a better way. Mr. *Hasenclever* had abused the confidence reposed in him, and expended immensely greater sums than were at first tho't of; they sent a gentleman to be first a check, and afterwards to supercede him, for he went beyond all bounds in drawing which would have still increased, (witness the navigation scheme) had he not been put a stop to—his bills were protested,—an unfortunate circumstance both to the proprietors, and the holders,—and although the first could not otherwise stop his career, yet the latter who purchased his bills on the faith of his former credit, fell into an unhappy dilemma, which was further increased by his giving them the slip, and breaking his most solemn parole of honour; he has the modesty however to make a merit of travelling 2000 miles to avoid them: The New-York gentleman had the benevolence to trust him at large on his protestations that all the money had been expended on the works, tho' he did not think it convenient to wait the proof here; now at last he pretends to produce evidence to this fact, in his pamphlet—but who are they?—why the very *negligents* to *say* no worse again, whose faults it was his honour and interest to repair, whose expences he reduced one third, and whom he himself blames so highly—a justification from such a quarter, has so much the appearance of a mutual release, that it can have very little weight, either in a court of equity, or with any thinking person.

I never saw the *manufactured books,* as one of the proprietors with justice call them; therefore cannot tell whether the many hundreds nay thousands expended in the *salt petre* scheme, the *turning flax into silk,* the *silver mines,* the *tin mines,* the *wood cutting on Lake Champlain,* the sums advanced to FREDENBERG, to the ficticious Count APRAXIN, and to numberless other needy adventurers, schemers and projectors, who found him a ready gull to swallow any bait; as I have never seen the manufactured books, I say, I cannot tell whether those numberless expences are carried to account: Mr. HASENCLEVER however being silent in his pamphlet with respect to all those articles, makes it seem highly probable, that neither do they appear in his books of account, unless couched under some general terms similar to that article where he charges 2166l. for his private expences, or very probably they may be included in the many thousands charged by the lump *for making of roads.* I am bold enough then to enforce Mr. ATKINSON's idea of his books being manufactured, and have perhaps more to alledge than has come to that gentleman's knowledge; of this much I am certain that immense sums of money were spent, not at the works, but in profusion, extravagance and dissipation, this the whole Jerseys can witness—need I add any more—I could bring proof the sums of money have been paid by some of the managers from handfulls of bills carried loose in the pocket, without either acknowledgement or receipt,—how is it possible then the books could be otherwise than *cooked,* that the money can be fairly accounted for, or that Mr. HASENCLEVER has the least shadow of right to charge the expence of all his mad projects to account of the proprietors of the iron works, in several of which they were to have no share, and many of them I suppose, never came to their knowledge.

Robert Erskine [7]

The above scathing arraignment was not published until well nigh a month after it was submitted to the editor; maybe because the typesetter was loath to tackle the job, or more probably because the editor was a bit wary of subjecting himself to the likelihood of a suit for criminal libel. It appeared, however, in the issue of August 9th, 1773.[8] That Erskine had a penchant for preparing newspaper articles we know. Yet doubtless he was a man open-minded and willing to be convinced, else why should he have advertised in the following strain? Had Faesch's preference for German workmen been ill-advised, Erskine would scarcely have solicited their services as he did in the "want ad" inserted in the *New-York Gazette* of July 12th, 1773, several months after Faesch had relinquished his position and begun business elsewhere:

FORGEMEN.

A few good forgemen, may hear of constant employment and sure pay, by applying at Charlotteburg iron works, New-Jersey.

N. B. Those who are Germans, or who can work in the German way, shall be preferred.[9]

[7] *New Jersey Archives*, Vol. 28, pp. 586–92.

[8] Erskine's letter drew fire from one of the former managers under Hasenclever, a Captain D. Wrisberg. Erskine answered rather curtly that his "deductions" had been only general ones. Wrisberg replied with some heat that the explanation was not satisfactory. Erskine wrote again, in a somewhat more conciliatory tone, saying his intent had been only to expose Hasenclever's "absurd pamphlet." The correspondence was printed in the *Gazette* of September 6, and may be found in *ibid.*, vol. 29, pp. 7–11. Mr. Heusser apparently overlooked this correspondence. H. S.

[9] *New Jersey Archives*, Vol. 28, p. 560.

Artist's conception of the original Ringwood Manor, which was razed or burned about 1807. When Abram Hewitt took up residence at Ringwood in 1857, he commissioned an artist to paint this picture from descriptions by people who remembered the old house. The original watercolor is at the present Ringwood mansion.

The anvil and triphammer on the lawn at the present Ringwood mansion are among the few remaining objects there associated with Erskine. The hammer, left, had a shaft made of a huge beam, which was raised mechanically and dropped by gravity on the anvil. The chain is not Erskine's; it is a spurious one purchased by Abram Hewitt.

The present marker near the tombs of Erskine and his clerk, Robert Monteith.

London 18th Feby 1766

Sir

In answer to your friends queries as he seems curious to know the nature of my Continual Stream Pump, I here give you a Sketch of the principles.

In this Pump there are four Valves A, B, C, D: E is the piston: F is a hole thro' which the piston-rod moves, Air and water tight.

Operation. When the piston is pushed down the Valves A and B open, when pulled up, C and D open, so A, B and C, D, open and shut alternately; Consequently which ever way the piston moves the water is Continually rising in the Tubes G & H. Hence this pump gives as much water as Two. or a double piston, and the friction of one piston is avoided.

As to raising the water to the Top, to assist the water wheel, if it is the Water wheel that works the Pumps, it is of no manner of use, for the water raised, cannot increase the power of the wheel in an equal proportion; to the force required on raising the water to the wheel, as the friction of the machine intervenes; I am therefore Clearly of opinion, it would be a disservice, and money thrown away

A letter describing Erskine's "continual stream pump," a device for unwatering sailing ships. It was for this invention that he was elected to the Royal Society. *New Jersey Historical Society*

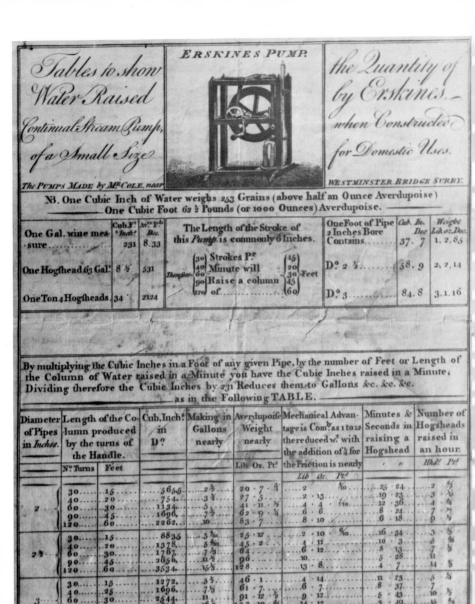

A circular advertising Erskine's pump. *New Jersey Historical Society*

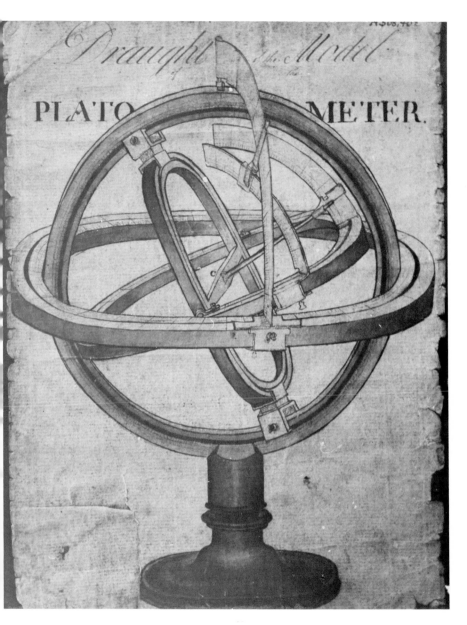

Erskine's drawing of his "platometer." *New Jersey Historical Society*

List of Goods belonging to Mr Robt Erskine Shipt on Board the Britannia Miller for New York Marked

R·E

Nº Fi	1 Case Tin Ware ✗ Value		4.4	
Fi	1 Cask Crucibles ✗		1.18	
Fi 3	Cases			
Fi 4 Dº	} Chemicals			
Fi 5 Dº				
Fi 6 Dº	Glass Retorts &c ✗			✗
Baggage	1 Flat Trunks Apparel Value	100		✗
Dº	2 Do Dº	50		✗✗
Dº	3 Do Dº Linin	50		✗
Dº	4 Bureau & Contents	20		✗✗
Dº	5 Round headed Trunk Inst.	40		✗
Dº	7 Old Shirt, Books &c	15		✗
Dº 8	a Dº Sundries	10		✗
Dº 9 8	Case Soap	2		✗
Dº 10 Dº	Ores	5		
Dº 11 Dº	Jellys	1		
	1 Three Flat Cases	6		✗✗
Dº	1 Small p Mantua Trunks	10		✗
	1 Bag with Books	10		✗✗
Dº	1 Close Trunk not Matted	30		✗
No mark	Tea Bd Glasses Pictures ✗	1		✗
Baggage	In l Corded Together	11		361
Bedding	Bedding ✗			6.17
Baggage	1 Rule & Staves ✗			2.10
Box Marked J Mason ✗				5

List of goods brought by Erskine, his wife, and his apprentice, when they immigrated to the Colonies. *New Jersey Historical Society*

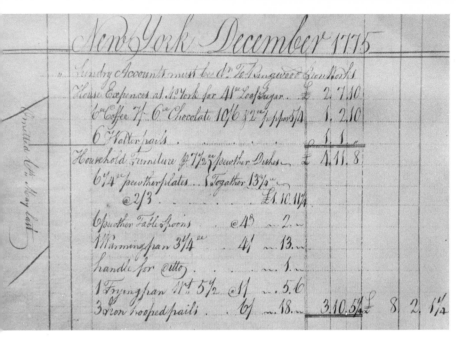

A page from the journal of the Bellgrave store. *New Jersey Historical Society*

page from Erskine's "Waste Book." *New Jersey Historical Society*

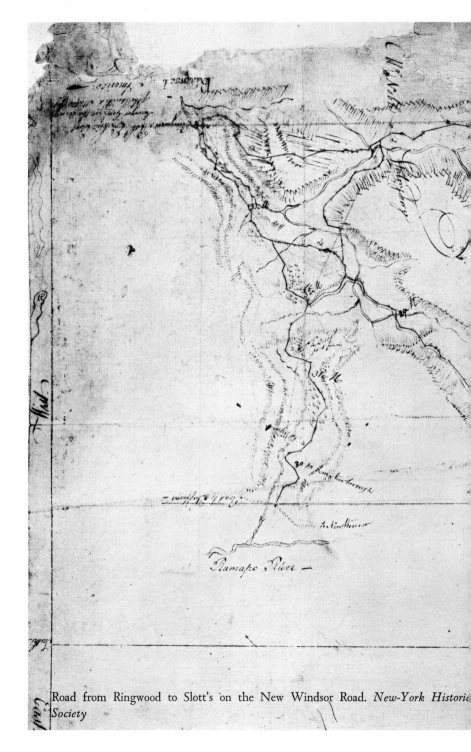

Road from Ringwood to Slott's on the New Windsor Road. *New-York Historic Society*

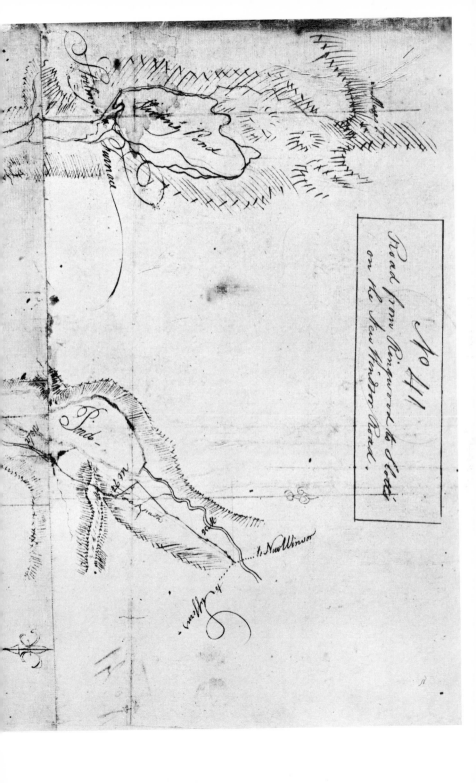

No 41
Road from Pomporet to Nott
on the New Hudson Road.

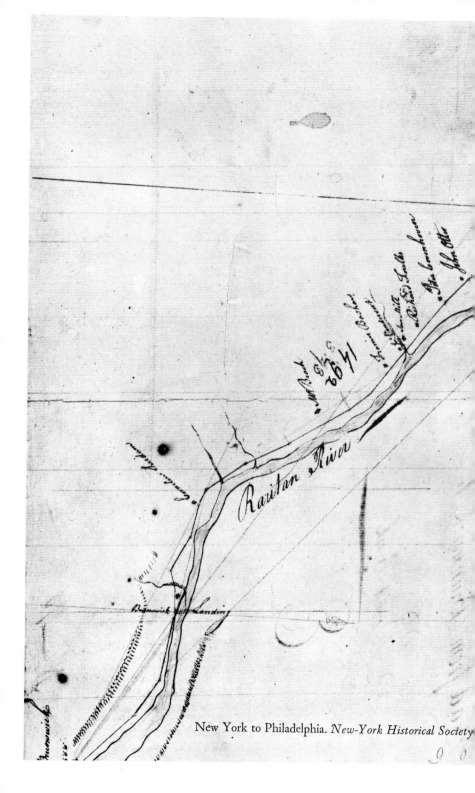

Raitan River

McBeak

1698

Francis Brokes

Mr Sandemonk

Mr Smith

Rahel Falls

Sir Cowenhoven

John Oten

Brunswick Landing

New York to Philadelphia. *New-York Historical Society*

Middle Brook

Sod Making
to Vanhoy

to Sommerville Course

valley
to Middle Brook hard the Maryland Court

Bound Brook Var. E ½ W

du North

to Quibbletown

No 70 E

No 70 W

Road from Brunswick to Bound Brook

"Road from Duyckinks Mill to the South Branch Garison's, Somerset Bound Brook, from South Branch to Reddington Brokaws & from near headquarters to S°. Branch." *New-York Historical Society*

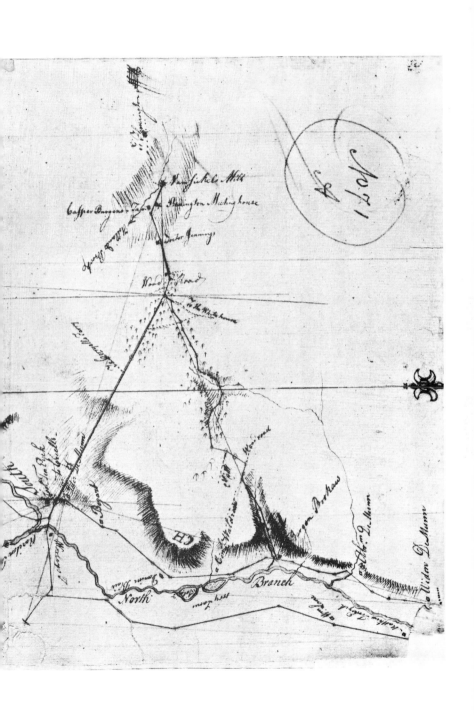

3 ¾ Km.

Perth Amboy

Strawberry Hill.

Mile Stone from N York

Second forking Paths

Port Road to Woodbridge

D

No.

CH

First forking Paths

Barracks

South Street

AM. BOY

Wide Street up for the Boat Road

The Sound

N° 4

Road from the Wh—
Woodbridge to Am—
Amboy towards b—

Wheat Sheaf to Woodbridge. *New-York Historical Society*

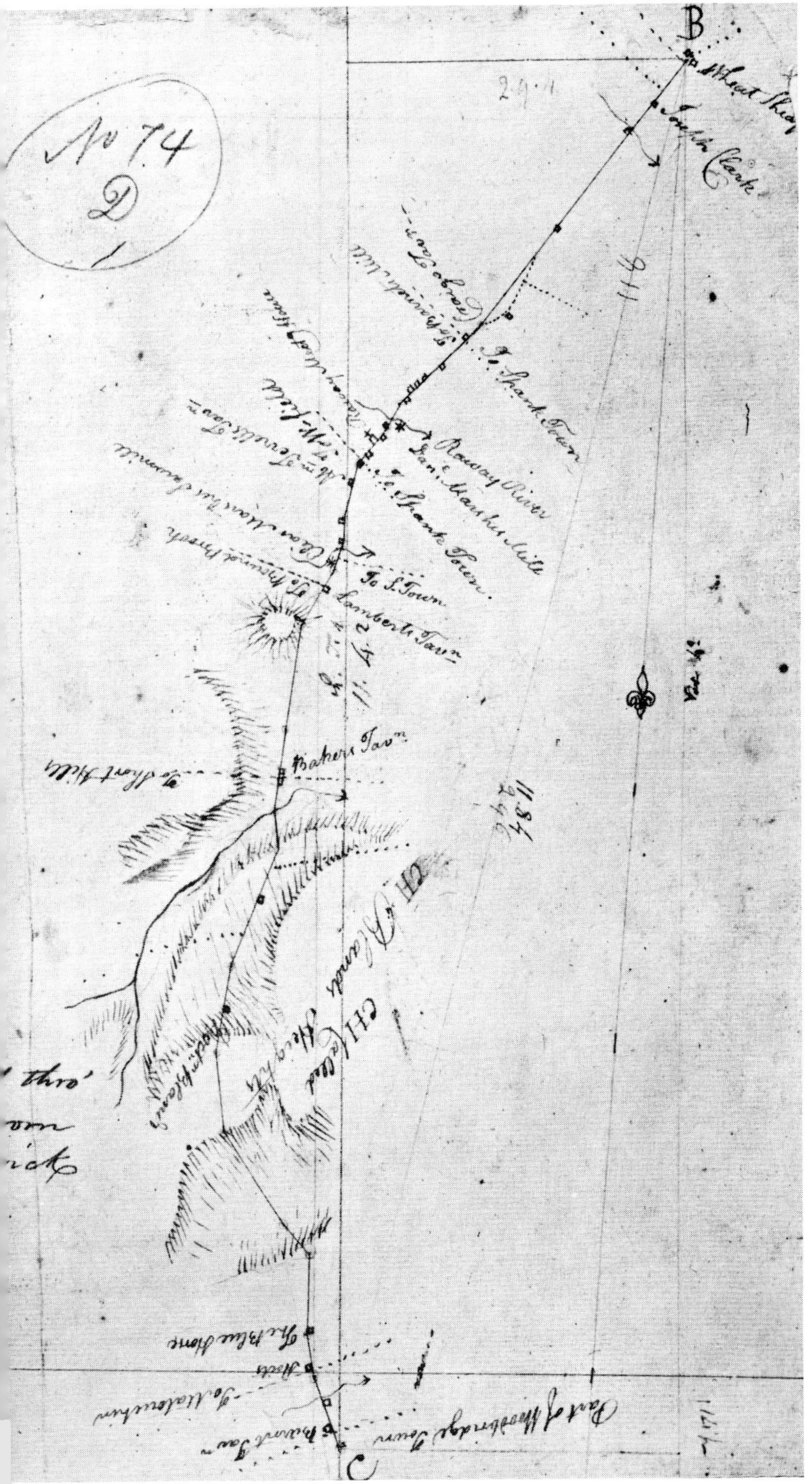

B

Wheat Sheaf

Smiths Clark

24.1

To Hawks Town

Rocaway River

Lane Maushu Mill

S. Hawke Town

To S. Town

Lamberts Town

11.84

Bakers Town

Short Hills

CLICKS Branch

thro'
town
rick

The Blue stone

Road of Woodbridge Town

Branch Town

To Woodbridge

C

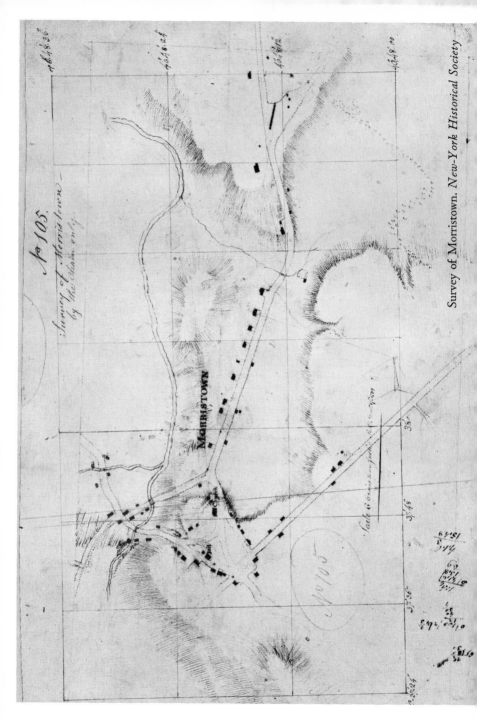

No 105.

Survey of Morristown —
by the Chain only.

MORRISTOWN

No 105

Survey of Morristown. New-York Historical Society

The closing months of the year 1773 must have found Erskine in a genuine dilemma. Apparently the English stock-holders had forsaken him because of his inability to perform the miracle of raising a torpid enterprise into life and activity. Thrown upon his own ingenious resources, we find him entering into an agreement with Curson & Seton, a firm of New York merchants, whereby they were to advance cash and goods to assist him in the maintenance of the works, while he was to supply their needs as regards iron, and go surety for whatever balances might accumulate in their favor.

From the original draft of this contract, in Erskine's hand, the following copy is given in its entirety:

We, Curson & Seton, Merchants in New York, & I Robert Erskine, hereby Covenant and Agree,

First

Robert Erskine, Manager & director of the Iron Works of Ringwood Charlotteburg Long Pond & Cortlandt by virtue of the powers vested in me by the proprietors of said Works and of my own free will and accord to hereby become bound unto Messrs Curson & Seton of the City of New York Merchants, and oblige myself by these presents to hold at their disposal and for their benefit and behoof, or to be delivered to them or their order when required, as much of the Proprietors Goods Consisting of pig & Bar Iron as shall upon the Sale thereof to be made by them, at a price not less than the Sum which may be drawn for on shipping viz £6.26 for Pig, or £21. for Bar Iron be equal to any actual advances they may at any time be under for the support of said Iron Works.

I further likewise bind & ingage myself to give security on the Proprietors said effects of Pig & Bar for the whole ballance of their account against the proprietors, whenever demanded to be disposed of as above, when ever their demands are reallized, and I further engage to hold at their disposal the other stock of goods moveable effect horses and cattle, should the pig Bar prove insufficient as above for their security.

Here Erskine has been deliberating as to the terms of the agreement, and has crossed out and rewritten the paragraph which was *first* worded as follows:

On the other hand, we, Curson & Seton, engage unto the said Robert Erskine—to continue assisting him in carrying on the Works as far as we can or untill our actual advances exceed £6,000 with cash and goods as the necessities of the works require, and by accepting his drafts from the Works.

His approved version of the agreement was, apparently, after this fashion:

Lastly, I engage thus by the foregoing articles to indemnify them in their just demands against the aforesaid proprietors to the utmost of my power, in preference to all others, except such of their creditors to whom I myself am personally liable.

On the other hand We, Curson & Seton hereby promise and engage, and by these presents obligate ourselves to Continue our support and assistance to the said Robert Erskine in Carrying on the above Works, by providing such goods as their necessities require by accepting his drafts, and advancing money in sums not less than two hundred pounds p^r month nor more than four hundred.

And it is hereby mutually agreed and engaged by the above parties that the foregoing agreement shall be deemed valid either in law or otherwise in witness whereof, we have hereunto interchangeably set our hands and seals this ninth day of Dec^r, 1773.[10]

[10] *The Manor and Forges of Ringwood,* II, 21. This is a rough working draft for an agreement, which may in the end have been quite different. H. S.

110 🖎

8

The Approaching Storm

M A Y we now, for a little while, forget the purely personal concerns of Robert Erskine and his business associates, and devote some attention to the trend of public events in the over-wrought American colonies. What the master of Ringwood thought and expressed in regard to the inevitable crisis is well demonstrated by his correspondence in the years 1773–1775. Indeed, some of his most interesting letters are those which deal with the political situation here and abroad just prior to the breaking out of the War for Independence. Before proceeding, I am constrained to digress sufficiently to explain that my readers must thank the late Rev. Joseph F. Tuttle, D. D.,[1]

[1] Dr. Tuttle, a native of Morris County, New Jersey, was at that time president of Wabash College in Indiana. The article alluded to, and from which Heusser copies verbatim, is to be found in the *Proceedings of the New Jersey Historical Society*, Second Series, Vol. II (1869), pp. 17–53. The spelling and punctuation of the Erskine letters which are quoted have undoubtedly been altered somewhat, but it seems probable that Tuttle was not as bad an offender on this score as Heusser himself. The latter's alterations have been changed back to the text as reproduced by Tuttle. H. S.

not only for the transcription of the communications which follow, but for the running comment. The present whereabouts of the original letters to which Dr. Tuttle had access I do not know. I herewith quote from the latter's elaborate essay read before the New Jersey Historical Society, May 20th, 1869. At the time he wrote he was probably unaware that many other Erskine letters were subsequently to come to light; but in one place he makes this significant comment, which seems as though it were meant for us of today: Let me indicate a few meagre facts about Ringwood . . . as possibly aiding someone who may attempt to write its history as it deserves . . .

I have in my possession the copies of letters of Mr. Erskine, in his own handwriting, to Mr. Walter Ewing and his "very dear cousin" Rev. Mr. Fisher.[2] The first is dated March 17, 1773, and the second March 18th, and both are written at New York. The first letter contains some items of interest concerning the extent of the London Company's business and Mr. Erskine's opinion as to its management previous to his taking charge. He speaks of its being "two whole years and upwards since I saw them"—(certain relatives in Scotland) . . . Mr. Erskine continues, ". . . But let me apologize for my partial silence and leave it to those concerned to find an excuse for their total. The concerns of the company for whom I am engaged are very great, the amount of their inventories at New Year in iron, goods, cattle and moveables alone was upwards of £30,000 currency; the annual circulation of cash and supplies is between £20,000 and £30,000. Before I came here this property was in the hands of a set of rascals, as I can now fully prove; the company suffered impositions from all quarters, many of which I have put a stop to, but not all. I have rid me of the greatest part of those who deserved no confidence, have discovered my predecessor in the management to have been

[2] Rev. James Fisher of Glasgow, the editor of Rev. Ralph Erskine's "Practical Works," 1764.

guilty of a most infamous breach of trust, confirmed under his own hand, and which makes it necessary to commence a suit in Chancery against him. The bringing things to the length I have done has required all my address. The affairs of my employers still require the whole of my attention. I am convinced the works may be carried on to profit were all those concerned honest. I have eight clerks, about as many overseers, forgemen, founders, colliers, woodcutters, carters and laborers to the amount of five or six hundred. The care of this centers in me, besides cash accounts of £1,000 or £1,500 per month, rendered monthly, to bring such an undertaking into a proper train of going on, is certainly not a small task. This is my apology."

The second letter, to his "Rev'd and very dear cousin," presents the writer in another phase and a better one, and at the same time furnishes a view of the conditions of society among the mountains as related to church privileges. "I heard of the loss of my Dear Cousin Mrs. Fisher (by Mr. Pajan's son,[3] who arrived here last summer), with no small concern. The God whom you serve has no doubt supported you and will carry you through this valley of tears with joy, but oh, my dear cousin, I beg an interest in your prayers. You will see by my letter of apology to Mr. Ewing for writing so seldom, how I am involved in the cares of this world. Were it not for a wicked heart, however, the business I am engaged in ought rather to lead me to God than make me forget him, as I have seen much of his Providence since I came here. There is no place of worship near where I live. Some German clergymen come only about five or six times a year. I have of late, however, procured supplies from the Presbytery here, and have agreed for supplies once in two months, which they promise to appoint. This expense I defray, and if the farmers and neighbors join in subscription we may have a clergyman once a month or oftener. . . ."

The difficulties of his position and also the manner of his

[3] Young Pagan later appears as one of the attesting witnesses to Erskine's will.

meeting them are set forth in his letters to his London employers during the years 1774, '5 and '6. They also present the
state of affairs and of public sentiment at that time as seen by
a very intelligent witness. Thus in June, 1774, he says: "I have
no doubt that a total suspension of commerce to and from
Great Britain will certainly take place. Such I know are the
sentiments of those who even wished a chastisement to Boston.
If in want of friends here, it will be difficult even with micro-
scopic search to find them. Gracious God! avert the consequences."

June 17 he writes: "The Virginians, who are the soul of
America, take the lead. We have not yet heard from the southward, but from what has appeared hitherto, the whole colonies
seem to look on that of New England as a common cause."

In August he writes: "The Southern colonies, as they are
more warmly situated, so they seem more warmly to oppose
the present measure; the Carolinians exceed those of Virginia,
if possible, but over the whole continent there is a feeling and
sensibility for the mother country. They have not yet forgot
their friends, their relations and their benefactors. These will
powerfully plead in the breasts of the Congress, and I hope in
a great degree counterbalance that warmth which injuries, real
or imaginary, naturally create. What is concluded on them
may be the dictates of necessity and not of resentment, and
therefore I think a non-exportation plan will be a dernier
resort and not entered into at present."

In October, 1774, he writes: "The Oliverian spirit in New
England is effectually roused and diffuses over the whole continent, which, though it is now pent up within bounds, a few
drops of blood let run would make it break out in torrents
which 40,000 men could not stem, much less the handfull
Gen. Gage has, whose situation is far from agreeable. The
masons and carpenters who began to build barracks have left
off work. Tradesmen of the same kind have been engaged here
—New York—but on second thought have refused to go. Were
he to come to extremities he no doubt might sacrifice thousands, but in the end would be cut off. I don't see, therefore,

how he can procure comfortable winter quarters without either abandoning the place or, like Hutchinson's addresses, publicly recant. The rulers at home have gone too far. The Boston Port Bill would have been very difficult of digestion, but not allowing Charters the due course of justice, and the Canada bills, are emetics which cannot possibly be swallowed and must be thrown up again to the bedaubing of the administration, who seem to have utterly forgot that they had the same spirit to contend with as at home, without the same advantages of turning it into a different channel by bribery and corruption. I have never disguised my thoughts to you or any subjects since I came to this country. You will therefore excuse my freedom on political concerns."

The rhetoric of the last letter was more forcible than elegant, but the writer is evidently in earnest in his attempt to arrest the unwise measures of the home Government. In October, 1775, he thus writes: "The communication with my native country may soon be cut off. The prospect is very gloomy and awful. God in his providence seems to have determined the fate of the British Empire, which is likely to be rent in pieces. I do not believe, however, that there is a man of sense on this continent who desires such a disjunction, provided they are not drove to it by absolute necessity, but if forcible measures are persisted in the dire event must take place, which may God in his mercy yet prevent."

In the same month he writes again:

"The situation of this country and my own makes me truly anxious . . . I shall add that the generality of people at home are totally wrong in their ideas of this country and its inhabitants, who being now in arms must by next spring be looked upon as equal to the same number of regular troops, not only to do them justice, but that their opponents may have proper ideas of the business they go upon if the enterprise of subduing them be persisted in, which, however, I hope in God will not be the case. Perhaps the petition of Congress may afford a proper opening for a negotiation. Should that be rejected, as the last, then God have mercy on us all. All hope of reconciliation will be cut off. That sword which has hitherto been drawn with reluctance will then be whet with rage, madness and despair, and the ports thrown open to all nations for assistance and trade, which it is impossible for the British Navy totally to prevent. Gracious Heaven prevent things from being brought to this pass, or that a total separation should take place between friends so dear!"

In the same letter Mr. Erskine speaks of: ". . . the general orders of Congress for all the colonists to be arrayed from 16 to 50 years of age, and of some inconveniences he is suffering at the works by 'several stout fellows going off and enlisting.' . . . It will be moved at the Congress to-night for the inhabitants of this place to provide for the safety of their wives, children and valuable effects. God knows, therefore, how long the communication with England may remain open and when you will have an opportunity to hear in a regular way again."

May 3, 1775, from New York, Mr. Erskine writes: "The people, as I have said before in private letters, are sincerely in earnest everywhere. I have even been applied to for gunpowder by the principal people of the County of Bergen in the Jerseys, in which your Iron Works are situated, where they, who till now hardly thought anything of the matter, are forming into regular disciplined bodies as fast as possible, which is the only business attended to at present anywhere. Gen. Gage is shut up upon salt provisions in Boston, from whence it is allowed he could not stir ten miles had he 10,000 men; for 20,000 men who now beyond doubt can fight, are entrenched without the town, and 30,000 more were sent home again as superfluous at present. But I leave particulars to the newspapers, and am sorry the times have furnished a subject so foreign to my former correspondence. The present subject I have adopted from the general voice which held it necessary that all who corresponded with England should be explicit in declaring the situation of this country, which is beyond dispute indissolubly united against the British Ministry and their acts, to which the Americans will never subscribe but in characters of blood; nor since blood has been shed do I believe a hearty reconciliation can again take place unless blood seals the contract."

A week afterward he writes: "Nothing now is attended to but arms and discipline. Even the Quakers of Philadelphia have taken arms, and two companies of that persuasion were formed last week. The seaport towns may be beaten down if the ministry think proper, but no force they can send will be able to penetrate ten miles inland. 'Tis perfectly astonishing they have carried things so far. The fishery bill, the allegations of cowardice, &c., have exasperated the whole continent to the last degree."

Again, of the 10th of June, he writes: "I beg leave to give you my sentiments respecting an accommodation, which there is not the least prospect of being effected by force of arms, soon if at all, for the universal diligence in learning and application given to military affairs must soon convert the people of this continent into regular troops. They have their eyes about them and are determined to be free or die. There is no doubt, however, that a hearty reconciliation would immediately take place were they put on the same footing as in '63 and the right of taxation given up, for independency is not their aim. Such a wish was never expressed or hinted at either in the last or present Congress."

In a letter May 23, 1775, he exclaims, "My heart bleeds for my native country." In August he writes, that "had the ministry designed to render the opposition to their measures as effectual as possible, they could not have hit upon a better method than the steps they have pursued." Sept. 5. "The people are in a general longing for intelligence from England, but however ardent and sincere their desires are for a happy and amicable reconciliation, they are in general prepared and preparing for the worst." Dec. 5th, he tells his employers that, whatever takes place: "I shall continue to act for your interests and the preservation of your property as well as I can."

Dec. 6th, he is in great trouble about protested bills in consequence of the troubles of the country, and then he exclaims: "Oh! my country! to what art thou driving? This gives me piquant distress indeed. How long will madness and infatuation continue? Oh God, justice and judgment are the habitation of thy throne; mercy and truth shall go before thy face. Excuse me, it is neither treason nor rebellion to wish the kings of the earth would imitate the Sovereign of the Universe. Civil war, subjects, and kindred blood shed, and for what? Because the Ministry of Britain have adopted the prejudices and resentments of a Governor and his petty partisans of one of the provinces. Heavens! what a figure the present annals will make in history."

On the 10th of February, 1776, he wrote to his London employers, among other things, that "brave Montgomery has fallen before Quebec and makes the third hero who has expired before its walls. We have some extracts from the English papers to the 17th of November; it makes me happy to see their complexion a little more favorable to a reconciliation. But shilly-shally undetermined procrastination and insidious maneuvers will not do. This country is too much on their guard, too well prepared and too much exasperated to attend to anything but plain English. It is the height of folly to hope to disjoin them. Unless the Ministry treat with the Congress they need not attempt treating at all, for were any colony base enough to break the Union, could they dare do it? No. Open on all sides, their being attacked on their skirts and sea-coasts by their European enemies is an happy alternative to that of being destroyed from all quarters; besides it is not in human nature to deliberate in the alternative, after engagements so short, in a quarrel that has gone so far, a fact so obvious that I hope all scrupulous punctilios will be got over and a cessation of arms and a repeal of the obnoxious acts take place, and then I trust Great Britain will regain the confidence and esteem of this country, provided she shows a hearty and speedy disposition to do them justice."

Under the same date he encloses his "Cash account" for January, and adds: "This—the profitable running of the Works—with a speedy settlement of the present disputes, would give me the highest satisfaction; but speedy the settlement must be if at all. A continuance of hostilities and another campaign and the burning a few more defenceless towns and such acts of wanton mischief, will most undoubtedly make the breach irreparable."

These quotations present the Ringwood manager in a light that reflects credit on him as one who clearly read the signs of the times and interpreted those signs honestly to his British employers. It is very evident that he desired the Revolution to be arrested by the honest retraction of their odious measures by the British ministry, and the faithful cession to the American colonies of the rights which they justly claimed. Were there no other sources of information than these letters, it would be evident that their writer was a warm advocate of the Americans in their dispute with the mother country; but, taken with other proofs, they fully demonstrate Robert Erskine's noble attitude in regard to the struggle which he predicted in such strong language, together with its issue.

Dr. Tuttle has truly and well appraised the character of the master of Ringwood in the foregoing digest of his over-seas correspondence. The actual fact is that Erskine had already thrown in his lot with the Americans, and —as will appear in the next chapter—had helped to organize and equip a company of Bergen County militia. Before referring to his military career, however, and to those distinguished services for the cause of America which were first to supersede and finally to obliterate forever his English ties, we ought, as becomes conscientious students of history and biography, to tell of the up-shot of his negotiations with Curson & Seton (the New York agents in co-operation with whom he hoped adequately to finance the concerns of the proprietors) and to make clear his exact situation, viewed from every angle, at the outbreak of the American Revolution.

It is to be regretted that there are almost no "personal memoirs" extant to provide intimate glimpses of Erskine in the flesh. In 1851, there was living in a little house upon the road between Rockaway and Mount Hope, a Mrs. Elizabeth ("Betsey") Doland, then in her 93rd year. As a small child she had been brought over from Germany with her father,—who was one of the workmen engaged by Hasenclever. She recalled Hasenclever and Faesch clearly. The former, said she, was lavish in his expenditures of money—especially when it came to providing luxuries for his own grand establishment or improving the houses occupied by his countrymen employed at the works; making them much more costly than was necessary. She lived at Ringwood during the regime of Faesch, and recollected Mr. Humphries, who assisted him in the management of the works. She remembered little concerning Erskine, but confirmed the generally accepted opinion that he was both prompt and resolute; and exceedingly thrifty, withal. According to her account, he had collected a large stock of goods and provisions at Ringwood during the months immediately preceding the outbreak of the Revolution, which he eventually disposed of at "an enormous advance." Mrs. Doland said that the man at whose house she was living gave Erskine 15 bushels of wheat for 1 bushel of salt. We cannot doubt her statement that "he had on hand a large quantity of rum and other articles deemed indispensable for times of war." The men comprising his regiment of militia, she adds, were kept employed around the works, but were ready for military duty should the emergency arise.[4]

[4] Rev. Joseph F. Tuttle, *Revolutionary Fragments, Morris County, New Jersey* (pamphlet, Morristown, 1896), p. 25. (Originally written in 1850 as columns in the *Newark Daily Advertiser*.) It seems likely that Mrs. Doland was thinking of the Bellgrove store as regards the large stock of goods. The price of salt was extremely high during the Revolution. H. S.

Unimportant and isolated as Ringwood seems to-day, it cannot be doubted that this settlement and the other iron-works villages were, a century and a half ago, centers of population and social life. In an ancient advertisement, appearing in the *New-York Gazette* of March 29, 1773, we find a small Ramapough farm offered for sale, with its favorable location offered as an inducement, because "it is situate . . . about 10 or 12 miles from Ringwood and Sterling iron-works, which are very good markets for all kinds of produce." [5]

Quite a little has been recorded concerning the Ringwood, Long Pond and Charlotteburg iron works of the American Company, because the sources of information are fairly numerous and well authenticated. Of the Cortlandt Furnace, we know much less. It is said to have been unprofitable; certainly it was too far removed from the New Jersey group of workings to be operated in any proper conjunction with them. The "Bellegrove Store," [6] a central depot and repository of general merchandise intended to supply all the works of the London syndicate, had been established in the old Ramapough section of Bergen County, near the New York line. It was so located for the reason that from thence there was good road communication with the great Hudson River and the upper tidewater shipping point on the Hackensack. Of this capacious old storehouse no trace remains, neither is its precise site known. It is not far from the truth, however, to record that it stood west of the present Erie R. R. station at

[5] *New Jersey Archives*, First Series, Vol. 28, pp. 469–70.

[6] *The Bellegrove Store*, as a base of supplies for all the Works, appears to have been exceedingly well stocked. Under date of *June 10th, 1774*, in Erskine's "Waste Book," we find a list of purchases totaling £363, "bought by Isaac Noble for Belgrove." Noble was probably one of the family who operated the Sterling Lake mines, and—if so—we may conclude that friendly and reciprocal business relations existed between these people and Robt. Erskine.

Mahwah, on the old road which passes under the railway and leads to the main highway running approximately north and south from Suffern to Oakland. A little below the intersection was the humble homestead of Andrew Hopper, erstwhile friend of Washington, which has been forever perpetuated in Revolutionary history as the "Bergen County headquarters," of the Commander in Chief in September of 1780.[7] Quite likely Erskine knew the house and its owner even better than did Washington, for he must have passed it often while en route from Ringwood to Bellegrove.

As has been intimated, Erskine kept his accounts with greatest care. Many of his books of original entry are preserved today in the vault of the New Jersey Historical Society at Newark, where they may be inspected by any inquirer. Old business records of this period are not excessively rare; but somehow or other those of Robert Erskine have a peculiar fascination as setting down the story of such routine transactions as visualize with especial clarity the every-day doings of the eighteenth century.

In the times of our fore-fathers (which seem to us so romantic after the lapse of years), people appear to have lived very much as do we of the present day. They were born and they died; they were married and given in marriage; they ate and drank; occasionally they were ill, even as you and I;—they had their times of famine and of plenty; they worked and played; some of them could put us all to shame when it came to mentality and culture. Life at Ringwood presented, of course, all of the striking contrasts common to those days. At the Manor House Erskine was the lord and the gentleman. In the cottages

[7] Andrew Hopper's inn has long since disappeared, though its site is still known and is marked by a State historical road marker. Hopper's grave is nearby. H. S.

of the tenantry and of the miners there was food and fuel aplenty—mayhap little else—but contentment reigned between master and men; for Erskine dealt justly and uprightly with his fellows.

I doubt whether many pages of imaginative fiction could be more diverting or more informative than the following items, culled from Erskine's "Waste Book," corresponding to the "blotter" used by old time book-keepers, which is now almost a relic of the past.

Erskine was pleased to give this book of original entry a very pompous heading:

"Waste Book
Commencing May 1774, By Robert Erskine, of
Ringwood, Longpond & Charlotteburg Iron Works New Jersey
& Cortlandt Furnace in New York Province &c.
Bellgrove Store New Jersey."

In it he sets down his purchases, with a columnar arrangement for debiting certain items to himself and others to the Proprietors of the Works. Quite evidently he made periodical trips to New York City, while there visiting the "city office" of the London syndicate, rendering accounts, writing letters to his principals, and—I suppose —going the rounds of the merchants and picking up bargains here and there. He did business with such people as Frederick Rhinelander, Thomas Burling, Jacobus Bleecker and Peter Goelet, all of whom have left names honored and familiar in the annals of the metropolis. Commenting prefatorily upon the items which are appended, taken at random during 1774 and 1775, let me say that the partners of "Lewther Pagan & Co." were distant connections of Erskine; that, in a subsequent letter, there appeared a passage condemning Hayman Levy as

being guilty of sharp business practice; and that I have
not multiplied the liquor items:

Ringwood, for wine	£ 11.12. 6
Cash for 9 [barrels] Cod Fish	11.14.
for 1 barrell Mackerel	1.12.
2 [hogsheads] N. York Rumm (257 Gallons at 2/7)	33. 3.11
9 Masqueraqde Waistcoat Patterns [at] 12/6	5.12. 6
5C. Fish hooks @ 16/pr. M	8.
50 lb. Allspice @ 10d	2. 1. 8
Bot. of Lewther Pagan & Co. 1525 galls. [rum] @ 2/7	196.19. 7
Cash paid Joseph Allicocke for 4⅞ gallons old F. Brandy	1.19.
1 doz. Lisbon Wine	25.
Bot. of Dennis McReady 5 bbls. Tobacco 188 doz 2/	18.16.
¼ hundred quills 2/—1 small paper book, 9s	12.
1 quire paper 1/6	1. 6.
Bought of Hayman Levy—2 Bear Skines @ 16/	1.12.
Bought of Samuel Loudon—1 Coppy of Roline 13 vos.	4.
Bot. of Thos. Bridgen Attwood,	

1 bottle Tincture Myrrh	1. 6	
2 lbs. Creamor Tartar @ 4/	8.	
	———	9. 6

Cash paid John Burch for . . . 1 Tin punched Lanthorn	4.
7½ lb. pewter Dishes 6¼ lb. pewter plates @ ⅔	1.10.11¼
Warming pan 3¼ lb 4/.	13. [8]

[8] The Bellegrove accounts are indeed interesting. They are those of a
store evidently used by people of the various iron works. Certain items
were charged against the works themselves. Occasionally Erskine autographed an item as being for himself personally. A more significant
sampling of items could be made. H. S.

It has been said that "the great American novel" has yet to be written. Might not the story of Erskine and picturesque Ringwood furnish an adequate background for such a bit of historic fiction? Even the prosaic entries above set down are replete with suggestion.

The high price of paper tells all too plainly of a British monopoly: [9] That Erskine was a book-lover is evidenced by his purchase of 13 volumes of Rollin's *Roman History*. The pharmaceutical items demonstrate that every well-ordered home had its "medicine cabinet." The "lanthorn" purchase tells in one brief word the story of days when candle-illuminated lanterns answered equally well the purposes of modern electric flash-lamps. And the last copied entry is very satisfying, for it conveys the impression that December must have made the need of a "warming pan" quite evident to the dwellers at Ringwood Manor, thus permitting the comforting reflection that cold feet are not a product of our present effete civilization.

There is yet one more published reference to Ringwood in the pre-Revolutionary period. True, it is but a newspaper item, telling that Erskine had been relieved of another horse; but it demonstrates that he still possessed plenty of energy and had ten dollars in ready cash:

Ringwood Iron Works, New-Jersey, July 10, 1774
Ten Dollars Reward—Lost, supposed to have been stolen from these Works about eight days ago, a ten year old black stallion, with his mane cut at the left side, short tail, and stands crooked on the near hind foot. Whoever secures the

---

[9] American paper manufacture did not begin until after the Revolution. Satirical as it may seem, almost all of the highly valued autograph letters of our patriot generals and statesmen during the war-period are written on British-made paper, some of the sheets bearing the watermark of the royal crown.

thief for conviction, or returns the horse shall be paid the
above reward and all reasonable Charges by

Robert Erskine [10]

Two purely business letters written by Mr. Erskine
must now be set down in full. Hereafter we shall refer
but casually to his position and responsibilities as the
agent for the English proprietors, but in order to comprehend just how unsatisfactory was his situation, and the
extent of the misunderstanding and hard feeling which
opposed his every effort to save the iron works from inevitable ruin, it seems that these last and final statements
deserve careful perusal.

In the first of these communications, addressed to Curson & Seton at New York, the Ringwood manager comes
out point blank in his expression of opinion that lack of
capital is the motive for the action of the New York house
in quibbling over details, and of subsequently falling
down entirely where matters of large financial extent are
concerned.

It seems that Erskine,—true to his policy of putting
the interests of his employers above all else,—had written
the home office in London, asking for advice. He had explained the attitude of Curson & Seton in regard to holding back payments and refusing to honor his drafts, and
had likewise expressed his concern over their heavy requisitions for iron. Already he was beginning to feel doubtful as to the stability of his newly-formed New York connections, and had offered, it appears, to handle the selling
end of the enterprise himself, providing the proprietors of
the American Company were able and willing to finance
him as occasion required.

[10] *New Jersey Archives,* First Series, Vol. 29, p. 419.

Curson & Seton had taken umbrage at some of Erskine's insinuations, which must have been transmitted to them, as they themselves had been corresponding direct with the London headquarters of the American Company. They had taxed Erskine with his statements of fact; and he, in rebuttal, contends that, in their anxiety to get ready cash, they had made at least one bad bargain in the sale of iron. Then, too, Erskine thinks that Curson & Seton have paid too much for supplies. Notwithstanding his annoyance, Erskine protests vigorously that he has thrown no aspersions on the honor of Curson & Seton, but has criticized merely their ability, business judgment, and financial worth, being genuinely concerned lest they were on the verge of bankruptcy.

In this connection, there emerges one of the most illuminating passages of the entire letter. Erskine had, it seems, offered to throw himself temporarily into the breach, and if the condition of Curson & Seton was as bad as he feared, to do his best to meet the obligations on which they had fallen down. He refers to himself as one who, having no posterity, could again face adversity. He states that he is willing to risk his own fortunes, rather than to jeopardize those of two families (presumably those of Messrs. Curson & Seton) with numerous children. Surely, after the unkind things they had said about him, this is a remarkable illustration of Christian charity:

New York, August 8th, 1774

Gentlemen

What passes in Conversation is frequently undeterminate and lyable to different Constructions besides several people, of whom I am one, have not the happiness of a quick recollection, or a ready way of Clothing their Ideas with proper words of hand, on these accounts, I beg leave to put what I have to say on paper, which has this aditional advantage, that what is thus said can neither be forgot nor retracted.

On recollecting our Conversation of yesterday particularly M^r. Cursons acknowledgment of writing M^r. Willis and of his being long dissatisfied with my Conduct to which I must own myself not at all a stranger for it was visible enough, I agree with you in thinking it necessary to come to a thorough explanation, which I shall now attempt. I shall endeavour to probe the matter to the bottom. The doing this and writing by the Lady Gage is as much as I can accomplish at present, for I find what M^r. Smith refers to was in different letters which I must defer Copying at this time as this is the less necessary because what you might think exceptionable paragraphs will appear in the course of this Exclaircissement.

If I mistake not the Commencement of that dissatisfaction on both sides Commenced at the time of your presenting me with a paper ready to be signed sealed and delivered, immediately, with my former obligation likewise ready to be given up, without previous notice, with this I acknowledge I was displeased, as well with the manner as the matter; as in recollection and perusal I found that by executing It I should divest myself of all right or share in the disposal of the Companies property any where, being made lyable to deliver up to you or your order any species of it what ever to be immediately sold and Converted into money, for what it would fetch. This would have been to fetter both my self and the Works in a manner to which I could not submit to, and carried all the appearance of distrust either of my head or my heart. I penned a Counter obligation in my eyes more equitable, the Conclusion of which Contained some restrictions on your part which M^r. Curson totally rejected in a manner which made it evident enough that an implicit acquiescence alone would give satisfaction and this further appeared by refusing me a small sum of Money £80. I think, when I was anxious to go up to the works, which I could not do without & which I borrowed, and should further have continued to shift as well as I could rather than have all the

Companies property and my self be under absolute Control of any one. This no doubt you perceived by my after Conduct in procuring & endeavoring to procure money without your intervention.

I told you yesterday that My Connection with the Company I looked upon as a primary object to which I think myself obliged to hold all other Connections in a secondary place[;] upon this principle I set out, and in this shall endeavour to Continue as long as I am in their Service. On this account then, it was that I renewed my Correspondence at that time with M^r. Atkinson as you might perceive by the Companies answer to your letter advising of your Bills for they mention your refusal of trifling sums of money, what I did not take notice of in the Company's letters, all of which you saw.

I commenced this Correspondence with reluctance; my duty to my Constituents forced me to do it and my regard and friendship for you made me carry it on with all the delicacy I was master of. This I think any of your friends would acknowledge were they to see the whole, where to want of Capital and to that alone I attribute your Conduct nor did I ever mean to convey any diffidence either in your integrity or honour, and if from hasty reading, misunderstanding or misapprehension of the same such a thing may be inferred I shall cheerfully do you justice by every means in my power, either by elucidating my meaning or acknowledging my error should I have used any unguarded expressions to which I think myself bound in equity and therefore be a pleasure. [B]ut to be more particular.

The palpable distrust commenced on your part naturally created a caution on mine especially as the subject which occasioned it was never revived. My First letter to Mr Atkinson stated the Facts as it appeared. I gave him the heads of your paper with the heads of my proposals, but sent copies of neither because I did not take a copy of yours—Then I mentioned your refusing me a trifling sum, which I attributed to my refusing to subscribe that paper. I mention this both to show you my inten-

tions and to give you an idea of the whole of the Correspondence. If in this or anything else I have wronged you or mistaken
your meaning I may not only acknowledge but repair my mis-
takes to the utmost of my power.

When I received a statement of your account with the Works
about the middle of Novem^r carried down only to October & the
November drafts left out, I conceived the idea of your exag-
gerating the Ballance, and mentioned that Circumstance ac-
cordly in a letter to M^r. Atkinson by the January packet; which
Letter I was induced to write because you did not inform me of
your intention of sending home your accounts by that packet
(for I expected they were to go with mine in February) till I
was just going out of Town, nor to my knowledge your intention of drawing at all.

M^r. Curson says that he told me of it as I was going out at
the door and I have no doubt but he did. I did not however hear
it or my attention being otherwise fixed; I did not attend to it,
which was the same thing for had I attended I must have taken
notice of it, as it was a measure I was averse to from the first
and instead of which I should have proposed others, mortgaging
or selling the pigs for money or goods and turning those goods
into money I would have rather preferred if possible; however
that you did not look on my Concurrence as necessary appears
from the next Bill, of which I knew nothing until March. M^r.
Seton was at Ringwood either before or soon after the February
packet on asking told me you either had or would not draw by
that packet but mentioned nothing of your intending to draw
the middle of the month. I acknowledge that when I found you
had done so I was greatly vexed, and wrote that letter to M^r.
Atkinson in which were the expressions about paying the piper.

I then alleged that, at that time, you were not a farthing in
actual advance, for which I gave my reasons as follows

Your Bills Drawn this year were then about £2325 Sterling,
which was about £4168 Cur^{cy} which deducted from my gross
Ballance at New Year of £8745 rem^d £4577 odd [,] that the
acceptances outstanding were March 1st £2068, that by your

letter in Jany you reckoned the Iron outstanding (which amounted to 2/3 of the whole, or about £2400) equivalent to debits for goods not due [;] that as the iron was usually sold at 3 months it was now nearly all due, which I supposed was not the Case with dry goods, especially, which I usually get at 12 Months credit; [G]iving this reason that, as you were aware of an unavoidable advance since last October you would not needlessly increase it when it might be so easily avoided.

I likewise mentioned that this drawing perplexed me so much that if you drew any more extra I should think it my duty to break off all Connection with you till I heard from home. I likewise said that I had no doubt I could get other houses to take the business upon them but as I offered to do it myself with an occasional Credit of £3000 Sterling, I would defer Conecting my self farther till I heard from home. The paying the piper was thus applied. I concluded that the Rivers were now open & M^r. Kittleton had received 20 Tons of his Bar Iron already and I suppose will get the whole in less than a fourtnight. There is therefore between 3 and 4 Pounds a Ton lost upon that Bargain merely because your agents could not spare £700 for a couple of months, which is all I have yet received on account of that Sale; thus the poor Works on this side as well as you on tother pay the piper. . . .

In this Calculation, the bills are supposed accepted, consequently I could not obstruct their being so. I possibly may be mistaken in my Calculations as I acknowledge it was wrote when I was fretted and vexed on account of your drawing. . . . That the Dry goods and other articles were generally dearer than when Yates supplied us whose example you did not follow in setting down the names of the persons from whom you purchased in the invoices furnished me.

This last paragraph, tho narrating a matter of fact, is the only exceptionable part of my whole Correspondence, which I now see and acknowledge might be twisted to your disadvantage. I frequently doubted your ability which you with Candour as frequently acknowledged but never your honor, not even where there was some appearance of reason, for when Kelso told me about the cloths I immediately assured him that I was Certain you had some way or other been imposed on. . . .

As I have therefore in my opinion pointed out the most nay, perhaps the only part of my Correspondence from whence an improper Inference might be drawn at least, so it appears in my eyes I beg leave to assure you I shall be happy to do you all the justice you think necessary in the most effectual way which can be devised.

When I drew the Bills on the Company through M^r. Atkinson, I set forth in the Clearest manner I could my reasons for taking that step, and the principal force of my arguments lay in the Consideration that if the bills returned protested you could not stand it, which Mr. Seton acknowledged, the Consequence of which would have been the ruin of the credit of your house. I therefore resolved at all events to place myself if possible in the gap, Considering that though your offers of assistance to me were voluntary, yet as I had unfortunately been the means of drawing you into this Dilemma, I was resolved rather to risque the fortune of one who had already been acquainted with adversity, for whom Providence has amply provided hitherto by his own industry, and who by the Will of God has at present no posterity to provide for, I say I rather choose such an one should run the Risque as far as he could, rather than that two families with numerous Children should be involved in ruin. No other Consideration than this would have induced me to take so disagreeable a Step, and therefore I candidly own that had I been previously advised that this Consequence was not likely to follow as happily it afterwards appeared I should not have drawn new bills. I would however have enforced the payment of the old ones on the principle of the Companies advancing £3000 on account of themselves or whoever else took the advance reaping the profits of the agency which I had no doubt they would assume since they found that at any rate they must risque the advance.

My subsequent letters contain nothing more material than

my account of my offering to take the burden of you by doing the business my self which though at the time you declined you afterwards unexpectedly gave up. I mentioned one circumstance; that in June when you gave up the business, that you proposed I should draw for the Iron in future which has not been done but which however is very immaterial, as I advised of my having received £611 on that account. Duplicates of the last letters, both to the Company and M^r. Atkinson I have enclosed on the last of which I beg leave to observe that I made the agency an advance of £800 upon 430 Tons of pigs because in May & June I drew £1500 on that gentleman each month over and above my drafts in your favor; I am, gentlemen,

With real regards

Your most obed^t humb. Servt.

P. S. In Case there should be want of time I think the best way will be to transmit this with your observations of it, only furnishing me with a Copy at leizure, and I give you my word neither to write to M^r. Atkinson or the Company without your knowing the Contents, provided you come under the same restrictions to me in your Correspondence with M^r. Willis, so far as it shall relate to myself and the Works.

R. Erskine [11]

That matters grew from bad to worse is evident from Erskine's personal letter to William Seton a month later. Here, with his back literally to the wall, the master of the mines stands entirely alone and on the defensive:

Ringwood, September 10th, 1774

Sir

Whether the favour from your house of the 8th Ins^t., excites most my Contempt or my pity, I cannot fully determine; persons who are guilty of the injustice done me by such low sus-

---

[11] *The Manor and Forges of Ringwood*, II, 23. As quite often, especially when perturbed, Erskine did not bother to punctuate very much in his first draft. The paragraphing is that of Heusser. H. S.

picions deserve both. I call your Letter a favour therefore, as it really is; for thereby you have given me an opportunity of knowing, not only the sentiments you are pleased to entertain, but also of acquitting myself from Charges so base as those of falsehood, of fraud and of villainy.

It would be the height of meanness to think of, much less to attempt a justification to you; besides, to persons so prejudiced the attempt would be as futile as mean. But there are many Gentlemen in this Country whose friendship I hope does not depend on that precarious tenure by which I held yours, and who, uninterested in the event, cannot view the doing justice to my employers as a Crime; to such I can shew, that it was not from fancy and conceit or a design to injure you that I commenced and continued the Correspondence at which you are so much offended: no Sir, it was from stubborn facts by which I can prove that I was justly alarmed at the situation of your house; that notwithstanding this, I treated the matter with all the delicacy and friendship I could consistant with justice; that I made known the Contents, but to two, in America, and that, very partially, to one only so much as was necessary to show the probability of the payment of some bills I drew; the other had some right to enquire and be satisfied with the propriety of my Conduct; but neither I am sure could or would make use of my Communications to your prejudice, and when I mentioned in my last letters which passed through your hands & which are the only ones I have wrote home since mine to M^r. Atkinson you perused, when I mentioned, I say, the referring to our differences to your Correspondent whom I would not supposed prejudiced and one of the proprietors, I meant it for your sakes, not my own; I am totally indifferent should all the World know my proceedings, and it is a matter equally eligible to me, whether the differences in our accounts are settled on that or this side the Atlantic; your making choice of the latter will enable me to clear myself the sooner from the stigma under which you have laid me.

I shall shew, and have it Certified by Gentlemen of Credit

and honour, that from a minute inspection of our accounts, from the testimony of the people to whom I gave the drafts, their Companions, the overseers & the Clerks, that they are justly credited for work done on our Books, that the sum due for the bills you refused to pay were due *Bona fide* to the respective people *ab origine.*

Conscious of my innocence and integrity in this as well as every other transaction, and of my ability to refute with the Clearest demonstration any Calumny of so base a nature, I can look over the paragraph with disdain, and can speak of it with temper, which perhaps would not be the case were there any justice in your allegations. To some of the new people I advanced money on their drafts, Three of them are Master Colliers, worth some hundred pounds carried here, who voluntarily left them in my hands for safety and begged me to receive the Cash for them that they might be saved the trouble of going to New York. I brought them for acceptance, and they have been in my hands ever since, for their use, nor did I recollect their being due till a few minutes before M^r. Hayes set off, when the sending for the people out of the woods to have them endorsed would have delayed him too long, I therefore told him it was a matter of indifference whether they were endorsed or not, and he might either leave it alone or do it himself. I have received money for such Drafts without endorsement both from M^r. Yates and you, and surely my discharge or that of my Clerks is a sufficient voucher for paying money for which you had both debited the proprietors and been Credited for in our accounts. I could not possibly have imagined that such a pretense for their non payment could have entered your thoughts, much less that you would confirm on paper your thus coinciding with M^r. Curson's ungenerous Suspicions both of M^r. Lewis and myself, which Suspicions so easily proved totally groundless may be a detriment to the Suspectors—not the suspected.

To your other reason for their non payment the deficiency of iron I can only say it appears by the Carter's receipts, that there went to the Landings of:

Bar Iron from Charlotteburg in July	16.12.0.18	
Do Ringwood Do	15. 7.1.10	
Do Long Pond Do	9. 2.0.19	
		41. 1.2.19
Bar Iron from Charlotteburg in August	14. 6.3.10	
Do Ringwood Do	17.12.2.21	
Do Long Pond Do	8. 4.1.00	
		40. 3.3. 3
		81. 5.1.22

Since, therefore, you have received only 41 Tons for June July and August, there must be a Considerable quantity not come to hand for I suppose the sales in that time does not exceed 10 Tons: my knowing that the above quantity was gone in the two last months and only asking for the value of 10 tons that you might have 30 Tons a month for 6 months as I proposed in my letters last May, showed both my inclinations and willingness to serve you.

I observe in your account Current, two bills dated May 16th of £250 Each to Joseph Wharton, which I suppose are those you mention as protested (I have received no letters by last packet, and therefore can only speak from conjecture respecting the bills you say are protested). This I own surprises me, and I can account for it in no other manner than by the engagements under which they accepted one of your £500 Bills due (I suppose, about the time) to your correspondent Mr. Smith, wherein he engaged for you, as advised by his letter you read me, that you should remit Iron to them without drawing for it equivalent to that Bill. My bills were of May 7th, you have not been pleased to tell me whether they have been honoured or not; by your silence I suppose they have.

Your Drawing for the pigs shipt which I should have been glad for your own Credit had all gone on account of my Bills, might likewise have had some influence. This Fabric however is none of my raising, and if by my proximity to it I should be bruised with the ruins, I must bear it as I ought, Conscious that however deficient in my duty to God, I have not designedly injured or done injustice to man. Be it as it will, I can yet thank God, erect to save me from being quite Crushed an arch Composed of 1000 tons of pig metal and abundance of other solid materials, should even the portended fall take place.

Mr. Hayes informs me that besides your refusing payment for the accepted Bills in his Custody, you told him you were sorry to have paid £80 to the Morris town post, from whence the Conclusions that you mean or that you must stop payment is natural. I have done and shall do all I can to prevent the Works from being either the real cause of such a misfortune, my knowing the fate of my Bills and this is a circumstance is then important both to yourselves and the works of which therefore I shall be glad you would apprise.

Gentlemen,

Your humble servant,

Robert Erskine

To Mr. William Seton.[12]

Here the curtain finally falls: no more is known, nor are there other letters in existence to enlighten us as to what happened between Ringwood and New York. Henceforth Erskine assumed the entire responsibility of trusteeship; he carefully gathered in whatever was to be gotten in the way of profits or moneys outstanding, and took upon himself the burden of payment of all legitimate obligations due or thereafter to be incurred.

[12] *Ibid.*, II, 28. This is apparently a copy of the letters sent rather than a first draft. The paragraphing is Heusser's. H. S.

9

Erskine the Patriot

ROBERT Erskine has justly been given the credit for organizing one of the very first companies of patriot militia in the Province of New Jersey. Reading the signs of the times as he did, he made early preparation for the coming struggle. He himself drilled the greater portion of the younger men employed at Ringwood and the neighboring works under his control into a remarkably efficient body, and soon placed them at the disposal of the New Jersey Legislature. In August of 1775 that body suitably acknowledged his patriotism by issuing to him an official commission as captain of his own contingent.

Interesting confirmation of the historic record that this company of rural provincials actually existed, is found through an examination of Erskine's books.[1] Undoubtedly they were outfitted and armed at his own expense. Under

[1] Erskine Papers.

date of July 17, 1775, we find the following charges for
money expended by him at New York City:

```
Boᵗ of Francis Lewis & Son—
    25 Guns @ 28/              £35.—.—
     7 ditto @ d/                  9.16.—  £44.16.—
Boᵗ of Edward Annely Gunsmith
   ·12 Guns & Bayonets @ 45/  £27.—.—
     2 ditto & ditto               4.10.—
     6 ditto & ditto         41/  12. 6.—
     5 ditto                 36/   9.—.—  £52.16.—
```

These figures would suggest that Erskine's little army
numbered about sixty. Under date of July 19, 1775,
there appears:

```
Boᵗ of Daniel McCormack 14th Ultimo—
    1 pᶜ Green Coating, 80 yds. @ 4/9      19.—.—
```

Were Erskine's men, like the outlawed band of Robin
Hood, clothed in "forest green"? A further scrutiny of his
tell-tale "Waste Book" reveals other expenditures for
saddler-work and 24 pairs of shoes, then, on October 10,
1775:

```
Boᵗ of John Bailey 1 Gun           £ 4.—.—
    3 Swords, Silver mounted @ £7 10/ ea.  22.10.—
    2 pairs Swivals, @ 8/           —.16.—  27. 6.—
```

These latter items, coming after Erskine's appointment
as Captain, would seem to indicate that he was by no
means averse to equipping himself and his lieutenants
with handy but dignified sidearms for the coming fracas.

In a communication dated December 2, 1775, to the
"Colonel and other officers of the 1st Battalion of Con-

tinental Troops raising in the Jerseys," Mr. Erskine transmits a copy of his own commission, which deserves to be reprinted.

In Provincial Congress, Trenton, New Jersey, 17 August, 1775. This Congress being informed by John Fell, Esq., one of the Deputies for the County of Bergen, that Robert Erskine Esq., hath at his own expense provided arms and accoutred an independent company of Foot Militia in said County, do highly approve of his zeal in the same, and do order that he be commissioned as Captain of said Company. A true copy from the Minutes.

Wm. Paterson, Sec'y.[2]

This commission Erskine copies in order to have the higher officers of the battalion rectify the irregular proceedings of one Yelas Meade, who was enlisting his men contrary to the exemption of Congress; such enlistments seriously interfering with the business of the Works.[3] He says his company "consists of forgemen, carpenters, blacksmiths and other hands, whose attendance is daily required. I dare say, however, that there is not a man belonging to it but would lend his aid in a case of extremity, when every consideration must give way to the salvation of the country." He further says, "I have been at a very great expense in arms, uniforms and discipline," and he closes his letter "with the sincerest wishes of success to the friends of the British Constitution and the Liberties of America." [4]

[2] Later the Governor of the State of New Jersey. The City of Paterson was named in his honor.

[3] After the war had begun, Erskine applied to the General Congress, and later to Washington himself, to have his men exempted from field duty, except in cases of special exigency.

[4] The previous two paragraphs, including the quotation, Mr. Heusser "lifted" from the article by the Rev. Joseph F. Tuttle, "The Early History of Morris County, New Jersey," *Proceedings of the New Jersey Historical Society*, Second Series, Vol. II (1869), pp. 33–34. H. S.

Somewhat amusing now, although serious enough to the parties concerned a century and a half ago, is the "Hoff-Erskine controversy," a neighborly squabble between rival iron-masters in the Jerseys, which occurred while the actual military operations of the war were going on in New England, and the patriots hereabout had yet a little while to dispute among themselves before the common cause of liberty demanded a more noble spirit of coöperation.

At the outbreak of the Revolution, Joseph Hoff was the active manager of the iron mines and furnaces at Hibernia, N. J., owned largely by Lord Stirling. The following series of combative notes, copied from the Hoff duplicate letter-books now preserved at Washington's Headquarters at Morristown, N. J., give interesting "side lights" on Erskine's character, demonstrate the shortage of powder in the colonies in 1775, and indicate, moreover, that there were disputed mining rights and much ill-feeling between the rival iron masters. Lord Stirling seems to have claimed "half a dollar a ton" royalty from both Erskine and Col. Samuel Ogden on all the ore raised from a certain vein in Morris County which he believed to be his property. It is also quite evident that Erskine had indeed formed his henchmen into a little army, whose efficiency was known among his neighbors; and, from what Hoff has to say, it is apparent that the former had gained the reputation of being "resolute" to a point of stubbornness. Quite likely, however, the master of Ringwood knew that he was justified in his contentions regarding the right to take ore from Hibernia, and was reluctant to part with the powder which his own forethought had laid by for times of need; especially as Hoff made his first request in rather a blustering manner. The incident, nevertheless, shows Erskine's state of preparedness; and reminds one of those virgins of the Scripture—five of whom were wise and five foolish,—the latter "having no oil in their lamps."

The first letter from Hoff to Erskine opens the battle of words:

Hibernia, May 7th, 1775

Robert Erskine Es^{qr}.

Sir:—I lately received a letter from Messrs Murrays, New York, informing me that all the powder in that place had been procured for the safety of the province in case matters were to come to such desperate lengths as that they must have recourse to blows with the parent state. Alarmed at this piece of news, I went immediately to New York, to know what was to be done with the works; they being lately put in blast, a large stock of wood cut and great numbers of hands employed at the Coaling and other business, and not more than five weeks Oar now raised. They assured me that although the most diligent search had been made for powder not a single pound was to be had, but that a little before the General Stoppage took place ¾ had been sent for us to Elizabeth Town, which they hoped would serve as a temporary relief till more could be had. I went immediately to Elizabeth Town, where I found the committee of that place on all the powder we had there, and would not suffer it to be removed. In this emergency I wrote Lord Stirling to know what was to be done, and have received the enclosed letter for answer, which you will be pleased to consider and favor his Lordship or me with your pleasure thereon. I doubt not your willingness to assist us to the loan of a couple cwt. of that article. It shall be thankfully returned as soon as it is to be had, or if as agreeable I will give you a bill on Murray, Sanson & Co. for the am't, payable at sight.

If the powder is not to be had, the great distress we are in for Ore will oblige me to adopt the measure prescribed by his Lordship. As you will see by his letter, he expects you to stipulate in writing to pay him half a Dollar per tonn for every tonn of Ore raised at the Hibernia Mine at the upper part commonly called Lord Stirling's vein,—under Col. Ogden's or any other person's pretentions to rights there, whatever. If this is not complied with, he has enjoined it on me not to suffer the Oar to be moved, which I can't fail to observe. I hope, nevertheless, I shall not be drove to taking an acting part in this affair, as the requisitions made by his Lordship will appear to you as highly just and reasonable.

My brother will wait on you with this, by whom you'll be pleased to favor me with your answer. I am Sir, with due respect, your most humble servant.

Joseph Hoff

Quite evidently, Erskine's answer was a definite refusal, for upon the reverse of the letter-book page from which the above is copied, we find the following notation in Hoff's hand-writing:

May 21, 1775.
Wrote Lord Stirling an account of what Mr. Erskine said to my brother, and sent him a copy of my letter to Mr. Erskine. Wrote him also that no information could be obtained of Col. Ford's [5] advancement to the town. That 70 tons pig were made, and that I should observe his directions, if Wighton had the Castings."

Hoff's second letter is to his Lordship, the Earl of Stirling, and shows the writer to be conscious that he has been lacking in diplomacy in his request to Erskine. He asks what next is to be done:

Hibernia, May 25, 1775

My Lord,
Yours of the 15th ins't received and till then yours of the 4th of May did not reach me. I was at some time at a stand what

[5] Col. Jacob Ford, Jr., owner of the Morristown forge and the house wherein Washington established his famous headquarters of 1779–80.

methods to take to obtain the powder from Mr. Erskine and finally concluded I could not in any other way so well make your orders to me known to him, as by enclosing your letter on that head, which I accordingly did and sent by my brother Charles, therewith. Mr. Erskine told my brother that had he been applied to in a more modest manner he would not have refused the powder, but that he was not to be threatened into compliance. That, however, he was then on the way to Boonton and on his return would send a definite answer. I am sorry I did not apply to him in a different manner, but it can't be helped now.

If I have taken a wrong step, I daresay your Lordship will view it as an error of judgment. I only thought it would prove to be the most effectual measure to answer the purpose. I must now beg to know how I must proceed. I wish proper steps by law were taken to prevent any further invasion on this property. Violence, I think, will be both illegal and dangerous, for they are resolved to repel force with force, from what I can find out.

Mr. Erskine has bought the ore of Col. Ogden,[6] who must deliver it to him and prevent any persons from molesting him in the transportation of it to the Works. I shall, in your name, forbid any person removing it, as they'l answer the consequences, and if they are obstinate, I'll take an account of the names of the carters and send them to you immediately. The consequences of these works are greatly diminished by these working in the mine, not only from the quantity of ore raised from it, but from the irregular manner in which they carried it on. I'm not able at present to give you any account of Col. Ford's advancement towards the Dam, but will apply to him for it if your Lordship thinks proper.

If you have done with the accounts I sent you, I sh'd be glad to have them sent the first opportunity. I shall observe what you say about the carting, if Wigton's employed. I thank

[6] Col. Ogden was one of the proprietors of the original Ringwood Company (1740-1764) who had subsequently established himself at Pompton.

you for magazines and chronicles lately sent me. They shall be taken good care of and duly returned.

I want next year to go into some other business for myself, less perplexing and as profitable as possible.

Your humble servant,
Joseph Hoff

The third letter sounds the note of warning from employee to employer: "Erskine is ready to fight," intimates Hoff, and he, for one, is not going to burn his hands by pulling Lord Stirling's chestnuts out of the fire:

Hibernia, 27 May 1775

To the Honorable, the Earl of Stirling

My Lord, I have received your letters of the 21st and 24th inst. I was, till now, in hopes some other methods would be found out to settle the Despute about the mine. Your Lordship told me an action would be commenced against Mr. Ogden in the name of Messrs. Murray, and this I have expected for some time past.

I would willingly go any farther justifiable lengths to serve your interests or obey your commands, but to enter into a dispute as serious as I am satisfied this would be is what I can't think of, nor your Lordship expect of me. Mr. Erskine, with Col. Ogden, is resolved to make the most vigorous resistance. Their numbers are 2 to 1, nay 3 to 1; which is great odds, and at any rate I would declare against the measure. There certainly will provide other and better methods, which will produce more salutory effects.

I shall in your name forbid every person from removing the Oar, and will send you exact acc'ts of all matters. If Col. Ogden has no right to the mines, and there is no other way to prevent him from raising the Ore but by force of Arms, he will both keep possession and the property,—for his strength (with Mr. Erskine's Long Pond and Charlottenburg troops) is far too superior to ours. However, if I could see it ever so equitable to us, it is not the case. I would not engage in a thing I could not go through with. Messrs. Murray know nothing of this dispute. I think they ought to be informed of them. Nothing more to add.

Your humble servant,
Joseph Hoff

Thus endeth the correspondence. Joseph Hoff died in 1777 and was succeeded in the management of the Hibernia Works by his younger brother, Charles Hoff, Jr. Lord Stirling and Erskine eventually arrived at an amicable solution of their business differences, or at any rate they put them aside for good and all; both of them thereafter devoting every energy and resource to the cause of American liberty, which soon took precedence over all else.

Perhaps the first attempt of Erskine to devote his mechanical talents to a purely patriotic service for the American cause was his construction of a model "chevaux-de-frise" for the obstruction of rivers and harbors. Much has been written concerning the schemes for defending the Hudson River during the Revolution, but not one word of credit has ever been given to Erskine. Yet it was he who first suggested the contrivance of spiked beams and cofferdams which was employed on several occasions—unsuccessfully, it is true, between Forts Washington and Lee, but with better results farther up the river during the later years of the war. In 1920 the writer came upon Erskine's own autographed copy of a communication which he had forwarded to General John Morin Scott, of the New York Militia (together with a cleverly executed model of the contrivance) soon after the publication of the Declaration of Independence, wherein the struggling provinces had thrown down the gauntlet to Great Britain.

Fully to understand the circumstances under which Erskine's letter was written, let us refer to contemporary history. On the 28th of June, 1776, the British fleet had arrived from Halifax and had discharged thousands of troops upon Staten Island, threatening New York and New Jersey with the prospect of a speedy and formidable invasion. On July the 12th, five of the enemy's ships of war had passed the patriot batteries at New York City and Paulus Hook, and were, at the time of Erskine's communication, snugly anchored in Tappan Bay near Haverstraw. Acting promptly, Erskine hurriedly put together the model of his proposed entanglement (to which he was pleased to give the geometrical name of "Tetrahedron") and at once forwarded it to the authorities in charge of New York's defenses. Personally, I regard this letter as the most important "find" in my biographical quest:

Ringwood, July 18th, 1776

Dear Sir:—When I heard that some ships of war, with a fair wind and tide of flood, had passed the batteries with little or no damage; I could not help regretting that the Channel was left open. I know it has been proposed to stop it up, but the present exigency requires some contrivance, that shall be both speedily executed and effectual. After canvassing this matter a little time, an invention which I beg leave to call a Marine Chevaux-de-Frise occurred. Of this I have sent you a model by the bearer, Platt Smith, one of my carpenters, a person I can confide in as a friend, and I trust a true friend to his country, America.

May I here interrupt the continuity of the letter to divulge an interesting revision?—a rather enlightening glimpse of Erskine's ideas of the social system. In the original draft from which I quote, the master of Ringwood had written: . . . "Platt Smith, a gentleman I can confide in, etc." . . . Then he scratched out the "gentleman," and revised it so as to read "one of my carpenters"; showing that he preserved some of the old-world ideas of gentility,—possibly arguing that a worthy and honest carpenter, though he might be a patriot, was scarcely entitled to be called a *"gentleman."* But we must remember that this was in the eighteenth century, and that Erskine —before coming to America—was wont to distinguish between gentle folk and artisans:

Supposing, therefore, the Model to be before you, you will observe it consists of six pieces; it is made to a scale of half an inch to a foot. The pieces then represent beams a foot square and about 32 ft. long. If they were 13, 14 or 15 inches square, so much the better. The nails which join the pieces represent bolts (with a head on one side, to be keyed or screwed with a nut on the other), about 1-½ inches thick.

The Carpenter work is very little, each piece having only two notches, bevelled 60 degrees, or the angle of an equilateral triangle, and cut on one side about one-third of the thickness. A spare piece I have sent will show what carpenter work is required, better than a tedious description. Any carpenter may line, square, notch and bore such pieces without knowing their use; in the same manner the blacksmith may be directed to make the bolts, and shoe them with sharp round iron, which is represented by the black upon the model. The beams could be shod all along like the spare piece, as then the iron would render it specifically heavier than water, but if the points are only shod, it will be necessary to plank in the . . . Tetrahedron, to contain pig iron or stones sufficient to sink it.

There is but one right way of putting the model together, which makes it necessary—though it appears simple—to observe it attentively and comprehend its construction before it is taken to pieces; when the construction is well understood, its putting together is very easy; if the pieces are all of the same dimensions and the notches alike—which they should be—they will fit any way. But to give a true practical idea of taking it to pieces and joining it again, please observe that the Tetrahedron has four horned corners, numbered 1, 2, 3, 4, and three horns to each corner. Place corner No. 1 uppermost.

Then Mr. Erskine goes on to explain the construction of his model and the portability of the contrivance, the timber of which "a sloop might carry, and rigg them up out at sea." "I beg you to excuse me," he continues, "in being thus minute, I intend by it to give a workman a thorough idea of the construction; tho it appears simple when joined, it would prove puzzling to put it together if the construction and position of the beams is not perfectly understood."

Mr. Erskine then explains that the contrivance is about 26 feet in depth, and that, if sunk in a channel of 42 feet of water, it would lie 16 feet beneath the surface. That a ship of 400 tons draws more than this, and therefore frigates would "more than touch it." "The consequence of a vessel running against it must be either to be staked upon it" or "make a hole in her bottom." Mr. E. then makes himself more explicit:

Any vessel being swept upon horns within 14 feet of the surface, would strike it, which must be attended with some of the following consequences: She would either be staked upon it, or her velocity over-set it, the other horns would then rise and take her in the bottom (which probably would make holes through her and oversett her too), or else she would break the "Chevaux-de-Frise" by her weight, which no ship could do without receiving such material damage as to render her unfit for service.

The writer then furnishes data as to the length and the number of units necessary to obstruct a channel the width of the Hudson.

But I need not further enlarge. I shall be happy if it could be put in practice soon enough to incomode our enemies at New York; if too late, then it may be practical elsewhere, particularly to prevent the approach of ships to the forts up the river.

It will naturally occur that this "Fence" should be placed in a channel commanded by a battery to prevent boats weighing them. Two "Chevaux-de-Frise" would reach about 60 feet or 10 fathoms, 20 would make over a channel of an hundred fathoms. Were they scattered here and there in a harbour or anchorage ground, it would render it very unsafe. I shall be happy if this invention could be put in practice soon enough to incommode our enemies at New York; 20 or 30 carpenters and a proper and able number of blacksmiths might finish as many as needful in 30 days. Those ships which have got up, however, may be fenced in at Kingsbridge, or elsewhere. They may be used to prevent ships approaching the forts in the Highlands, but—excuse me—I need not enlarge to a gentleman who now gives his attention to the salvation of his country, in the success of which most heartily joins, dear sir,

Your most obliged and humble servant,

Robert Erskine

His Ex. Gen. J. M. Scott.[7]

As has been recorded, the "chevaux-de-frise" idea was carried into effect as an adjunct to the land defenses of Fort Washington, and the descriptions given by such minute historians as Mr. Reginald Pelham Bolton link the work done at this point with Erskine's plans by words so singularly identical that we cannot doubt the relation. If you will go down to Jeffrey's Hook to-day you may still see some of the iron rings, solidly embedded in the rocky

[7] The original of this letter was once preserved in *The Manor and Forges of Ringwood*, I, 65. The space today is empty, except for a penciled note, "To Scotty," which no one can explain. We must content ourselves, therefore, with Heusser's copy. H. S.

promontory, by which the contrivance was fastened to the New York shore of the river. Because of the fact that it was never fully completed from shore to shore, the British vessels passed and repassed the barrier, but this was no fault of Erskine's. That the contrivance was deemed of real worth is proven by the fact that it was again employed, in 1777–1778, between Polopel's Island and the west shore of the Hudson north of Cornwall. At Washington's Newburgh Headquarters may be seen one of the iron-shod ends of a heavy beam dragged up from the bed of the river in 1836, which is tangible proof of the "Tetrahedron" as a reality. History, moreover, confirms the fact that, under Captain Thomas Machin, such a barrier was laid across the river below New Windsor.

An interesting letter of this period, addressed to Robert Erskine, at Ringwood, well illustrates the manner in which business was transacted by the merchants of the beleaguered city:

N. York 19th Aug^t, 1776

Sir, I am sorry I had not had the pleasure of seeing you when I was at your house—as I should have been glad of Setling a Correspondence with You—but have enter^d into an agreement with M^r. Gordon, in youre behalf—and Paid him for 20 Tons of Good Refin^d bar Iron, for which have given Directions—Who has engag^d to Deliv^d it at Powlass Hook Ferry by the First, of Sept^r, but in Consequence of the Communication being Stop^d between the Jerseys & N Y he has engag^d to return the money, and Likewise in Case the North River should be Cleare has Engag^d to Deliver it at Burling Slip New York—which will be much to my advantage, as I have Left the Care of shipping of it with M^r. Robt. Totten. Please not to fail of Sending it at the Time, and please to Call on M^r. Robt. Totten, who is kind Enough to Take the care of it. Should the Communication be stop[d], as above please to Pay the money to Rob[t]. Totten, & his Rec[t]. will be youre Securaty.

From Sir yr Verry Hu[m] Sevt.

Luke Baker [8]

Notwithstanding the restrictions imposed by the British blockade of the port of New York, it seems clear from the following entry in Erskine's "Cash Book," dated August, 1776, that at least one small shipment of Ringwood iron had gone south, possibly in connection with preparations to resist the threatened British assault in that section of the country:

Received for 3 tons bloomary bar-iron, for
    Charleston, S. C., remitted for
    Peter Kittleton .... £81. 3.5¼ [9]

It was not, however, until the patriot army had been driven out of New Jersey, in the closing months of 1776 (after the disasters at Fort Washington and Fort Lee), that the British were free to prowl about among the rural districts of Bergen County. Even then the fastnesses of the Ramapo Mountains were by no means a safe nor a profitable field for marauders. Ringwood, by reason of its isolation, was a particularly secure place of refuge in these times of danger; the more so because Erskine was a fearless and energetic man and, besides, he had enough men at the home establishment and at the Long Pond Furnaces—only a few miles distant—to make up a respectable regiment; quite enough, plus the natural advantages of the country, to repel three times their number of redcoats. For these reasons, I suppose, no attempt was

[8] *The Manor and Forges of Ringwood*, I, 70. H. S.
[9] Erskine Papers.

ever made by the British Commander-in-Chief at New York to capture the Ringwood mines, although I have heard shadowy stories about Charlotteburg, which might lead one to think that, either through treachery or surprise, some portions of the works were burned, and charcoal pits in the forest hard-by hastily abandoned.

Robert Erskine's house, so it is said, was secured with heavy shutters and doors, well barred and bolted. In fact, he seems to have been fully aware that Ringwood must be made sufficient unto itself, not only because of the existing state of war, but by reason of the renegade robber bands which infested the Ramapo Mountains. It was, moreover, commonly reported and believed that many persons living in New York City, feeling the insecurity of their residences against the depredations of British and Tory enemies, carried their plate to Ringwood for safekeeping.

In an article by the Rev. Joseph F. Tuttle which appeared in the *Newark Daily Advertiser* in 1850, the reminiscences of Mrs. Elizabeth (Betsey) Doland (elsewhere mentioned) touch upon this subject. The writer of these memoirs says:

She was living with a Mr. Walmsley at Pompton, an innkeeper, who did much toward entertaining our soldiers during the war. [V]ery frequently gentlemen would stop for refreshments, and would display great caution and privacy about certain boxes, or trunks, as to justify the suspicion that they contained articles of value. These gentlemen were generally on their way to Ringwood. Mrs. Walmsley would frequently call Betsey's attention to these things, and would say: "Betsey, do you know what is in these? They are full of silver, and they are going to Erskine's for safe keeping." [10]

[10] Rev. Joseph F. Tuttle, *Revolutionary Fragments, Morris County, New Jersey*, p. 27. H. S.

Reports such as this, eagerly circulated throughout the wild mountain region, could not fail to make Erskine's house a tempting bait for the thieves and robbers who infested the hills. Perhaps the most famous of all those rascals who gained notoriety because of their propensities for wholesale stealing was Claudius Smith, the so-called "Cowboy of the Ramapos," to whose myrmidon career I have devoted several pages in volume two of my *Footsteps of Washington*. Whether he had anything to do with the robbery at Ringwood, about which Mrs. Doland refers as she proceeds with her recollections, we have no means of ascertaining; but we will put the blame elsewhere. Smith has already had enough charged to his account, which he finally settled on a scaffold at Goshen, N. Y. (where he was hanged after being wounded and captured)—a dramatic climax to a long series of crimes.

References have been made in the *Proceedings of the New Jersey Historical Society* to another looting of the Ringwood mansion some years later by the Babcocks and their confederates, but Mrs. Doland's account deals with an episode occurring during the lifetime of Erskine. She says:

The gang being very numerous, it is not unlikely that they had some reliable spy in Erskine's employ, to give information when the force at the works were weak, and the family off their guard, especially when the strong man, Erskine himself, was away. These conjectures are corroborated by the facts. Long safety had led the family to be fearless of robbery; and many of the men, with Mr. Erskine, were away in the Army. Be this as it may, a strong band of mounted robbers about midnight stole silently into the settlement and, it is said, were so fortunate as to get hold of a clerk belonging to the concern. Perhaps he was the very spy who gave the information. They tied the young man and ordered him, as he valued his life, to go to the door of the house and wake up the family, telling them that there were some gentlemen from New York, friends of Mr. Erskine, who had just arrived, and would be glad to share in the hospitalities of the family.

The trick succeeded, and the door being unbarred, the robbers rushed in and took possession. Mrs. Erskine by this time finding that the house was taken, put a valuable gold watch into a slipper, and threw it carelessly under the bed, where it would have escaped, had the lady possessed sufficient nerve to carry out the concealment. But the men seemed to know she had such an article of value, and threatened to kill her if she did not go and get it. She was accustomed afterwards to say laughing, "I was so frightened, that I did not dare to refuse, and went and brought the watch to them with my own hands."

Mrs. D. says that they made clean work of all the valuables in the house and it was said secured plunder to a large amount, and then made off. After this, a strong guard was kept about the establishment and no more invasions of this kind occurred.[11]

In 1880 the same writer, Dr. Tuttle, gives the added information that "the robbers induced the clerk to open the store on the pretense of getting medicine for someone sick, and then forced him to go to the house and get admittance." [12] This may have been an elaboration born in the imaginative brain of the writer after thirty years, but that Erskine's house was actually plundered is proven from a notation made by him in 1780 (March 17th) on an inventory sheet, "600 Continental Dollars, property of the Proprietors, taken when the house was robbed." [13]

In June of 1777, Erskine journeyed to Philadelphia; mainly—so it would seem—for the purpose of collecting money due him from the Continental Congress for iron

[11] *Ibid.*

[12] *Proceedings of the New Jersey Historical Society*, Second Series, Vol. VI, p. 164.

[13] *The Manor and Forges of Ringwood*, I, 76. H. S.

furnished for some of the earlier Hudson River defenses. That this trip had anything to do with the map making which was soon to occupy so much of his time is extremely doubtful, although he may have made some cursory observations of the territory in the neighborhood of the Quaker City, being aware of the threatened investment of that place by the British. Nor is it likely that he had any special reason for communicating with or receiving instructions from Washington, then quartered at the Wallace House, Somerville, N. J., although, as will afterward appear, his reputation as a topographer was known to the Commander-in-Chief because of certain of his surveys which had already been placed at the disposal of the patriot leaders in the Jerseys.

In his "Cash Book," [14] Erskine gives an itemized list of his "Expenses to Philadelphia." Besides indicating the route over which he traveled, it furnishes several interesting bits of information as to his character, his habits and his tastes. The tabulated figures represent, of course, pounds, shillings and pence:

Jacobus'	—.12.—
Veal Town	—. 5.—
N. Branch	—. 3.9
Correll's Ferry	1. 8.—
Bogart's	—.13.9
Billet and Board	2.17.—
Germantown	1.12.—
Horses	11. 4.—
Bethlehem	3.12.—
Ink Powder	1.16.—
300 quills	1.12.—
Peter the Great (History)	—.—.08

[14] Erskine Papers.

Ramsay's Poems [15]	—.—.08
Cato	1.04.—
Wine	—.17.06

Business good, & pay*ᵐᵗ* for iron from Gen*ˡ* Mifflin.

It may be explained that "Veal Town" corresponds to modern Bernardsville, and "Correll's Ferry" is Lambertville, N. J. Erskine's return journey, by way of Bethlehem, Pa., probably led him homeward through the Moravian settlement of Hope, N. J., thence to Ringwood via Sussex Court House (modern Newton).

In his cash-book extensions, Erskine deducts from his total expenses the items for "horses, board and travel" and charges the residue to the Proprietors of the Ringwood Iron Works, clearly indicating how closely he drew the lines of demarcation between what he regarded as his legitimate services for the struggling colonies in the capacity of patriot-American by adoption, and as manager, in trust, for the property of his English employers. He seems to have calculated that the expenses of this journey were occasioned by his service to the patriot cause, while his outlays for physical sustenance entailed an obligation necessarily to be met by those in whose interest he had come to this country.

The most surprising fact in connection with this bill-collecting jaunt of the worthy Erskine is the circumstance that he was successful in inducing Congress (in the person of self-respecting General Mifflin) so promptly to disgorge. Considering that this phenomenon occurred at a period when the securing of ready money from our poverty-stricken governing body was a thing almost unheard of, one wonders just what "influence" contributed to the result.

---

[15] Allan Ramsay (1686–1758), one of the lesser poets of the 18th century, and, of course, a contemporary of Erskine's youth.

This settlement, which Erskine notes with evident satisfaction, was undoubtedly a liquidation of the charge against "the United States" which is debited in his books under date of March, 1777, "Chevaux-de-frize . . . £1022.17.6 . . . eleven tons." [16] A careful study of existing records leads the author to the conclusion that this item had to do with the secondary obstruction (somewhat after the fashion of the abortive Fort Washington to Fort Lee barrier), constructed near Polopel's Island, south of Fishkill and north of West Point,[17] to which reference has already been made.

Viewed, however, from the personal and sentimental standpoint, the business connected with Erskine's Philadelphia trip fades into the background as we conjure from the long-vanished past a picture of Erskine, the man. Place, perhaps, the old "King of Prussia" tavern at Germantown. Time,—eleven o'clock or midnight. Setting, an alcove in the deserted tap-room. Cato, negro body-servant, sleeping peacefully without; tired horses snugly stalled; Erskine reading. "Ink-Powder" and quills (destined for future use in lining out the by-ways to be trodden by the path-finders of liberty)—tucked away in saddle bags not far away—are, for the moment, forgotten. The story of Peter the Great and his semi-barbarous civilization has likewise been relegated to a far corner of the oaken table to permit ample elbow-room for successive refillings of the sparkling goblet from the capacious flagon; while Erskine, in the seventh heaven of peaceful and delightful exhilaration,—forgetting wars and rumors of wars—and all unconscious of his own nemesis (only some thousand nights distant), is in communion with the poetic spirit of

[16] Erskine Papers.
[17] See pp. 84–85, E. M. Ruttenber's *"Obstructions to the Navigation of Hudson's River,"* J. Munsell, Albany, N. Y., 1860.

Ramsay, his fellow-Scot. 'Twould be interesting indeed could we see the lines he read. Ramsay's "love song" might well have turned his thoughts to hill-girt Ringwood and his waiting spouse:

> *To a' our haunts I will repair,*
> *By greenwood, shaw, or fountain,*
> *Or where the summer day I'd share*
> *Wi' thee upon yon mountain:*

Or the more pertinent lines of "Lochaber" (wherein is set forth the resolve of the heroic swain to win the love of his highland "Jeanie" by brave deeds of glory) may have caused him to wish that the veil of his own future might be momentarily lifted and a glimpse of what was to be vouchsafed:

> *Though borne on rough seas to a far, bloody shore,*
> *Maybe to return to Lochaber no more!*

Erskine! for thee verily there is to be no returning to the banks of the Clyde. Better thy wine and thy dreams of long-continued happiness than a vision of the bitter truth! Just man that thou hast proven thyself to be, thou art ready for either life or death;—perchance the latter may bring thee greater peace after all, and the enjoyment of thy reward the sooner!

10

Geographer and Surveyor General

T H E first personal meeting of Washington and Erskine occurred at Pompton, N. J.,—whether by circumstantial accident or prearrangement we do not know.
The Commander-in-Chief was quartered at this hamlet on
July 11th to 13th, 1777, being detained by inclement
weather while en route to the Ramapo defile (Smith's
Clove) in consequence of Burgoyne's advance from the
northward and the necessity of protecting the region of the
Hudson Highlands. Well authenticated tradition has it
that he lodged at the little frame cottage of Captain Arent
Schuyler, situated at the road intersection where now
stands the commemorative monument,—the house itself
having long since disappeared.

Erskine's letter to Washington of Nov. 24, 1777 (which
will hereafter be set down), refers to the interview "at the
cross-roads" as being of an introductory character, but
Washington's own communication to Congress,—in which
he suggests that Erskine's ability and worth should be

given official recognition—implies that the latter had already rendered services of signal importance to the patriot cause. The logical inference is that Washington,—being aware of Erskine's reputation as a skilled topographer,—met and conversed with him at Pompton, and entered into a tentative agreement then and there.

The government records show that Erskine was commissioned Geographer and Surveyor-General to the American Army, July 27th, 1777, indicating a surprising promptitude on the part of Congress in complying with Washington's request. The letter of the Commander-in-Chief which brought about this result was written at Suffern's Tavern on July 19, shortly following the interview between himself and the Ringwood iron-master. It was addressed to the members of a committee of the Continental Congress.

A good Geographer to Survey the Roads and take Sketches of the Country where the Army is to Act would be extremely useful, and might be attended with exceedingly valuable consequences. He might with propriety have the chief direction of the Guides who must have a head to procure, govern and pay them. If such a person should be approved of I would beg leave to recommend Mr. Robt. Erskine who is thoroughly skilled in this business, has already assisted us in making Maps of the Country; and has (as I am informed) uniformly supported the Character of a fast friend to America.[1]

General Washington, upon the 28th of July,—losing no time, as will be observed—communicated the confirma-

[1] Washington Papers, Library of Congress. This note is part of a much longer communication, which has been reproduced in Fitzpatrick, John C., ed., *The Writings of George Washington*, Vol. 8, p. 443. See *ibid.*, p. 372 n., for a quotation from the *Journal of the Continental Congress* of July 25, noting that Washington was empowered to appoint Erskine or "any other person that he may think proper." H. S.

tory resolution of Congress to Mr. Erskine, accompanied by a brief note as follows, dictated to his young aide, Alexander Hamilton:

> Flemmington, 28th July, 1777
>
> Sir: In consequence of my representations to Congress of the advantage that might be derived from having a good Geographer to accompany the Army, and my recommendation of you for that purpose they have come to the inclosed resolution authorizing me to appoint you or any other Gentleman I shall think proper to act in the capacity therein Specified; and to determine the allowance of pay to be annexed to the Office. I shall therefore be obliged to you to let me know without delay the conditions on which it will Suit you to undertake it, and shall be glad to see you as soon as possible at Head Quarters to fix the matter upon a footing, and put everything in a train for the execution of it. If you engage, your entrance upon the business will be immediately necessary, as there can be no time in which your Services will be more useful than the present.[2]

Washington had now set his face toward Philadelphia, well-nigh certain that Howe had decided to strike for that prize, although, as he wrote to Gates, he could not help casting his eyes continually behind him, marveling at the strange abandonment of Burgoyne. It is, therefore, not at all surprising that he desires Erskine's prompt coöperation. Howbeit, his "headquarters"—for the next three months—were as shifting and transitory as the proverbial tent of the Arab, and the desired personal and detailed conference was long delayed. From Flemington the Commander moved rapidly to Coryell's (Correll's) Ferry on

[2] Washington Papers, Library of Congress. Reproduced in Fitzpatrick, Vol. 8, 495–96. Fitzpatrick credits its penmanship to Robert Hanson Harrison, rather than Alexander Hamilton. There is a photostat of the original in *The Manor and Forges of Ringwood*, V, 16. The Fitzpatrick version is used here and in the other Washington letters which follow. H. S.

the Delaware, and from thence to Philadelphia; at which place he probably received Erskine's interesting and cordial letter of acknowledgment:

Ringwood, August 1st, 1777

May it please Your Excellency

Your favour of the 28th ult, concerning the office of Geographer, I had the honour to receive yesterday at Pompton. The distinction you confer upon me, I beg leave to acknowledge with graditude; and shall be happy to render every service in my power to your Excellency, and to the cause in which the rights of humanity are so deeply interested: on these accounts it is necessary to be explicit; both by laying before you my ideas of the whole subject at once, and likewise by setting forth how much time and attention I can immediately bestow on the proposed department.

It is then perhaps proper to begin with a general view of the nature of the business in order to shew what may really be accomplished by a Geographer, that more may not be expected than it is practicable to perform; and that an estimate may be made of the number of assistants required should the Map of any particular district be required in a given time. It is obvious that in planning a country a great part of the ground must be walked over, particularly the banks of Rivers and Roads; as much of which may be traced and laid down in three hours as could be walked over in one; or in other words a Surveyor who can walk 15 miles a day may plan 5 miles; if the country is open, and stations of considerable length can be obtained, then perhaps greater dispatch can be made; very little more, however, in general can be expected; if it is considered that the Surveyor, besides attending to the course and measuring the distance of the way he is traversing, should at all convenient places where he can see around him, take observations and angles to Mountains, hills, steeples, houses and other objects which present themselves, in order to fix their site; to correct his work; and to facilitate its being connected with other Surveys. A Surveyor might go to work with two

Chain-bearers and himself; but in this case he must carry his own instruments, and some of them must frequently traverse the ground three times over at least; therefore, to prevent this inconvenience and delay, as men enough can be had from Camp without additional expense, six attendants to each surveyor will be proper; to wit, two Chain-bearers, one to carry the Instrument, and three to hold flag staffs; two flags, indeed, are only wanted in common; but three are necessary for running a straight line with dispatch; and the third flag may be usefully employed in several cases besides. From what one Surveyor can do, it will therefore appear that in making a plan, like all other business, the more hands are employed in it, the sooner it may be accomplished; likewise, that the director of the Surveyors will have full employment in making general observations, and connecting the different surveys as they come in, upon one general Map; and, at any rate, that a correct plan must be a work of time.

A great deal however may be done towards the formation of an useful Map, by having some general outlines justly laid down; and the situation of some remarkable places accurately ascertained; from such data, other places may be pointed out, by information and computed distances; in such a manner as to give a tolerable idea of the Country; especially with the assistance of all the maps in being, which can be procured: and this, perhaps, is as much as can be expected, should plans be required to keep pace with the transitions of War.

Navigable Rivers, and those which cannot be easily forded, and likewise the capital roads, should be laid down with all the accuracy possible; but, in the Map of a country, the general course of fordable rivers need only be attended to; it not being practicable to express small windings but on large scale, the same accuracy not being required here which is necessary to ascertain the quantity and boundaries of private property. In general, therefore, the adjacence to, and intersection of, such rivers with roads, will determine their course with sufficient exactness: the situation of woods and mountains, too, may be remarked in a similar manner.

Young gentlemen of Mathematical genius, who are acquainted with the principles of Geometry, and who have a taste for drawing, would be the most proper assistants for a Geographer. Such, in a few days practice, may be made expert surveyors. The instrument best adapted for accuracy and dispatch is the Plain-Table; by this, the Surveyor plans as he proceeds, and—not having his work to protract in the evening —may attend the longer to it in the day. One of these instruments, with a chain and ten iron-shod arrows, should be provided for each of the Surveyors it may be thought proper to employ.

But I ought not trouble your excellency with the minutia of the business, it is time now to proceed to my own situation. I was engaged for America on purpose to superintend the Iron Works under my direction; in conjunction with another Gentleman; who, not choosing to comply with the orders of the Proprietors was dismissed from their service, which developed the charge of the whole upon me. The great confidence my employers have all along placed in my integrity and honour, has demanded my best endeavors on their behalf. These, however, have been very partial and uneffectual, from unavoidable causes, and of the immense sums which had been sunk and expended for them before I arrived, very little now remains but their Lands, which, I suppose, if sold at the best market, would not make up the money they have lost by £60,000 Sterling. The Owners, who reside chiefly in London, have been well acquainted with my sentiments concerning America from the first of the dispute. As they have been totally silent respecting my political opinions, I have reason to believe that my conduct—which in other respects they have fully approved— has not, in this case, met with their disapprobation. These circumstances, however, I mention only by the by; for, whatever be their private sentiments, and whatever feuds and differences take place between States and Nations, yet these cannot alter the nature of justice between man and man, or cancel the duty one individual owes to another. I, therefore, hold myself as much bound as ever to be accountable for the trust reposed in me. Such being the case, I cannot relinquish the concerns of which I have the charge till I have brought them to a proper conclusion. Moreover, the suspension of intercourse with my principals has obliged me to become personally answerable for all the contracts I have or had made in their behalf; and thus I have in a great measure, become a principal myself, and invested my own property to the amount of some thousand pounds in their stock.

These particulars I have troubled you with to shew that I cannot at present devote my whole time to the Department you have obligingly offered, having got between £20,000 and £30,000 moveable property to dispose of, and accounts to a large amount to settle and discharge. My present business is now, however, so far circumscribed that I can employ at least half my time in the Public Service, and by the opening of next campaign, perhaps the whole; concerning, which, too, I beg leave to add, that I can fully depend on your candour; and that I can very soon attend to the proposed Department for such a length of time as shall be sufficient to make a beginning of the business, which afterwards may be carried on under mine or another's direction, as shall be thought proper.

Having thus far encroached on your Excellency's time with regret, I request your kind indulgence finally to observe, that the stated terms upon which myself and others of my profession used to do business in England, were a Guinea a day and all reasonable expenses, such as travelling charges and the hire of laborers and assistants.

I hope, if it please God, to have the honour of waiting on you early in the week after next: meantime, I have the honour to be, with the greatest respect and esteem.

May it please Your Excellency,

Your greatly obliged, and most obedient hum[1] servant,

Robert Erskine

His Excellency, General Washington.[3]

[3] Washington Papers, Library of Congress. There is a photostat of the original in *The Manor and Forges of Ringwood*, V, 17–19. H. S.

To one so familiar with Erskine's profession as was Washington, the details of what the former proposed to do must have met with a thorough and understanding approval. In his own youthful days (in the wilderness of Lord Fairfax and the Valley of Virginia) he too had stretched the chain, and planted flags, and outlined the tortuous courses of rivers: of the difficulties incident to this sort of work in a broken and mountainous country he was fully aware. That he acquiesced in Erskine's plan, and availed of the part-time arrangement, is understood; although three months now elapsed without any further written communication between them. This is natural enough; as the swift-following events incident to the lost battle of the Brandywine, the complicated maneuvering around Philadelphia, and the abortive attempt to dislodge the British from Germantown, were amply sufficient to occupy the time and thoughts of the Commander-in-Chief.

From the temporary headquarters of Washington at Whitemarsh, Pennsylvania (the house of George Emlen, Upper Dublin, where he had been since Nov. 2nd and remained for five weeks) came a letter to Erskine in the hand of Col. Tench Tilghman, Washington's aide. The fact that it was directed to "Wm. Erskine, Esq.," would give the impression that the members of the headquarters staff were either overwhelmed with work, or else that the master of Ringwood was not personally known to Tilghman. The existing duplicate copy among Washington's papers bears no signature, but the original was, most likely, signed by the General, as the wording would indicate.[4]

[4] Fitzpatrick, Vol. 10, p. 63 n., also credits the handwriting of this communication to Tilghman. It is reproduced on the same page. There is a photostat of the original in *The Manor and Forges of Ringwood*, V, 21. The Fitzpatrick version is given here. H. S.

It will likewise be noted that the "office" upon which Erskine is to enter is referred to in so guarded a manner that no one would suspect its importance. This vagueness is intentional, without doubt. Bearers of letters were always liable to capture by the enemy, and the shrewd Commander was taking no chances of having his plans for a Surveyor-General nipped in the bud:

> Head Quarters, Whitemarsh, 14th November, 1777
> Sir: I shall be glad to know, by return of the Bearer, whether the portable ovens bespoke last Summer, are finished. If they are, you may send them down to the Army if you can procure Waggons; if you cannot, let me know and I will order the Qr. M. General to send for them.
> Be pleased to let me know when you think you will be able to enter upon any of the duties of the Office which I spoke to you about last summer.[5]

Happily for Erskine's reputation for strict attention to business, the ovens were ready and waiting,—as we shall presently learn. And the interesting part of this transaction comes to light when we consult his Cash Book. Therein we find that he had already succeeded in collecting from General Mifflin a goodly sum on account of the work, having made a secondary journey to Philadelphia for the purpose. That Erskine could again induce Mifflin to make such prompt payment, at a time when Philadelphia was upset with uncertainty and the Continental treasury in a more than usual impoverished condition, speaks volumes for his Scottish thrift and powers of persuasion. Yet here we have the entry in August, 1777, as proof sufficient:

[5] Erskine Papers.

"Sales—Rec'd of Coll. Mifflin on acct. ovens £533.6.8" [6]

A very delightful character-study of Robert Erskine came to the attention of the biographer through the discovery of the appended memorandum in his minor account book (which is also at the N. J. Historical Society), having direct reference to his trip to Philadelphia on the above occasion. He appears to have mingled business and pleasure whenever possible, being ever on the look-out for books with which to stock his Ringwood library. He was like a prosperous countryman coming to town, and I suppose carried with him several lists of needed articles. That he remembered Mrs. Erskine, and that either she or himself possessed a "sweet-tooth" seems obvious. Surely, on this particular journey, attention was again paid, in equal measure, to the wants of body, soul and spirit:

Expenses going and returning to and from Philadelphia for payment of Ovens, etc.:

27 sheets Drawing paper	4.. 1.—
Brushes	.16. 3
Snuff	.10.—
Sewing Silk	. 8.—
14 vol., Nature and Art	20.—.—
4 vol., Nature and Art, Displd.	8.—.—
8 vol., Spectr. [Spectator]	12.—.—
Walker's Sermons	. 9.—
Compass	1.12.—
Making Breeches	1.16.—
Sugar Candy, 2 lb.	2.—.—[7]

Finding himself, therefore, some months ahead of the Commander-in-Chief in the matter of the ovens (of the completion of which Washington was evidently unaware)

[6] *Ibid.*
[7] *Ibid.*

and having already applied himself to the matter of military surveys, Erskine could answer, with assurance, as follows:

Ringwood, November 24th, 1777

May it please Your Exc'y:

The twenty Ovens ordered last Summer, concerning which I have your favour of the 14th inst., were delivered as follows: four to Col. Mifflin, as the army passed Pompton; fourteen were sent after it to Morristown, by seven waggons employed for that purpose; and two large and two small ones remained here, when I was at Wilmington, which I mentioned to Col. Mifflin; who ordered me to send four, (viz. two large and two small) to the care of Major Taylor at New Windsor, which was done; and to keep the rest here till further orders.

From the time I had the honour of speaking with you at the Cross Roads, I fully resolved to enter upon the proposed office next spring, should it then be vacant; and, God willing, I shall devote my whole time to it, if your Exc'y thinks proper, by the beginning of next April; meanwhile, I have the satisfaction of giving some part of my time now to the public service; Gov[r]. Clinton having accepted of my assistance at New Windsor; where I have been taking Surveys and Levels of the ground near the Chevaux-de-frise, for a Fort; which is erecting under the direction of the French Engineer Your Excellency sent to Fort Montgomery. I am happy to assist a gentleman of skill in his profession, from whom much of the art of practical Engineering may be learnt, and I shall return to the North River again in a few days, to finish some surveys at New Windsor, Forts Constitution, Montgomery, etc., Copies of which shall immediately be transmitted to your Excellency by

May it please Your Excellency,

Your most obliged & most obed[t]. humble servant,

Rob[t] Erskine [8]

[8] Washington Papers, Library of Congress. The letter is mentioned and summarized in Fitzpatrick, Vol. 10, p. 63 n. There is a photostat of the original in *The Manor and Forges of Ringwood*, V, 24. H. S.

True to his promise to Washington, Robert Erskine contrived to mingle business affairs with Army matters during the early months of 1778. The Commander-in-Chief was struggling through at Valley Forge; the British were living upon the fat of the land at Philadelphia. The Hudson Highlands were once again under patriot control,— the British having withdrawn down the river to New York after failing to effect a junction with Burgoyne before Saratoga.

In the letter which follows, Erskine speaks in terms of warmest praise of the French Engineer, Colonel La Radiere. He was one of four engineers who had served in the French Army; and whose services had been secured for the Continental cause by Silas Deane and Benjamin Franklin, the American Commissioners in France, upon the authority of Congress, and with the sanction and encouragement of the French government. Duportail, Laumoy, Radiere and Gouvion all served with distinction. Duportail was afterwards promoted to a Brigadier Generalship. Radiere died in the service at the beginning of 1780. Lossing's *Field Book of the Revolution* gives many details as to the fortification at West Point, and makes interesting reading in conjunction with this letter of Erskine's:

Ringwood March 26th 1778

May it please Your Excellency

The Enclosed plan is so far from being worthy your attention that I have delayed sending it till now, in hopes of making one more compleat, by taking in a greater scope of the North River, at least between the Chevaux-de-frise and West Point, where a fort is now building; but as I find Col. La Radiere, who is now here on his way to New Windsor, has not been furnished with any further surveys, from which I expected to copy, I have presumed to transmit this, though very imperfect on account of the small space it comprehends.

When I went to survey at New Windsor, I proposed to make a map of the river from thence to Haverstraw, which would have comprehended all the highlands, and pointed out, without dispute, the most proper situations to fortify; but this I found impracticable, both on account of the season of the year, and the time required to settle my private concerns in such a manner as to attend Your Excellencie's commands with satisfaction to myself, should you require my services the ensuing campaign. I am, with the greatest respect and esteem,

May it please your Excellency:

Your obliged and most obedient hum[1]. Servant,

Robt. Erskine

His Excellency, George Washington.[9]

Washington's acknowledgment (written at the Potts' House, Valley Forge) is an unmistakable compliment to Erskine's skill as a topographer:

Head Quarters, 11th April, 1778

Sir

I rec'd yours of the 26th, March inclosing an elegant draft of part of Hudson's River. If your affairs are in such a situation that they will admit of your attendance upon the Army, I shall be glad to see you as soon as possible. Captn. Scull, who is intended for one of your assistants, has been for some time employed in surveying the Country adjacent to the Camp.

Robert Erskine, Esq., Ringwood

To the care of Col. Taylor, New Windsor.[10]

[9] Washington Papers. Library of Congress. There is a photostat of the original in *The Manor and Forges of Ringwood*, V, 26. H. S.

[10] Washington Papers, Library of Congress. It is reproduced in Fitzpatrick, Vol. 11, p. 246, which version is here used. There is a photostat of the original in *The Manor and Forges of Ringwood*, V, 27. It is reproduced in Fitzpatrick, Vol. 11, p. 246. In a letter to Capt. Scull on June 5, Washington stated that Erskine was at Valley Forge to organize his department and ordered Scull to report to camp. Fitzpatrick, Vol. 12, p. 21. H. S.

Robert Erskine and George Washington met face-to-face for the second time at Valley Forge, when glorious spring was busily bedecking the uplands bordering the Schuylkill with gorgeous blossoms; and the patriot army was all a-tingle with animation at the prospect of administering a drubbing to the British who were known to be meditating an immediate evacuation of Philadelphia after a winter of more or less demoralizing inactivity.

Shortly following this conference, and even while the events immediately preceding the battle of Monmouth were shaping themselves toward a climax,[11] Erskine endeavors to get into touch with Simeon Dewitt (later to become famous and honored as the Surveyor General of New York State), whom he has decided upon as his chief lieutenant. The following communication, bearing the superscription, "On Public Service. To Mr. Simeon De Witt, at Dr. Andrew De Witt's, Rotchester Township, Ulster County," explains itself quite fully:

Ringwood, June 20th, 1778

Sir

As I have got a Commission from his Exc'y. Genl. Washington for Geographer and Surveyor to the Army, and have his permission to engage you as one of my assistants, I beg leave to inform you that your pay, in that capacity, will be two dollars per day, an horse and one ration when at Camp, and travelling expenses when employed at a distance from it, which terms I have no doubt will be agreeable. I shall therefore be glad if you will come here as soon as possible to accompany me to the army, to which I propose to set out again next Friday.

June 23d 1778

Sir:—Above is a copy I sent by express to your uncle, Genl Clinton, to be forwarded to you. An opportunity offering, I

11 On the 20th of June, Washington was at Doylestown, Pa., and on the 23rd at Hopewell, N. J. On the 28th of June, the Battle of Monmouth was fought. H. S.

send a duplicate: it may perhaps be Monday next before I set off; should I go sooner, I shall leave directions where you shall follow.

Sir,

Your humbl. Servt.,

Robt. Erskine

Mr. Simeon De Witt.[12]

[12] Papers of the Continental Congress, Library of Congress. There is a photostat of the original in *The Manor and Forges of Ringwood*, V, 28. H. S.

11

The Hudson River Chains

T H E extent of the services rendered by Robert Erskine and the quantity of the material supplied by his Ringwood Iron Works toward the making of the famous Hudson River chains seems to be a subject inviting debate. The first obstruction was, of course, the chevaux-de-frise between Forts Lee and Washington. Of this, which cannot properly be denominated a "chain," we have already spoken.

In discussing the many perplexing circumstances connected with the chains of 1777 and 1778, we must bear in mind that an intentional secrecy surrounded these operations. Our chief sources of information relative to the chain stretched across the river from Fort Montgomery to Anthony's Nose in the spring of 1777, as well as that at West Point a year afterward, are the official papers of Governor Clinton, as digested by Ruttenber.[1] Under the

[1] E. M. Ruttenber's *Obstructions to the Navigation of Hudson's River.* J. Munsell, Albany, N. Y., 1860.

orders of a "Secret Committee" from the New York State Assembly, work was commenced upon the Fort Montgomery project during the summer of 1776. After various experiments, it was determined to utilize the chain originally intended for the obstruction of the River Sorel near Ticonderoga on Lake Champlain. This was brought down to Poughkeepsie, and there assembled and added to by Van Zandt, Lawrence and Tudor. When finally it was drawn across the river, late in March, 1777, it comprised an elaborate barrier, the heavy chain being supported upon wooden floats placed beneath it at frequent intervals; the whole being protected on the down-stream side by cumbersome wooden booms. Although it gave promise of great defensive possibilities, it was fated to suffer ignominious capture in its entirety. When the formidable British expeditionary flotilla under Vaughan and Wallace passed up the great river in early October to effect a junction with hard-pressed Burgoyne (then struggling to maintain himself north of Saratoga), they wisely came to a halt below the barrier. But, after successfully engaging the land forces which but half-garrisoned Forts Clinton and Montgomery (which they did on the 6th of October), the enemy found themselves at liberty to remove the chain at leisure. Their enterprise completely failing in its main purpose,—for Burgoyne's situation was already beyond relief—it may be imagined that the dejected British derived peculiar pleasure in possessing themselves of the aforesaid chain upon their return journey down-stream. So highly did they appreciate its quality and workmanship that it was sent across the Atlantic as a trophy of victory, and for many years it did service at Gibraltar, where—along the mole—it served as a protection to vessels riding at anchor behind Britain's impregnable fortress.

The patriot officer who had most to do with the abortive Fort Montgomery obstruction was Captain Thomas Machin (1744–1819), an engineer attached to Gen. Knox's artillery, who had been temporarily assigned to serve under Col. George Clinton. As to the source of supply for the incidental materials employed in elaborating and placing the contrivance in position, I am of the opinion that almost all the iron-works in the region contiguous to the Hudson contributed their quota, great or small, as the exigencies of the situation demanded. There were many alterations in the original plans; the chain parted once; small iron, such as bolts, bars and spikes, was repeatedly needed upon short notice; and altogether there is nothing to prove that any one concern monopolized the work. There is preserved at Newburgh, in the Museum Building adjoining Washington's famous headquarters, the following original bill, in the holograph of Erskine himself, which constitutes conclusive evidence that he had a not inconsequential part in this undertaking.

Messrs. Thomas Machin & John Nicoll
   For the United States of America
     To Robert Erskine, Ringwood, Dr.

1777		No. of Clips	No. of Links	No. of Bolts	By Whom Carted	Weight
August	21, to	27	18	..	Henry Cole	1– 0–1– 0
Sept.	8, "	..	11	..	Ditto	4–0–21
	9, "	19	18	..	Robert Devenport	16–1–21
Oct.	2, "	18	27	18	Patrick McDougald's	
					Negroe	19–2– 0
	4, "	14	21	14	William Clark	15–0– 7
	6, "	16	15	16	Richard Goldsmith, Jr.	15–2–14
	" "	18	30	18	Ditto	1– 1–1– 0
	" "	..	42	..	Jonathan Whyte	15–0–21
	" "	24	..	24	Ditto	15–0– 7
	" "	16	24	16	Coleman Curtis	18–2– 7

" "	14	21	14	James Runels	15–3–14
7, "	28	12	28	David Sutherland	1– 0–3– 0
" "	30	..	..	John Mandevile	15–1– 0
" "	28	..	27	Henry Vandousar	15–3– 7
Novem^{r.} 1, "	51	37	22	At Ringwood	2– 1–1– 0
				Waste	1– 7–0– 0

303	276	197	Tons	14–17–0– 7

```
46 Setts of Clips, Bolts & Chains ⎫
      Compleat ................. ⎬ 14–17–0–7
29¾ Setts Clips & 3¼ Setts Bolts .... ⎭
101 Bars 2 Inch Chain
       Iron ............ 3– 8–0–21
100  do 1½ Inch Ditto . 2–10–1– 7    5–18–2–0
     (for mooring chain.)
```

Tons	20–15–2–7 @ 14/
T. C. Q. Lbs.	£2908–18– 9
To Making 14–17–0–7 of Bar Iron into the ⎱ above Clips, Bolts and Chains .... ⎰ @ 14/	2079– 8– 9
To Carting the two First Loads Wt. 1–4–1–21 @ 10/	12– 4– 4½

£5000–11–10½

By Cash Received in part of Capt. Machin's Order
on Capt. Nicoll for £2,000 ....   1300– 0– 0

Balance £3700–11–10½
N. B.   This Account shall be further credited with
the above 5–18–2–0 of Iron made for the Boom &
Mooring Chain if not wanted by the States,
Amounting to 829–10– 0

which will reduce the Balance to £2871– 1–10½

Again, Erskine's "Cash Book" preserves the record of
other interesting debit and credit items; among which
the following are, I think, of a significance similar to the
bill at Newburgh: the last item being the precise sum
credited thereon:

1777—July, To Proprs. Recd. of Genl. Mifflen
   for 37 Tons of Bar Iron Deld. Peekskill   £2960.—.—
1777—Augt. Pr. Proprs. Sales, Recd. Machin.   303.17. 6½
1777—September, Recd. on account Boom
   Irons   1300.—.—   [2]

Why was bar iron delivered to Peekskill if it were not for the river obstruction? And for what other purpose could "boom irons" have been used, if not for the same object? To my mind, these entries prove conclusively that Erskine's iron manufactory at Ringwood performed its due share of the labor incident to the Fort Montgomery chain and boom, the total cost of which was estimated to be £70,000 sterling.

The order for the second or "West Point" Chain, was placed with Noble, Townsend & Company (proprietors of the Stirling Iron Works) February 2nd, 1778, by Hugh Hughes, Deputy Quartermaster General of the Army of the United States. This chain was completed and swung across the river between Constitution Island and West Point on April 30th, 1778, at a point where it turns sharply and narrows greatly in width. As originally specified, the links were to be constructed of iron "about 2¼″ square"; each link about 2 feet long; the length of the chain required stated as 500 yards. Some authorities maintain that portions of the chain were actually composed of larger and heavier links, but this is debatable.

The West Point chain was protected by booms much after the fashion of that at Fort Montgomery, and was completed in much less time because of the experience gained in the former undertaking. Happily, it was destined to remain in useful service until the end of hostilities; during the intervening winters (when the river was

[2] Erskine Papers.

frozen), being drawn up beside the shore. When the war was over, it was taken apart, and many of the links are to be found to this day scattered here and there throughout the country, particularly in the Highlands.[3]

In 1906 a memorial tablet, imposed upon a rugged boulder, was unveiled at the Stirling Iron Works, at the foot of the lake of that name in Orange County, N. Y., telling the passerby that here the West Point chain was made. But this again is only a half-truth. As in the former instance, several works coöperated in the endeavor, Ringwood among the number; for the relations between Robert Erskine and the proprietors of the Stirling mines and iron works were close and friendly. The labor involved in the construction of such ponderous chains must have been very considerable. Mr. Macgrane Coxe, who made the principal address at the ceremonies in connection with the Stirling memorial, told of the various processes of mining the ore and smelting it into pig-iron, which in turn must be forged or wrought into bars. It was from this bar iron that the links were made; in many instances the bending and welding being done beside the Hudson. The links (or bars of sufficient length for that purpose) were conveyed by cart or on mule-back over the rugged country to the river. In one of my rambles in the vicinity of New Windsor I came upon a monument beside the Moodna Creek very much like that at Stirling, telling that here formerly stood one of the forges where the chain was put together. Upon one of Erskine's maps it is noted as "Brewster's Forge."

Little wonder then, when all these operations of manu-

[3] In 1928, two links of the West Point chain were in the N. Y. State Library at Albany, seven at the West Point Military Academy, one at Stony Point. Two were formerly in the possession of Prof. Peter Townsend Austin, of Staten Island.

facture are taken into consideration, and the added fact remembered that speed was a vital element in the operation, that joint and concerted effort on the part of many patriot iron-men was indispensable. It is not surprising, therefore, to find in Erskine's cash book, under date of May 14th, 1778, another heavy charge:

"To Quarter master general in full for
    Boom Iron acct.   £3860.17.2½" [4]

It will be noted that this date is but a fortnight after the placing of the West Point chain, and, if circumstantial evidence counts for anything, this entry (coupled with those referring to the Fort Montgomery chain) proves beyond a doubt that Robert Erskine, in his private capacity as iron-master, as well as in his official position as Surveyor-General, was not found wanting.

When the Hon. Abram S. Hewitt took up his residence at Ringwood Manor, the former owner, Peter Ryerson, called his attention to two rusty chain-links found on the premises by his father in 1807, which were unquestionably "left-overs" from the operations of 1777 or '78. In 1876, these links were sent to the Centennial Exposition at Philadelphia, as a part of the historical exhibit of Cooper, Hewitt & Co. They were never returned to Mr. Hewitt, and their present whereabouts is unknown. Much as this is to be regretted, we have Mr. Hewitt's testimony that they existed on the estate in 1853. We may, moreover, derive some consolation in the fact that the anvil and trip-hammer, which are now mounted before the Manor House, are actual relics of Erskine's day —probably the very tools used in executing the government contracts. The nineteen ponderous links comprising

4 Erskine Papers.

the great chain at present stretched across the beautiful lawn at Ringwood are, however, of a period much later than Revolutionary times; having been placed here by Mr. Hewitt as being not only decorative but suggestive of Erskine's part in two of the greatest engineering accomplishments of the War of Independence.

The story of the Indian atrocities along the upper Delaware River, the battle of the Minisink, the massacre at Cherry Valley, and the exploits of General Sullivan's expedition against the redskins under Joseph Brant and the Tory Colonel John Butler, do not properly form a part of Erskine's biography. Yet the fact that he was concerned with these events, more or less directly, is proven by a letter written by Captain Wm. Gray of the 4th Penna. Regiment, and dated Schohara (N. Y.), October 28th, 1778. It is addressed merely to "Robert Erskine, Esq.,— Headquarters," causing some speculation as to why, in those days of military punctilio, the official title of Erskine was not employed; and giving added weight to the theory that Erskine's duties were regarded as matters of extraordinary secrecy.

The letter concerns the so-called "Expedition of 1778" —Col. Wm. Butler's march to the Indian villages, Oct. 2nd to 16th,—which was but a minor enterprise when compared with the activities of the following year; yet it afforded an opportunity for obtaining some accurate knowledge of the country now embraced within the counties of Schoharie, Otsego and Delaware (N. Y.). It is quite evident that Erskine based many of his maps upon field work actually performed by subordinates; in this instance we find Captain Gray communicating some of the details which the Surveyor-General later incorporated into his own beautifully executed surveys.

Schoharie, as it is now called, lies some 18 miles southwest of Schenectady, while the "Headquarters" to which the letter was addressed was the transient covert of Washington, at Fredericksburg, N. Y., some thirty miles east of the Hudson and near the Connecticut line. Here again we have proof that Erskine was often to be found close to the Commander-in-Chief.

For the benefit of those of my readers who have not delved into the complexities of the border warfare of the period, may I say that William L. Stone, in his *Border Wars of the American Revolution*, gives a most complete and unbiased narrative. In the spring and early summer of 1778 (the year succeeding the dispersion of St. Leger's motley force at Fort Schuyler), occurred the atrocities in the Wyoming Valley of Pennsylvania and the destruction of the Springfield settlement in New York, with similar terrors constantly threatening every one of the outlying communities. Small expeditions of reprisal having proved abortive (like that of which Captain Gray writes), General Washington eventually found it necessary to send General Sullivan into the very heart of the Indian territory. Marching from Wyoming (Pa.), July 31st, 1779, he joined General James Clinton at Tioga Point. On the 29th of August they fell upon a mixed force of Tories and savages at Chemung (now Elmira, N. Y.), and then pushed on to the Genesee River, where the work of retaliation was begun. By Oct. 20th, General Sullivan had thoroughly punished the tribes of the Six Nations, having driven them from their villages and "laid waste their dwelling places."

Captain Gray's letter may be regarded as typical of this phase of the Revolutionary struggle, and as being indicative of Erskine's coöperation with his subordinates and the other branches of the military service:

Schohara, Octr. 28th, 1778

Sr. I recd. yours of the 20th Inst., & understand the Contents & have accordingly sent you a Draught of Part of Schohara, Part of the West Branch of Delaware & part of Susquehana which is all that I Can Colect. I Shewed your Leter to Col. Butler who has Promised to Let me Have Leave & Men to Assist me to Survay the Roads you mentioned If possible which I Doubt not but it will. If So, I Shall write to you as Soon as I begin. I had Neither pencel or Indian Ink to Shade the Hills which are Very Numerous as there is nothing Else after you Quite the waggon Road, too you can Reach Unendilla the Road or path from thence Ononaughquaga is much Better as it gos all the way along the River.

As to my finding out the Varyation at this place I imagan that it will be very Difficult, as Sun is not to be seen for at Least one hour after he Rises, & an hour before he Sets. However I will try my Best.

I Shall now give you an Account of our March & Expedition to the Indian towns as well as I can. We Marched from Fort Defiance on Friday, 2nd ult., with a Party of men Consisting of the 4th Pennsyl. Regt. Part of the Rifel Chore, & some Militia in Number about 260—Officers Included, along the Line you see Marked on the Draught, without anything Worthy Notice to we Came to Unendilla which we found Evacuated from thence we Marched Down the River Susquehana for Ononaughquaga the Chief Indian town where we thought to atact a Party of Savages & Torys By Surprise, but we Happened unluckiely to be Discovered by some Scouting Savages who made the best of their way, & as they knew the path Better than we did & had got the Start So far we Could not Come up with them though our Scoting Party traveled all Night, to no purpos. We got to Ononaughquaga on Thursday the 8th ult about 10 o Clock at Night which we found Evacuated also the Greatest Disorder. Everything Seemed as if they had fled in the Greatest Haste. Next morning we set the town (which Consisted of About 30 or forty good Houses) in Flames, Destroying therein great Quantities of Household Furniture &

Indian Corn. After the Burning of the town two men of our party went out to Search for Some Horses that were Lost, & not minding to take their Arms with them, were fired on from a thicket by some Lurking Indians who wounded one of them (that is Since Dead of the Wound) on which Col. Butler Ordered Capt. Parr with a Party of Rifel Men to go in Search of them, but they Could not Come up with them though they Marched five or Six miles Down the River, Seting fier to a very Large Indian Council house in their Return, The Same Day About 2 o Clock, we marched from Ononaughquaga up the River to Another Town called Cunahunta (burning Some Indian houses & Corn on the Road) from thence we Marched Next morning Early Leaving it in flames, but that Night & the Day Raining so terrably that it Rendered Every small Run both Defficult & Dangerous in Crossing, but when we Came to the River below Unendilla (as pᵣ Draught) it was Dreadful to See So Large a Stream to the Mens Breast & very Rappid Rising at the Rate of one Inch pr. Minet, but by the Pressing Desire of the men to Get over & the Deligence of the officers with their owne & the Pack Horses they were all Got over Safe which if we had been but one houre longer we Could not have Crossed & God only knows what would have been the Dreadfull Consequences.

We marched that Evening up the East Side of the River as far as the Scotch Settlement burning all as we went along that could be of any Use to the Enimy. We Could not March thence on Sunday by Reason of the great Rain, on Munday we Marched burning some Tory Houses before we Set out & encamped in the woods that Night. Marched early Next Morning, but when we came to Delaware we Could not Cross it but was obliged to March up the N.W. Side of the River, & the Pilot not knowing the Road & Night Coming on we Lost our Road about five or Six miles & had to March over two very Large Hills before we Could get to the River again. However the Party Got Home on Saturday the 16th ult. in Good Spirits After a March of Near 300 Miles in such Terrable Weather Almost barefooted & naked. We suffered a good Deal for want of Bread, as we had not any of that usfull Articles for four Days. You Doubtless May See a more Particular Account of this at Head Quarters but I have Endavoured to Give it as True as I Could. Present My Best Compliments to Capt. Scull & the Rest of the Party & Let them See this, & I am S[r]

Your very Hu! [humble] Serv[t]

W[m] Gray

P.S. If you see Col. Stewart Shew him this, my Compliments to him, and I Desire that he may Leave my Accts. with you as I hop to See you My Self Soon.

To Robert Erskine   On Public Service
Head Quarters [5]

We learn from the New York State publication, issued in 1887 (which gives minute details as to General John Sullivan's campaign against the Six Nations), that among the "Erskine Maps," quite a number were made from the preliminary surveys of Lieut. Benjamin Lodge, who, with compass and chain, surveyed the route of the army from Easton over the mountains to Wyoming; and from present Sunbury, Pa., along the Susquehanna to Wyoming, and thence to the Genesee River, including the return route of Col. William Butler along the east shore of Cayuga Lake. Lodge was promoted from Ensign to Second Lieutenant, Oct. 16, 1776; and from Second to First Lieutenant, Oct. 11th, 1777. He is often mentioned in the journals as "Captain" Lodge, but the index of the Erskine maps designates him as "Lieut. Lodge."

Besides Capt. Gray and Lieut. Lodge, who on occasion gave special assistance to Erskine, Simeon De Witt,[6] his

---

[5] New-York Historical Society.

[6] Simeon De Witt, who ultimately succeeded to Erskine's position as Geographer General, was at first a private soldier in the Continental Army. Upon the recommendation of Gen'l James Clinton to Gen. Washington in 1778, he was, as we have recorded, appointed assistant to Erskine. Under date of Dec. 4th, 1780, in the Proceedings of Congress, we find:

regularly-appointed understudy, soon began to take a hand in the business of the Surveying Department. A careful examination of the "rough-draughts," the finished large-scale maps, and the "general contractions" now treasured at the New-York Historical Society will reveal the workmanship and individuality of several draftsmen, displaying varied degrees of skill. Map No. 26, for instance, dated August, 1778, is the work of Capt. John W. Watkins, A. B., a patriot school-master of the type of Nathan Hale; while No. 40, a Connecticut survey, is based upon preliminary work done by "Mr. Porter, surveyor of Farmington," in 1765.

Nevertheless, Erskine was the one man, above all others, who was sufficiently trained and temperamentally fitted to coördinate and utilize the abilities of the willing striplings who were so eager to do their best for him and for the cause; and to turn to good account all the other maps and surveys upon which he or they could lay their hands. Methodical in his arrangement, and so artistic that —when time permitted—he could execute a colored map of unusual beauty, it is easy to appreciate the value of his services to the American army; and it is a matter of no wonder that Washington and the members of his staff soon came to regard him as one of the inner circle.

According to Ebenezer Erskine (the nephew who had come from Scotland to assist Robert Erskine in the management of the ironworks), "His services in the cause of liberty were highly valued, and . . . he received visits

---

"*Resolved*, That Simeon De Witt be appointed Geographer to the Army in the room of Robert Erskine, deceased."

On Dec. 16th, 1780, De Witt was ordered to headquarters and continued to be attached to the main army until the end of the war. On the 16th of May, 1784, he was commissioned as Surveyor General for the State of New York, which office he held for fifty years, until his death at Ithaca, Dec. 3rd, 1834.

from General Clinton, Colonels Morris and Stewart, and other persons of consideration." [7] Yet were it not for the survival of his maps and the information to be found in the Erskine Papers at the Newark headquarters of the N. J. Historical Society, he would, most likely, have gone to his grave to be forever unrecognized by his country,— as was many another confidential agent of Washington who was willing to submerge himself and his identity for the ultimate welfare of the cause. The meager and infrequent references to Robert Erskine (even in our most detailed histories) give no suggestion that he was actually one of the great men of the American Revolution, and demonstrate how completely any tell-tale records of one person may be covered up, when such a course is demanded by policies of public safety.

[7] From Rev. Donald Fraser's *Life and Diary of Rev. Ralph Erskine.*

12

Man in the Shadow

F O R a year following the battle of Monmouth, there were no important military movements to demand the attention of the army under Washington's immediate command. During the summer and fall of 1778 the Commander spent most of his time in the region of the Hudson Highlands, but in early December he settled down at his former headquarters in Middlebrook, N. J., from which point he was free to wait upon Congress as occasion required.

From thence there came to Erskine in early February of 1779, the following surprising and somewhat peremptory summons to leave sequestered Ringwood and permanently to attach himself to the army: [1]

Head Quarters, 10th Feby. 1779

Sir: As I think you are much exposed in your present situation, to the enterprises of Refugees acquainted with the Country, and the work in which you are employed unquestionably

[1] The copy of this letter (also in the "Washington Papers" at the Congressional Library) is in the handwriting of young John Laurens, the son of Henry Laurens, one of the Commander's dearly beloved aides.

makes you an object with the enemy; I desire that as soon as possible after receipt of this letter, you will remove to quarters more safe by the vicinity of the Army. You will of course dismiss your guard, and direct the Serjeant to march it immediately and join Col. Clarke.

P. S.—It will naturally occur to you to remove with you all your surveys that might be of any use to the enemy.[2]

To one in Erskine's position,—practically that of a landed proprietor, serving voluntarily in an adopted cause,—this message must have caused a measure of chagrin. That he dearly loved his home-life is certain; it is to be imagined, also, that his business affairs might be expected to suffer further neglect through his prolonged absence at the cantonment of the army; therefore it may be assumed that this was an unwelcome command. Were it not for the correspondence which follows, we might be led to speculate as to the motives behind Washington's order; as it is, we have evidence that he acted with discretion. And Erskine, putting his duty above all else, made the sacrifice.

As to the exact words of Erskine's reply we have no knowledge, for the letter is not among "Washington's papers" at the Congressional Library. Of its purport, we gather something from a letter in the writing of Tilghman, reiterating the original suggestions and urging an immediate compliance therewith. Moreover, it enlightens us as to the reason for Washington's concern:

Head Quarters Middle Brook, 3ᵈ March 1779
I am favd. with yours of the 26th ulto. by Colo. Malcom. Notwithstanding the many conveniences that would result

[2] This letter is reproduced in Fitzpatrick, Vol. 14, pp. 93–94, and it is this version which is given here. There is a photostat of the original in *The Manor and Forges of Ringwood*, V, 30. H. S.

from carrying on your work at your own House, I am still of opinion, that convenience is overballanced by the danger you are in, should the enemy think the draughts on which you are engaged worth their attention. I can assure you, your Work is no secret to them. Some of the Convention officers who were at your House, saw the Maps and mentioned the accuracy and great Value of them. Altho' a small guard, assisted by your own people, may be sufficient to keep off the small parties of Villains who infest your quarter merely for plunder, it would probably be otherwise with a party sent expressly to take your papers, which from the desultory kind of War they now seem inclined to carry on would be infinitely valuable to them.

I must therefore repeat my desire of your removing as near to the Camp as a convenient situation will admit. You will be as perfectly safe any where in the Rear of the Army as if you were in the midst of it, the people being to a man well affected, and a chain of Guards so posted that no parties can penetrate undiscovered. I cannot think your family will be in danger after the objects that would probably tempt an enemy are removed, but of this you are the best judge. Colo. Malcom delivered the two maps safe.[3]

In acknowledging this final decision, Erskine diplomatically reassures the Chief as to his loyalty, and asserts that he has committed no intentional act of carelessness. What he says, moreover, about the "robbery" at Ringwood is completely confirmatory of the facts elsewhere recorded:

Ringwood, March 20th, 1779

May it please your Excellency:—

As the Supreme Court is now sitting near Pompton, for the trial of Criminals, some of whom were concerned in the rob-

[3] Washington Papers, Library of Congress. Reproduced in Fitzpatrick, Vol. 14, pp. 182–83, which version is given here. There is a photostat of the original in *The Manor and Forges of Ringwood*, V, 32. H. S.

bery of my house, I have no doubt of your excuse for not coming along with the papers and drawings of my Department, to provide Quarters; I have however, sent them all by Capt. Scull, who will look out for accommodations as convenient and agreeable to your Excellency's directions as possible. They should have been sent sooner, had I not been delayed a greater while at Albany than I expected, where I was under the necessity of going to receive interest, and to deposit some Called-in Currency at the Loan Office. Col. Malcom therefore returned about a week before I got back.

Meanwhile, while at Albany, I enquired after maps and surveys which might be of service. —One surveyor has engaged to compile a Plan of Albany County, from his own and other surveys in his possession; besides which I expect to procure several other useful plans, particularly copies of the North and West Branches of Hudson's River, surveyed to their sources; a survey of the same river taken on the Ice, from some miles above Albany to about 40 miles below it; a map which belonged to Sir William Johnson, along the Mohawk River to Oswego, compiled from actual surveys, etc. All of which I took the liberty to say would prove acceptable to your Excellency, as from them perhaps a better Plan of the northern parts may be formed, than any hitherto extant.

With respect to some Convention Officers seeing the Maps, I beg leave to observe that should it have been so represented to your Excellency as if I had made a public Exhibition of them, my prudence, at least, might well be called in question. The fact, however, was far otherwise, and is simply this. The Only Convention officer I ever saw was a Majr. Noble, aid-de-Camp to Genl. Phillips, who last winter was recommended to the civilities of my house in his rout to your Excy's. Quarters: he enquired for me, and was shown into the room where I was drawing, without his being known for a British officer, till he introduced himself. I happened then to be laying down the road from Chester to this place, which he had just traveled over, and speaking of the distance he had come this morning, he cast his eyes over my drawing, (which was the contraction of two miles to an inch) and observed it was the only plan he had seen which bore any resemblance to the face of the Country. The only map of mine, therefore, he saw was that before me; for on his inquiring further into his rout, and the distance he had to go, I produced him Montresor's and Holland's Maps, which he had often seen before: he staid dinner, and went as far as Pompton that evening.[4]

Few letters which I have seen bring the facts recorded on the pages of history so near to being reality as the above. The British officer, journeying "on parole" to quarters assigned to him; the enjoyment of wayside courtesy and refreshment at hospitable Ringwood;—the human nature displayed on both sides, and the frankness of Erskine's recital,—these are far more comprehensive and appealing than many pages of exhaustive digest concerning those "great events" of which we are accustomed to read.

We are justified in believing that Erskine did, for a time, attach himself quite closely to "headquarters" as requested; but the ensuing day-to-day intimacy seems soon to have removed from Washington's mind any lurking doubts which he may have had concerning the absolute reliability and loyalty of his Surveyor-General. Ere long the latter came and went as heretofore, much as he chose, and—in June of 1779—had the pleasure of entertaining his superior in his own spacious manor house at Ringwood.[5]

On Sunday, the 6th of that month, Washington wrote from Ringwood to the President of the Continental Congress in reference to the capitulation of Verplanck's Point-

[4] Washington Papers, Library of Congress. There is a photostat of the original in *The Manor and Forges of Ringwood*, V, 34. H. S.

[5] Gen. Washington on a trip from Middlebrook to West Point, spent the night of June 7, 1779, at Ringwood. See Fitzpatrick, Vol. 15, p. 285 n. H. S.

on-Hudson. He had come up from Middlebrook, on his way to New Windsor and West Point, the better to guard against any pending movements in that direction on the part of the British. It is likely that he arrived at Ringwood on the 5th of June and that he spent one night only beneath Erskine's roof, for we find him at "Smith's Tavern" on the seventh.

It seems that some of the troops followed him by way of Ringwood on this expedition, for we find this rather sarcastic item in the *"Royal Gazette"* (New York's pro-British periodical), June, 1779.

> Mr. Washington, by our latest accounts, was on the 8th instant still *serenely embowered* at Smith's Clove, most of his artillery at Ringwood, and about 300 of his dragoons at Kakiate . . .[6]

Ringwood Manor, in Washington's time, was not substantially different from the Ringwood Manor of the present day. True, the homestead of the Hewitt family (an enlarged and beautified expansion of the Ryerson mansion,—erected 1807–1810, following the demolition of the older house where Hasenclever, Faesch and Erskine abode in old-time elegance) is set a few rods back from the location of the original residency; but the outlook is now very much as it was a century and two score years ago. The lower story of the carriage house, a pre-Revolutionary structure near at hand, reveals ancient hand-hewn beams of an age long past; and although greatly remodeled, the building retains much of its ancient picturesqueness. Then there is a tiny building—a dear little cot beneath a beautiful oak tree—which was the smithy

---

[6] *New Jersey Archives*, Second Series, Vol. III, p. 470. Dr. Thatcher, in his "Military Journal," states that the army passed through Ringwood on the 7th.

of Revolutionary days. Here it was that Washington's horses were re-shod on several occasions by Greene, the blacksmith; for, as will later appear, the General was neither content nor justified in passing this way but once.[7]

In the present instance, however, the patriot leader—much as he may have been inclined to tarry longer amid these pastoral surroundings, so much in keeping with his own ideas of life at its best—was obligated to the more urgent call of duty. And it is not at all unlikely that, as he pursued his way toward the Hudson, Erskine comprised one of the party which augmented his regular staff.

Washington arrived at New Windsor on June 21st, where he remained for a month, then removing to West Point. During this interval, Stony Point was taken by General Wayne; and, in August, Major Lee executed an equally brilliant enterprise in the surprise and capture of the British post at Paulus Hook (Jersey City).[8] After these noteworthy episodes, however, there followed another protracted period of watching and waiting; affording Erskine ample time for the prosecution of his map-making.

The following letter of his, written to Baron Steuben, is very interesting, despite its brevity:

New Windsor July 3ᵈ 1779

Sir:

Pursuant to His Excellency's orders, I beg leave to transmit you the enclosed Draught of the adjacent Country—at the same time His Exy. desired me to mention it as His particular request that no Copies whatever be permitted to be taken of it.

Robert Erskine

[7] The reader should recall that Heusser's account was written in 1928. There have been some changes at Ringwood since. H. S.

[8] In actuality, Lee did not capture the central redoubt, in which the British commander, Major Sutherland, and a few of his troops held out. Lee retired at once with 159 prisoners. H. S.

The original of the above is the only letter of Erskine's which the New-York Historical Society possesses. Another, however, worded and dated exactly as is this, but addressed to General Wayne, is in the Pennsylvania Historical Society's cabinet at Philadelphia, together with the map which accompanied it,—the latter being a magnificent layout of the Hudson Highlands. Here we have a practical illustration of the workings of the Surveying Department: two of the most eminent generals of brigade being supplied with maps identical in character, and each being admonished to refrain from copying the precious drawings.

Washington's headquarters at West Point from July 21st until November 28th, 1779, was at "Moore's House" (now long since vanished), but then standing upon the grounds now belonging to the Military Academy. From thence he dispatched the following note to Erskine:

West-point, August 7, 1779

Sir,

Are the cross roads between the Sussex and Morristown Roads Surveyed? If they are I wish to have them laid down on my pocket Map as soon as possible; if they are not, no time should be lost in the completion of this necessary work.

If you have any Assistant with you, unimployed, he may Survey the Road from Stamford to Hartford by the way of Norwalk Fairfield & New Haven, & come back the most direct Public Road from Newhaven to Bedford.

G°. Washington [9]

Rob[t] Erskine, Geographer

[9] Washington Papers, Library of Congress. There is a photostat of the original in *The Manor and Forges of Ringwood*, V, 36. The letter is printed in Fitzpatrick, Vol. 16, p. 60. In this case, the original was copied here rather than in Fitzpatrick. All evidence is that Heusser was right in believing that the letter was written by Washington himself. H. S.

196 ☞

The above letter is entirely in Washington's autograph. It is his original draft, found among his military papers and now in the Congressional Library. We do not know whether Erskine was, at this time, with the army or at Ringwood; but there can be no question, after this, of Erskine's standing with Washington in point of recognized professional ability. Rather a unique distinction, indeed, to have one's handiwork carried in the pocket of America's first character!

There is, moreover, a second note of a similar intimate nature. This, too, is at the Congressional Library, being the customary "duplicate," but in the hand of Mc Henry. The proposed road (see below) was ere long laid out:

> *HeadQrs. West point*
> *16 Augt—1779*
>
> Sir
> Lord Stirling writes me that a very good road might be opened from Ringwood into the clove, about a mile below Galloway's, along the east side of Tucksets Pond. This will be a shorter route from Morris Town to New Windsor. You will therefore be pleased to mark out the road, and make the proper communication to Lord Stirling that it may be carried into execution.[10]

All accounts and traditions seem to agree that, during the progress of the Revolution, bodies of troops were frequently quartered at Ringwood. Being situated almost midway between Morristown and the Hudson River posts, it was an ideal halting place. Before the construction of

[10] Reproduced in Fitzpatrick, Vol. 16, p. 112, which version is given here. There is a photostat of the original in *The Manor and Forges of Ringwood*, V, 37. Washington wrote to Lord Stirling on the same day that Erskine would receive orders at once to mark out the road, and on Aug. 25 informed him that Erskine had left Morristown "for the purpose of laying out the road." *Ibid.*, pp. 110, 146. H. S.

the "new road" (in accordance with Washington's suggestion), the outlet from Ringwood into Smith's Clove was the old road through Eagle Valley. In 1777, some divisions of Burgoyne's captive army passed through the Ramapo Valley and Ringwood on their southward march to their concentration camps, and it is quite likely that they debouched by way of this same Eagle Valley road. Another ancient highway, and a slightly more direct route from the Ramapo Valley to Morristown, ran by way of Suffern, Oakland and Pompton.

That the Ringwood Iron Works were of considerable importance, and that their location was of sufficient security to warrant the establishment of a supply base at this point, is proven by documentary evidence. The following letter, between officers of the Quartermaster's Department,[11] tells its own story:

Pitts Town, September 27, 1779

Sir.

I have received notice of a considerable Magazine of Provisions ordered to be Formed at Ringwood Iron Works (but this to yourself) and that a Quantity of Forage will also be wanted there, which is Scarce in that Neighborhood; as you are the Nearest District to that of all, I have th. it best to order on what you can spare. I wrote Mr. Marsh not to press any more Hay in his District and to let a set of Hands go on to you so that it may be pressed & forwarded before the bad Weather and roads prevent it—You will let me know by the first opportunity what Quantity of Hay & Grass you think you can spare from your District that I may provide for that Post at Ringwood from other places.

By advice recd. from different counties and Districts in this

[11] Moore Furman was Deputy Quartermaster General of New Jersey. David Banks (1743–1820) was one of the assistants in the department, an officer of the N. J. Militia, son-in-law of Col. Josiah Ogden, of Newark. He was one of the men who crossed the Delaware with Washington in 1776.

State, I find they are now giving and offering Forty Pounds per Ton for best Hay Twelve Dollars for Rye Ten Dollars for Corn, & Eight for Oats & Buckwheat at which I think considerable quantities is and will be collected before Winter and I hope you will not be Obliged to exceed those prices in your District. I am sir,

Your Humbl Servt.

Moore Furman

To David Banks Esq., A. Q. M., Newark [12]

There is another letter, still extant, which makes mention of Ringwood and Erskine during the year 1779. In itself, it is of no great consequence, but—in conjunction with the facts of the case, as we now know them—it possesses considerable interest.

In the first place, it proves that Erskine, in his mountain retreat, was by no means unprovided with supplies. Secondly, it leads us to believe that the relations between himself and the Hoffs (operating the Hibernia mines) were now of a much more friendly nature than in 1775. This may be accounted for, in large measure, by the joint efforts and sacrifices of all the Jersey iron-masters in the patriot cause. As co-partners in the struggle for America's freedom, personal likes, dislikes and prejudices were bound to sink into insignificance.

Hibernia Furnace 15th Nov. 1779

Dear Sir,

Being solicitous for Mr. Erskine's answer respecting the exchange of Pigg metal for Salt at the price we yesterday talked, and the bearer, Peter Young, going near Ringwood on his own business, I should consider it as a particular favor if you'd

[12] The letter may be found in print in *The Letters of Moore Furman* (N. Y., 1912), p. 20. Pittstown was located in Hunterdon County, N. J., rather than in Pennsylvania as Heusser thought. Furman was the owner of a large tract of land there, to which he had moved when the British occupied Philadelphia. H. S.

write him fully on the matter by Young and let me have a satisfactory answer by his return. I should be willing that the quantity of salt exchanged for might be either 25 or 50 bushels.

I am Sir,
Your Humble servant
Charles Hoff

Mr. Wm. Harrison.[13]

It sometimes happens that the name of one great man so outshines those of his fellows that he alone is remembered. That no injustice may be done to any of the near neighbors of worthy Erskine by any such process of deduction, may I digress, in passing, to say that the name of but one other who dwelt in the immediate vicinity of Ringwood has come down to us as having served prominently in the patriot cause. That man was Captain Joseph Board, one of the sons of Cornelius Board, the pioneer iron-master of the region. A few facts as to his career have come down to us. A prosperous farmer at the outbreak of the Revolution,—having augmented his revenue from the fields by doing a considerable business through the hauling of Ringwood iron to tidewater at Acquackanonck Landing— he helped the patriot cause materially in the organization of a company of militia, and, as their captain, served with distinction in the New Jersey brigade. (On some of Erskine's military maps we see the location of his house clearly lettered: "Captain Board's." Joseph Board attained the ripe old age of ninety-four, surviving until 1832, an honored resident of the community.

As to the names of other officers and private soldiers from this part of Bergen County who served in the patriot army, there will always be considerable conjecture. The

[13] From the Hoff letter copy books, Washington's Headquarters, Morristown. One of Erskine's bookkeepers, Harrison's name appears many times in the Erskine Papers at the New Jersey Historical Society, Newark.

following, however, may be set down as a nucleus of a list which may be added to by some future historian:

Captain Peter Ward
" Crynes Bartholf
" John Vreeland
Adjutant George Ryerson
Lieutenant Peter S. Van Order
Sergeant Anthony Beam
Corporal Abram Vreeland
Privates: —
  George Anderson
  James Beam
  John Beam
  John S. Bertholf
  Cornelius D. Board
  Anthony Brown
  Thomas Burk
  Walter De Graw
  Isaac Fisher
  Peter Freeland (or Vreeland)
  John Green
  Michael Guillam

John J. Hopper
Samuel Lyon
Edo. Marcelles
Alexander Mc Donald
Garret Odel
Adrian Post
Martin G. Ryerson
Ryor Ryerson
Nathaniel Sisco
Peter Sisco
Peter J. Sisco
John Storms
John Taylor
Jacob Turse (or Tice)
John Turse (or Tice)
John Van Norden
Peter Van Norden
James Walker
James Ward
William Young

Mortality was high among bodies of encamped soldiery in olden times, largely because of inefficiency in sanitation, and lack of skill in the treatment of epidemic disease common to camp life. At nearby Hillburn, N. Y., in the locality still referred to as "the quarantine," large numbers of one of the Southern regiments succumbed to fever; and, so it is asserted, many of the Continental troops died at Ringwood during the course of the war and were buried in the cemetery a quarter of a mile from the Manor House. Mr. Erskine Hewitt pointed out to the writer many such soldiers' graves, marked only by uninscribed and roughly-fashioned slabs placed on end, or—in certain cases—merely large fieldstones. Some of these unknown dead were doubtless soldiers of Louis XVI, for—in the late summer of 1781—a portion of the French contingent (en route from the Hudson River to Yorktown, there to participate in the final and successful effort against the British) are known to have passed through and biv-ouacked at Ringwood, thence proceeding on their way through Whippany and Morristown.

There are no traces of fortifications or earthworks at Ringwood, but at Hillburn, north of Suffern, two bona-fide Revolutionary trenches exist in a surprisingly good state of preservation. The longer earthwork is near the "quarantine," and quite evidently guarded the southern entrance to the famous Ramapo defile: the smaller trench, to the northwest, seems to have been intended to defend a by-way leading to Ringwood, or may possibly have been designed as an inconspicuous observation post. At this latter site,—a position known as "Fort Sidman" during the war,—the Daughters of the American Revolution have placed a commemorative marker.

General Washington located himself at Morristown, N. J., on December 1st, 1779; there to remain for several months at the house of Col. Jacob Ford, Jr.; and, in the tarrying, to associate his presence with this region more inseparably than ever before, because fate has so ordained that the house which offered him hospitality should be preserved and venerated to this day as has been no other dwelling in all the region 'round. One letter to Erskine from this famous headquarters survives:

Head Quarters, Morris Town 9th Decembr 1779
Dear Sir

His Excellency is extremely anxious to have the Roads in front and rear of the Camp accurately surveyed as speedily as possible. He therefore wishes to see you immediately at Head Quarters that he may give you particular directions as to the Business which he wants executed.

I am, Dear Sir,
Sincerely yours,
T. Tilghman

Robert Erskine Esq., Ringwood . . .[14]

[14] Washington Papers, Library of Congress. The letter is reproduced in Fitzpatrick, Vol. 17, p. 240, which version is given here. There is a photostat of the original in *The Manor and Forges of Ringwood*, V, 38. H. S.

13

Last Days

WASHINGTON'S winter bivouac at Morristown (1779–1780) has come to be regarded as an especially trying period of the Revolutionary struggle, second only in its hardships to the Valley Forge sojourn. This opinion is well-founded, perhaps, for there were storms, privations and difficulties without number; to be endured, survived or conquered as occasion demanded. Yet it cannot be controverted that the vision of ultimate victory was already clearly discerned; and the temporary security of these Jersey uplands was recognized by private and Commander-in-Chief alike to be but a foretaste of the fully-recognized liberty that was to be. Hence it was a confident hope, rather than a dogged stoicism, which kept up the spirits of the snow-bound army of deliverance when the winds howled and hunger gnawed.

Robert Erskine, quite evidently, was more closely connected with Morristown during this period than the writer knew when he began this biographical chronicle.

And it is to Dr. David McGregor, writing in *The Master Mason*, that we are indebted for a considerable amount of valuable information anent this subject. In the March and April numbers of that publication (1927) wherein Dr. McGregor writes of Freemasonry at Morristown during the Revolutionary War, there are repeated references to Erskine which we unhesitatingly avail of as being both pertinent and appropriate.

Until the appearance of these articles I was unaware that Robert Erskine was a member of the Masonic fraternity, although the fact that his reverend father was prominently affiliated with this organization was set forth in the opening chapter. Dr. McGregor leads us to infer that Erskine became a Freemason while residing in London, and states that, when he came to America, he brought with him letters of introduction to a number of prominent Masonic brethren on this side of the water, among whom was the Rev. John Witherspoon, the president of Princeton College. Whether or not these fraternal ties had anything to do with cementing the friendship between Erskine and General Washington (who, as were so many of the Revolutionary leaders, was a Mason) I shall not venture to surmise.

Certain it is, however, that Robert Erskine was present at one or more important Masonic convocations at Morristown, at which also—in his simple role as a Master Mason—George Washington was likewise in attendance. In so far as the war of the Revolution was concerned with Freemasonry, it was in very fact a struggle of "brother against brother." Very many of the officers on both sides were Masons, and I think I am not going beyond the bounds of propriety to say that much of the fine courtesy which characterized the military intercourse of rival commanders during the long drawn-out and painful struggle was actuated by a spirit of fraternity which even the stern demands of political exigency could not entirely overrule.

Stormy December, 1779, moderated sufficiently to enable the "Masonic brethren" cantoned at Morristown publicly to celebrate St. John's Day (the 27th of the month) for which purpose forty members of the American Union Lodge and sixty-four visiting brethren from the various lines in the army congregated at Arnold's tavern, from whence they proceeded to the Presbyterian Church located on the other side of the green. Prominent in the procession, as representing the New Jersey line were: General William Maxwell, brigade commander; Colonel Elias Dayton; Lieut.-Colonel Anthony W. White; Colonel Jacob Arnold; Major Jeremiah Bruen; Captains Thomas Kinney, John Armstrong, John Sanford and Robert Erskine; Chaplain Andrew Hunter; Surgeon Jabez Campfield; Lieut. William Piatt.

Returning to Arnold's tavern after the religious services, the assemblage partook of a collation, and then adjourned to the lodge room above. The session which followed was one of the most vital in the history of the Craft in America, the chief subject under discussion being the advisability of "appointing a Grand Master in and over the thirteen United States of America," such a course being necessitated because of the unhappy separation from the Grand Lodge in Europe in consequence of the American struggle for independence. A petition to effect this result was then and there promulgated, to be circulated among the brethren of the various military Lodges represented in the Army.

Dr. McGregor, in his brief biographical sketch of Erskine's career, reproduces a map of the region contiguous to Morristown, executed by Erskine two weeks before the

St. John's Day celebration, "when surveying was seriously handicapped by two feet of snow on the ground." This was undoubtedly a portion of the work which Washington desired to be done when he dictated the letter referred to in the closing page of the last chapter. Dr. McGregor further states another interesting fact heretofore unknown to me, *i.e.*, that there is today in the library of the British Museum, London, a copy of a "book" written and published by Erskine, being "A Dissertation on Rivers and Tides," in which he advanced new ideas bearing on the construction of bridges. That he had written articles on this subject we have elsewhere stated; but it is pleasant to learn that his work was sufficiently expansive to warrant the making of a volume.[1]

About a month before the patriot army broke camp at Morristown to repel the threatening advance of the British toward Springfield, Robert Erskine penned a lengthy letter to General Philip Schuyler (one of the most staunch and conscientious among the truly great men of his time), partly in his own behalf, but more for the sake of the men who, laboring with him from day to day, had done so much for the common cause. The original, among the papers of the Continental Congress now treasured at the Congressional Library, bears, upon the verso, the brief notation in the hand of Schuyler: "From Mr. Erskine":

Morristown, May 7th, 1780

Sir:

In pursuance of your desire, I beg leave to lay before you a state of the Surveying Department, for the purpose of its being adjusted as shall be thought proper, by the Honble. Committee of Congress appointed to regulate the different Departments

[1] The original drafts are in the Erskine Papers. H. S.

of the Army, the Assistant Surveyors of which have represented their situation in a letter addressed to me, of which the following is a copy:

Morristown, February 12th, 1780

Dear Sir:

As the Directors of our affairs undoubtedly wish to do justice between the Public and its servants, we beg leave to request the favor of you, when arrived at Philadelphia, to represent the difficulties under which the Surveying Department labors at present, which, we flatter ourselves, only requires to be known to be redressed.

Formerly common Surveyors, whose acquaintance with the business was limited by the Needle and Protractor, were paid at least fifteen shillings per day, exclusive of their expenses; while persons of acknowledged abilities received from twenty to forty shillings and upwards; which was a considerable inducement for those whose genius pointed that way to qualify themselves for the profession; whereas, our pay at present is no more than two Continental Dollars a day, without any kind of allowance or emolument, except a ration and travelling expences, a charge allowed in every profession.

The officers in the line of the Army, have received a considerable addition to their pay, under the denomination of subsistance money; besides the benefit of State supplies: and the wages of other Departments of the Army, whose pay was formerly less than ours, has been greatly augmented; while we have been entirely overlooked, merely for want of having proper application in our behalf.

In the present case, we are far from wishing to raise fortunes by the calamities of our Country; but at the same time we believe our Country is as far from wishing us to present our fortunes to them, along with our services, without any prospect of reimbursement, which at present is the case. Our pay, so far from supplying us with clothes, has not been adequate, for these twelve months past, to the furnishing us with shoes, and now is not sufficient for washing.

If therefore the continuance of our Service be thought necessary, we have no doubt that the Surveying Department will be
so arranged, as in some degree to make up for the Depreciation; and fix our pay in such a manner, as shall prevent the
like inconvenience in future; the readiest way to do which, in
our opinion, would be to regulate it by the price of Specie.

We are, &c.   Signed,
                                          Simeon DeWitt
                                          Benjamin Lodge
                                          Asst. Survs.

Upon this letter I shall only beg leave to observe, that His
Excellency, Genl. Washington, has seen it, and is of the opinion
that the allegations it contains are reasonable: to which permit me the liberty of adding, that both my former and present
assistants, not only expect a recompense for Depreciation; but
that such as continue in, or return to this service, look for an
establishment on the same permanent footing with the officers
in the Line of the Army.

The number of Assistant Surveyors has varied from two to
six; the mean number employed for a Constancy, I suppose to
be one Assistant Draughtsman, three field surveyors, and
eighteen chain-bearers from the Line.

From Surveys actually made, we have furnished His Excellency with maps of both sides of the North River, extending
from New Windsor and Fishkill, southerly to New York; eastward: to Hartford, Whitehaven, etc., and on the west to Easton
in Pennsylvania. Our Surveys likewise include the principal
part of New Jersey, lying northward of a line drawn from
Sandy Hook to Philadelphia; take in a considerable part of
Pennsylvania; extend through the whole route of the Western
army under Genl. Sullivan, and are carried on from New
Windsor and Fishkill northward, on both sides of the River,
to Albany, & from thence to Scoharie. In short, from the Surveys made, and materials collecting and already procured, I
could form a pretty accurate Map of the four States of Pennsylvania, New Jersey, New York and Connecticut, and by the

help of a few Magnetic and Astronomical Observations, with some additional Surveys, a very accurate one.

The charges already incurred from this business have consisted in the Surveyors pay, of four, three and two dollars per day; chain-bearers at half a dollar, travelling expences; the purchase of provisions when beyond the reach of drawing rations; of forrage and horses, when they could not be had otherwise; and of Instruments, Maps, Drawing Papers, &c., &c.

The demands on the Department at present are inconsiderable, there being none of any consequence, except an years pay due to myself, with an allowance for extra Rations since I entered the service. Upon the whole, the money I have received from the Quartermaster General or his assistants for the above purposes, and to discharge about 1200 Dollars due on account of Surveying in Pennsylvania, before I had the Direction of the Business, amounts to 25,636 Dollars and an half, the balance of which remaining in my hands on the first instant was 320½ Dollars: the mean therefore of the expence of the Department, for twenty-three months, exclusive of the years pay due me, has been about Thirty-five dollars a day.

I must now trouble you with personal concerns, because necessary, although it is a task I enter upon with reluctance, for how ever much one may be supposed interested in this case, yet the setting forth any matters relative (to) self, are far from affording either pleasure or satisfaction in the Communication.

In the spring of 1777 I began to do business for the Public, by making a sketch of the Country for Genl. Lee; a map of the Jersies for His Excellency Genl. Washington from materials furnished by Lord Stirling; and a few trivial surveys at New Windsor: but did not engage fully in the Continental Service, or receive pay, till the first of June, 1778, when the Commander-in-Chief honoured me with a Commission as Geographer and Surveyor to the Army. At this time, on my pay becoming the subject, I observed that the stated price in Britain, which myself and others of my profession received, was a guinea a day and expences; but, as at this rate, such pay

would have exceeded that of a Major General; four dollars
and four rations were proposed with which I readily acquiesced; not only as I entered into the service without the view
of making a profit or a fortune, but because His Excellency
had left the determination of this point almost solely to my
own decision: however, it is proper here to observe, that I
looked on the four Dollars as a gratuity, which at some future
time would be equivalent to so much hard money; and I beg
leave to add that though, on a peace, I would not serve either
individuals or the Public at an under price, yet I shall be far
from expecting or desiring any augmentation while the war
lasts, provided my services continue to prove acceptable; and
the situation of my family and private concerns permit me to
continue to the end of it. On this head it is necessary to be explicit, particularly on this occasion. My family are situated in
the mountains, between New York and New Jersey subject to
the plundering Banditti from the enemy, by whom my dwelling house has been once robbed already; the situation, however, is inconvenient only in this respect; nor could I move
from thence, and continue in my present business, but to the
greatest detriment, or even the anihilation of my Fortune,
almost the whole of which is risqued in the Continental Funds;
and which, on acccount of the depreciation and their present
precarious state, has required, and must still require, more of
my attention than is consistent with the expediting of business,
particularly as I have no assistant draughtsman with me at
present, and only one Surveyor: It is an attention, nevertheless, I must now bestow, except I would render myself entirely
dependent on my Pay and the favour of the Public; a situation
by no means desirable, and which, I presume, all who have
the least acquaintance with history or the World, would avoid
if possible. From this representation it will be likewise apparent that I could not remove into a Southern Climate even supposing my Constitution would bear the change, which I am of
opinion it could not; because on that supposition, I must unavoidably subject myself to the risque I deprecate; and leave
a beloved wife a prey to cares, anxieties and Banditti, under

which she could by no means subsist; her health having been frequently impaired already from the troubles and solicitudes she has met with, though, thank God, hitherto her resolution and happy flow of spirits, with the little attention I could bestow, have in some measure helped to restore her.

I gladly now quit a subject that has given me pain in the recital, which the justice I owe myself rendered necessary, to observe; that the original protractions and plans already surveyed by the Geographers of the Army are contained in upwards of two hundred and fifty sheets of paper; that with a proper number of hands, which I suppose to be five surveyors and two draughtsmen, such additional surveys of the roads and rivers might be taken in the course of a year, as would afford sufficient data for the forming an accurate map of the middle States; and, that though there would be occasion, at any rate, for Geographers to attend the Army in order to survey and lay down particular districts on a large scale and other purposes; yet the best way to execute this general business with accuracy and dispatch, especially if extended to the other States, would be the establishment of a permanent office for this purpose, but still under the direction and disposal of the Commander-in-Chief during the war.

I have the honour to be,
Sir,
    Your obliged and Exd. most obedt. humble Servant,
Robt Erskine
Honble. Philip Schuyler, Esq.

Rather enlightening is this frank avowal of Erskine's sentiments. By inference we gather that it had been proposed to send him south, following the path of the war. To this suggestion he demurs. Another fleeting side light is vouchsafed in his references to Mrs. Erskine and his much-disturbed home-life at Ringwood. Man-like, he seems to have regarded himself as indispensable to the happiness of his spouse. Yet, as we shall see, when the very worst (as he imagined it), was to become an actuality, the beloved one was not to be left destitute in her grief nor to lack solace in the person of another protector. But so goeth the way of life, and such is the manner of womankind!

But—putting aside any small cynicisms which may be ascribed to the bachelor estate enjoyed (or endured) by the biographer—and reverting again to cold facts, let it be set down that Erskine was not urged to join the Southern army.

Washington, coming again into the Jersey hills after the Springfield encounter, progressed so far as old "Ramapough" (the site of Erskine's Bellegrove repository) and —in his Order Book, which contains the daily entries of happenings at headquarters,—thus refers to Ringwood:

Head Quarters, Ramapough, Friday, June 30, 1780. . . .
Colonel Livingston's regiment will take Post in the Clove near the old Barracks, and joined by the detachment of General Clinton's brigade, already there will furnish such Guards as may be necessary for the Security of the Stores at Ringwood.[2]

Upon another page of this manuscript volume it is noted that General Hand is to be sent from Ramapough to Ringwood and there quartered, with a strong body of troops, to protect the stores.

As to Erskine's activities during the early summer of 1780 there is not much available data.[3] A little survey of the Hudson which has come down to us indicates that he was still busily at work in this branch of the service. Al-

[2] Reproduced in Fitzpatrick, Vol. 19, p. 100. H. S.
[3] On June 30 and again on Aug. 12, General Washington ordered that men from the Army be detailed to act as chain bearers for Erskine and his surveyors. See Fitzpatrick, Vol. 19, pp. 100, 365. H. S.

though unpretentious, this Erskine map is of particular interest because it is the only specimen of his work which remained among the papers of Washington when he turned them over to Congress. It is now at the Congressional Library, and I believe it to be "No. 112," marked as being "missing" from the fine collection of Erskine's charts at the New-York Historical Society.

Among the praiseworthy episodes of the Revolution, in so far as sincerity of purpose is concerned, was the so-called "affair of Block-house Point"; yet, because of its partial failure, the incident brought forth from the Tory and British element in New York a storm of ridicule upon the heads of the patriot participants.

Three or four miles below Fort Lee, at the base of the Palisades, was a little village called Bull's Ferry. Just below the settlement, on Block-house Point, was a stockaded enclosure, occupied in the summer of 1780 by a British picket for the protection of the neighboring Tories. In the immediate vicinity, under this "Royal protection," were large numbers of cattle and horses, the capture of which seemed to General Washington to be an object of sufficient importance to warrant the sending of General Wayne, the hero of Stony Point, with some Pennsylvania and Maryland troops, to effect the business.

The little block-house proved to be too strongly fortified to be taken by assault, although the Americans sacrificed some sixty-four men in killed and wounded in the attempt. The live-stock, however, was captured without loss, and the herds driven away to the American lines by "Light Horse Harry" Lee's dragoons. It was this incident which inspired Major John André of the British army to write his exceedingly laughable poem, "The Cow Chase," which appeared in *Rivington's Gazette* a few weeks thereafter, at the very time, as fate would have it, that the unfortunate author was a prisoner in the hands of the Americans awaiting execution as a spy.

Charles H. Winfield, in his account of the Block-house Point incident, which appeared in the *Magazine of American History*, Sept., 1880, prefaces his article in part as follows, incidentally referring to Erskine:

> Assisted by Robert Erskine, Geographer of the Continental Army, Wayne visited Closter on the 17th of July, and carefully considered the possibilities of the British crossing the river from Phillips farm and pushing on to New Bridge by way of Closter Landing.

We are free to assume that Erskine came into frequent and almost daily contact with Washington while the latter was quartered at the mansion of Colonel Theunis Dey, at Lower Preakness, N. J., from July 1st to 29th. This fine old house, not so very far from Ringwood, but nearer to the present great city of Paterson, still stands in lordly isolation, privately owned, despite many efforts to acquire and preserve it for the public as an historic shrine.[4]

Of Washington's sojourn in this peaceful valley [5] much has been written, yet the fine colonial homestead made famous by his presence is one of the least visited of all his transient abodes. This may be accounted for by the fact that it is "off the beaten track," being situated on an infrequently used country road. Washington Irving, in his

---

[4] This statement is still true in 1965. H. S.

[5] During the summer and autumn of 1780, the main American army was encamped at Totowa, being ranged along the hills running parallel with the river Passaic. Practically all of this camp-ground may be said to be included within the present city of Paterson and its suburbs. The left wing, under "Light Horse Harry" Lee, lay at Wagaraw; the center was not far from the "great falls of the Passaic": and the right wing, in the neighborhood of Little Falls, commanded the approach through the "Great Notch." General Washington's headquarters at Preakness were well behind the center of the line.

Life of Washington has given us some delightful glimpses of life at the Preakness Headquarters, mentioning the visits of Lafayette and the Marquis de Chastellux, with an account of the daily routine, and the frequent conferences of Wayne and Knox and others among that notable band of immortals who shared the anxieties and now enjoy the glory of Washington. But here again has Erskine been forgotten. The "man in the shadow" must often have comprised one of the company around the table of the Chief. For some years he had been a near neighbor of Colonel Dey, and most likely was a frequent visitor at his home before the exigencies of war prompted Washington here to establish headquarters. Erskine himself has left not a word anent the doings at Preakness; history has likewise ignored any part he may have had in the councils of the patriot leaders. Again it is to an ancient periodical that we are indebted for a solitary reference to his name as associated with the Dey family; and then only because of the "war-work" in which his "better half" was engaged.

In an issue of the *New Jersey Gazette* of July 5th, 1780, there appears a list of the ladies banded together "in aid of the Continental soldiers in Bergen County," and among them are "Mrs. (Colonel) Theunis Dey, Mrs. Fell, Mrs. Kuyper, Mrs. Robert Erskine and Mrs. (Major) Dey."

Late September of 1780 demanded the presence of Washington in Connecticut, there to confer with the French allies. Then came the discovery of Arnold's treason and many bitter disillusions.

Robert Erskine was, however, not destined to know aught of these happenings, nor to participate in the closing events of the Revolution. Nor was he to see the resumption of peaceful relations between the land of his adoption and Great Britain. Whatever "after-the-war" plans he may have cherished for himself, for his employers, or for his foster-country, were never to be unfolded. Like many another great man and good, he was bidden to depart for the "far distant country" while yet in the midst of his labors.

According to the inscription upon his tomb at Ringwood, he died on the second day of October, 1780; a date which has been made notable because of the execution of Major John André, which occurred at Tappan, not many miles distant, that same afternoon. It has been current tradition in these parts for many years that Erskine's fatal illness was due to a fever, occasioned by exposure incident to some surveys he was making in the Hudson Highlands. His nephew, Ebenezer Erskine, has left the only known details. He says that, on the 18th of September, Robert Erskine "caught a severe cold and sore throat, which produced fever, and within the space of a fortnight terminated in his dissolution." During his last illness, according to Ebenezer, physicians were dispatched from the camp (then on the shores of the Hudson) to administer medical aid to him, and "his funeral was most respectably attended."

Ebenezer Erskine appears to have been most attentive to the dying man, being present at the closing scene, upon which he comments as follows:

Thus died my uncle, Robert Erskine. Through the whole of his life he strictly adhered to the principles of religion, honour, and justice; had a clear judgment, and a most sympathizing heart for the distressed, whom he was ever ready to relieve to the utmost of his power. Upon his death-bed he began to reap the benefit of such a life; for, when free of bodily pain, his mind was all calm and serene; and he is now in the full enjoyment of bliss in the realms above. Poor Mrs. Erskine is in the greatest distress. Never, I believe, was a couple more firmly united by the most sincere esteem and tender affection for each other.[6]

What I myself know, positively, is this. Among the Erskine papers which have passed through my hands there was a half-sheet of foolscap, torn and much bescribbled. It was a memorandum of accounts, for the most part in Erskine's own writing, but showing a disjointedness of thought and great feebleness of hand. It is headed "this 2nd of October" and appears to have been the brave attempt of a stricken man to arrive at a final balance,—to leave a concise statement of his affairs before he died. It was never completed, nor was it signed. This seems to indicate that the illness of Erskine was neither so protracted as to have permitted him properly to wind up his business affairs, nor so sudden as to have robbed him of consciousness and intellect at one fell swoop; hence corroborating his nephew's statements.[7]

Without a doubt Washington attended the funeral ceremony, which occurred a day or so later; but it is my private opinion that the Commander-in-Chief was at Ringwood on the day of Erskine's death. Historians agree that Washington was not present at the execution of Major André, while it is further recorded that the headquarters at Tappan appeared to be forsaken on that tragic day. Until further evidence be adduced to establish the whereabouts of Washington on the 2nd of October, 1780, I am satisfied to believe that he had already set out from Tappan before the execution, in the knowledge that his friend was nigh unto death. Such an errand of mercy would

[6] From the journal of Ebenezer Erskine, quoted in Rev. Donald Fraser's *Life and Diary of Rev. Ralph Erskine.*

[7] The document alluded to is in *The Manor and Forges of Ringwood*, I, 75–76. H. S.

have furnished him with a welcome excuse to absent himself from an ignominious spectacle.

The distance between Tappan and Ringwood does not exceed twenty miles, and Washington could have covered it with ease in a long afternoon. Indeed, I should imagine that the flight of hours mattered little to the care-burdened general at this particular time. Those who love the personal Washington and appreciate the real warmth of his friendship for the men in whom he confided, may understand something of his return from Ringwood after the laying away of his friend. Admirer of nature though he was, the gorgeous woodland surely wasted its charms that day. Abstractedly he must have turned his face toward the Hudson; scarce noticing the fast falling leaves of russet and crimson which bestrewed his path, the conversation of the staff-officers who rode beside him, or even the proffered attentions of devoted black "Billy" who cantered behind. Rather were his thoughts upon his erstwhile friends—Benedict Arnold, who had "gone to the enemy," and Robert Erskine, who had gone to meet his God—both lost to him forever! And who can doubt that there was much of kindly pity for poor André, "more unfortunate than criminal!" [8]

The last resting-place of Erskine is marked by a respectable brick table-tomb, topped by a marble slab.[9] I have heard it said that Washington himself caused this monument to be erected. But this is highly improbable. Ebenezer Erskine is authority for the statement that his uncle's prosperity in the new world fully equaled his

---

[8] The present editor can only regard the above as a pleasant myth. Had Washington been at the funeral or at Ringwood before Erskine's death, it seems likely that Ebenezer Erskine would have recorded the fact. H. S.

[9] The present stone, bearing the inscription, is a replica of the original, which—having become broken and defaced—was replaced some forty years ago by the Hon. Abram S. Hewitt, owner of Ringwood Manor.

expectations, and,—while this assertion may be discounted to some extent,—it is certain that Robert Erskine did not die in circumstances bearing any semblance to destitution. Mrs. Erskine was amply provided for, without a doubt; and Washington—as is well known—was not given to the expenditure of money without occasion, although ready enough to aid the poor and needy. Therefore, we may discredit this far-fetched tradition about Erskine's tomb. But there is a prettier and truer story.

Upon the occasion of a subsequent visit to Ringwood, in 1782, Washington planted an elm tree beside the grave of his faithful geographer. For over a century it shaded the tomb, until—a few years ago—it was blasted by lightning. What remains of it is now carefully preserved in a corner of the ample portico of Ringwood Manor House.

The making of Erskine's coffin-plate, according to his nephew's account, was a labor of love performed by his devoted friend and assistant in the Surveying Department, Simeon De Witt. Upon it, neatly inscribed in "gilt letters," was the following legend:

In memory of
R O B E R T   E R S K I N E ,   F .   R .   S .
Geographer and Surveyor General to the Army of the
United States of America.
Born Sept. 7th, 1735.   Died October 2d, 1780.
Aged 45 years and 25 days.

The same words comprise the epitaph upon the marble slab of the tomb, with the added sentence: "Son of the Rev. Ralph Erskine, late minister at Dunfermline in Scotland."

The place of Erskine's burial is surpassingly lovely, by reason of its situation upon a slight rise bordering the miniature lake, beside the farther shores of which, nestled among tall trees, are situated the present palatial Manor House, and the older out-buildings of the Ringwood Estate.

Around this peaceful retreat, where Erskine has lain undisturbed these many years, a tiny graveyard has grown. Many of the humble folk among the villagers and workmen whom he knew, have here been laid away beside him for their last long sleep. Then too there are the soldiers' graves to which we have referred. These brave hearts also rest forever in the quiet sanctity of God's acre.

But Erskine's closest companion in death is Robert Monteath, his youthful scrivener, like himself a son of the Land of Heather. Of this young man nothing is known save the fact that his name occurs with more or less frequency upon Erskine's books and among his papers. He died in 1778, aged 33 years, and was (so I am inclined to think) the predecessor of Ebenezer Erskine as the accountant and assistant of the Surveyor General, looking after much of the routine work of the iron manufactory during the absence of the master of the mines. Excepting the monument of Robert Erskine, that of Monteath is the only table-tomb in the cemetery. It closely resembles that of Erskine himself and is in its original condition. Were nothing else known concerning Robert Erskine of Ringwood, this tomb of "Robert Monteath, born at Dunblain in Scotland, Clerk to Robert Erskine" would speak volumes. Erskine, it cannot be doubted, was possessed of a natural spirit of kindliness and a grateful appreciation of faithful service; and it was he himself who erected this memorial to his young accountant, little dreaming that, ere long, he, too, was to keep him company in that long silent watch, "until the day break and the shadows flee away."

Surely so notable a man as Erskine is entitled to a ghost, through the medium of which (or "whom") to revisit his quondam haunts. And, according to some of the older Negro residents of Ringwood village, such a spiritual visitor has actually made his appearance more than once,—a military figure, so they assert, sitting upon the tomb and musing beside a flickering lantern with a bluish and sepulchral flame. I think I should like to meet this unearthly apparition; there are so many things about which we might converse with profit. This spectre ought surely to be interested in hearing of the happenings of the intervening years; and I doubt not that he, on his part, could clear up for us a great many puzzling historical queries.

Nevertheless, I am persuaded that hours of darkness are times inopportune to attempt communication with the spirit of Robert Erskine. The rather do I seek him in the sunny morn, when the light—coming up over the hills behind the site of his old forge by the dam—bathes his lowly tomb in the glory of a newborn day. Or when, more often, I stand eagerly beside his grave when the stone whereon is chiseled his worthy name is shadowed with leafy tracery and the sun is high. And yet again, at the close of day,—when feathered songsters render for him their sweetest evening carols,—I, too, have come to say good night.

The life of Robert Erskine has been to me an inspirational study and a source of joy. Having been led, as I believe, into an intimate knowledge of the little known circumstances attending his career, I have become convinced that it is a sacred duty to tell his story, because it is an example well worthy to be followed. Moreover, it were a pity indeed that the name of one so true and steadfast should sink into oblivion.

14

What Happened Afterward

IN the *New Jersey Gazette* of Wednesday, Oct. 18, 1780, appeared the following brief but appreciative obituary notice:

Died the 2d instant, at his house at Ringwood, ROBERT ERSKINE, F. R. S. and Geographer to the Army of the United States, in the 46th year of his age. A man in whom were united the Christian and the gentleman. His integrity and unbounded benevolence have rendered his death a loss to the publick, and a subject of sincere regret to all his acquaintances. He made the laws of justice the invariable rule of his conduct, and upon this principle espoused the cause of America, in which he served his country with approbation and universal esteem.

In a letter to the President of Congress, bearing date the 26th of November, 1780, General Washington (writing from the Dey Mansion at Preakness, N. J.) says:

The death of that useful and valuable Officer, Mr. Erskine, Geographer to the Army, makes it requisite that a successor should be appointed. I beg leave to recommend Mr. Simeon De Witt. His being in the Department gives him a pretension, and his abilities a still better. From the character Mr. Erskine always gave of him and from what I have seen of his performances, he seems to be extremely well qualified.[1]

Washington, while paying tribute to Erskine in the above communication, gives us a last "side light" upon the character of the departed, who in having always spoken well of his subordinate (for Dewitt, as we know, had been his assistant in the surveying work of the army) displayed thereby a spirit of appreciation not always to be found in present-day heads of military departments.

Simeon Dewitt served acceptably in the capacity of Surveyor General through the concluding years of the War for Independence. Into his custody came the precious maps of Erskine (at least the major portion of them) and, when the troublous times had passed, they appear to have been treasured by him to the end of his days as personal possessions. You may see them to-day in the library of the New-York Historical Society, into whose possession they came many years ago from members of the Dewitt family.[2] A consummate artist and draughtsman, as well as a surveyor, Erskine has injected so much personality into his charts that one can unfailingly recognize his work. Rich in color are some of them, too, showing that the labor was not that of a hireling, but that their making was a task of love and a source of profound delight. A few other scattered maps of Erskine are known to be in

[1] Reproduced in Fitzpatrick, Vol. 20, p. 400. Washington had already refused to recommend a nominee of Gen. Anthony Wayne on the grounds that "in justice" he must recommend Dewitt, of whom he had often heard Erskine speak "in very high terms." *Ibid.*, p. 387. H. S.

[2] They were presented to the New-York Historical Society in 1845 by Richard Varick DeWitt.

224 ✍

existence. Mr. Erskine Hewitt of New York City has several fine specimens; another is in the J. P. Morgan Library; and the writer was once called into the map room of the New York Public Library to identify a choice specimen of Erskine's work hitherto attributed to one of the French engineers in the service of the Continental Army. Unquestionably it was "an Erskine," and a beauty, at that, bearing all his peculiarities of lettering and those unmistakable and artistic touches which individualized his work.

If, by a perusal of these pages, any of my readers have come to appreciate the labors of Robert Erskine, fail not to visit the library of the New-York Historical Society and personally examine his maps. Consider also, as one by one you turn them with reverential tenderness, that great Washington himself has done likewise. Doubtless his fingers, time and again, have traced the lines of the mountain roadways; his deep-set eyes have looked upon the very sheets over which you pore; some of the folds and rents we see to-day may have been made while these charts were being hurriedly stuffed into his saddle bags, for all we know to the contrary.

I regard Erskine's maps as his tangible legacy to the American people. More and more frequently will they be consulted as time goes on, and their existence and value become universally known. It is eminently fitting that they are so well housed and cared for. In the possession of the New-York Historical Society they are most truly a part of our public records, and are accessible to any inquiring student.

Erskine's disposal of his worldly effects, though purely a personal matter, is certainly a part and parcel of his biography. And as such, the last will and testament of the erstwhile merchant of London, iron-master of Ringwood, and geographer of America's struggling army, seems to round out his life story. It is an epilogue after his own design, in his own words, and as he himself would have it.

The document, now preserved in the office of the Secretary of State at Trenton, N. J., is an autograph copy of the complete original with codicils. The first draft, which appears to have been executed at New York City, in January of 1776, must, in some way or another, have come to grief, else why the necessity of a "copy"? The British occupation of Manhattan may have had something to do with it.

The preamble of Erskine's will comprises a most striking and evangelical confession of his religious faith. To those unfamiliar with ancient documents of this character it may seem high-sounding and pharisaical, but I can bear witness to the fact that many another testator of these olden days, far less righteous than Erskine, has prefaced the directions for dividing his property with a theological discourse of much greater length. In the present matter-of-fact age, these devotional introductions (after the manner of our prayers, I fear) have been much curtailed, yet—as a people—we are probably as truly devout as were our forefathers, having—despite all that may be said to the contrary—the same firm and abiding faith. Happily, the substance of Erskine's will proves his sincere goodness. First of all he provides for his life-partner; then (as the years bring added prosperity) his codicils mention his old creditors beyond the sea:

A Copy, through the mercy of God, wrote this 28th day of March 1779, by Robert Erskine.

I, Robert Erskine, son of the Rev'd Ralph Erskine, author of the "Gospel Sonnets &c"; by the Providence of God at present in America, for the purpose of directing, conducting and taking charge of several Iron Works, and other lands, belonging to Gentlemen in England, who stile themselves the Proprietors of the New York and New Jersey Iron Works, being now in good health of body and sound in mind, make this my last will and testament as follows:

When it shall please my Gracious and Merciful Father, God Almighty, to call me hence after my days are completed (the number of which he knows), my body I commit to where his providence pleases to deposit it till the resurrection of the Just, and my soul flies now (and at the hour of death I trust will be enabled to fly) to the merits of my Gracious and merciful redeemer, our Lord Jesus Christ, for protection against the wrath of a justly offended God. He came to call sinners to repentance; blessed be the name of the father, son and Holy Ghost, One God, that I ever heard the call, that I ever felt myself inclined to obey it, through the influence of his Blessed spirit. Oh! may me & mine and all that belongs to me hear and know the joyful sound, let the whole earth be filled with the glory! let my Mediator's Kingdom extend from sea to sea! May he go forth the conquering and to conquer poor miserable sinners to himself!

Before I proceed to the disposal of all my worldly effects, I think it proper to premise what follows with respect to my former and present circumstances. God, in his providence (and I trust by his Fatherly Chastisements) was pleased to deprive me of the patrimony bequeathed by my parents, which I lost in trade; [3] it appearing by my Books forever that had I got payment from my debtors, I would have satisfied my creditors, they in general gave me a Letter of Licence for 2 years, on my giving up all my bond, note, and book debts; they not requiring my household goods and the whole of my effects, upon oath, as, in case of bankruptcy; none of them thought proper to renew their demands during the space of 7 or 8 years afterwards, and their demands became outlawed. They looked for

[3] Reference is here made to the failure of "Erskine & Swinton."

payment to a person abroad in whose hands the greatest part of their and my effects lay, who has made them some remittances.[4] Being thus deprived of my patrimony, what I have now of worldly goods has been obtained by my labour as a surveyor and Engineer, since my quitting the mercantile business, and the present Emoluments I enjoy for conducting the Iron Works.

My personal estate in this country is trivial at all times, often little or none; and whatever engagements I am under on account of the Proprietors or their works, they, their works & property in America are indebted to me for the Amounts, and they are fully able to answer all demands upon them, should it please God to take me to his mercy before my connection with the works is terminated, the business relating to them will be found in my Books in New York and theirs in the Country, which I have endeavored (and shall, if it please God, to continue) to keep as clear and distinct as possible; this much I have thought necessary to premise. And now with respect to my worldly effects:

I hereby give and bequeath all my worldly effects and debts due me, of whatever nature, to my dearly beloved and loving wife Elizabeth Erskine, my true and faithful friend and companion of my sorrows and my joys; all my effects I give and bequeath as aforesaid, consisting at present in household goods and other goods, Negroes and Servants, and debts and balances due me from the Iron Works, both on account of my own proper Salary & likewise on account of my transacting all the business as Agent.

All which and what it may please God in future to confer on me, I give and bequeath unto my beloved wife Elizabeth Erskine, appointing her my sole Executor and Administrator and heir to all my property, to be disposed of as she sees fit:

Excepting that I have directed her to apply part of the money arising from the agency commissions mentioned in the

[4] Swinton, Erskine's former partner, who is said to have emigrated to the Colony of Virginia.

228 ↩

Schedule annexed on the other side of this writing, And as I have been author of several Inventions which may prove of benefit to the country (but which have produced little or nothing to myself but the making me known as a person of some Genius, which no doubt recommended me in business) I follow therefore, though I should reap no benefit from the said Inventions in my lifetime, yet if it is thought an object worthy of notice to do justice to my memory by some public reward for the encouragement of others, particularly for a Machine called Centrifugal Engine and the consequent improvement of pump Work in Navy I bequeath ½ of such reward to the Creditors of Erskine & Swinton in gratitude for their indulgence, and the other half to my said heir and Executor.

In Witness this being my last will and testament wrote by my own hand, I have signed the other side and have signed and sealed and published and declared this to be my last will before witnesses in New York this 11 day Jan. & 1776 year of our Lord and Saviour Jesus Christ.

Robt. Erskine   (wax and wafer)

Signed, Sealed and ⎱
delivered before us: ⎰

Will Pagan [5]
Robert Mercer
Robert Monteath [6]

Philadelphia April 27th, 1779
Acknowledged before us:

Robt. Aitken ⎫
John Thornson ⎬ witnesses
Robert Smith ⎭

The original Sealed with the same seal of wax & wafer as above by Robt. Erskine.

[5] A kinsman of Erskine.
[6] Erskine's clerk, now buried beside him at Ringwood.

Schedules and Codicils

(A) Commissions from June 1774 to Jan. 1777; on money at 2½ per cent, Sales from 3½ per cent, & goods purchased at 5 per cent Amounts to about £1000 Curren^y; please God, when the Books are closed for last year, this shall be further elucidated. About the above Sum however is due me, as the proprietors have thrown the whole of this concern upon me without granting any credit or assistance for transacting this Business. Should it please God to take me to himself, therefore, I would have my dear Ex^{rs} dispose of it as pr Ca:—   (R. E.)

To Richard Atkinson	300.—.—
Robert Muir	47.–5.—
Wm. Graham Taylor	100.—.— [7]

God in his mercy grant me health and strength further to my own satisfaction, & that of all my Concerns, for my Saviour Jesus Christ's sake:

Ringwood Jany 1776
Robt. Erskine

(B) *Ringiwood, May 28th, 1778.* The Balance due me the first of the year was £3764.3.8 and is now about £4500. Exclusive of Cash for the use of the works, there is deposited at Ringwood £10,040 in Continental Loan Office certificates for the payment of my own Balance, for what I owe on account of the proprietors, and the rest for their use or order. My own property of whatever kind I freely give and bequeath to my sincere friend & Dearest wife Elizabeth Erskine as above in the foregoing will.

Robt. Erskine

(C) *Ringiwood April 5th, 1779.* By the Providence and blessing of God I am favoured with the opportunity of adding what follows, Thanks to his Mercy:—

The effects I now possess, besides Servants, household goods &c. Consist in Loan Office Certificates amounting to £6600 New

---

[7] Three members of the London Syndicate who were Erskine's special patrons. He had corresponded with them frequently, before and after his arrival in America.

York Cur^y, the interest of which is payable in Bills of Exchange upon France. My personal account with the proprietors being nearly upon a balance.

Concerning which money, I recommend to my dear Executor, Elizabeth Erskine, to remit the above specified Sums amounting to £448 [8] (Bills of exchange can be purchased at 200 pr ct or under), and likewise one hundred pounds sterling more at the same exchange of two hundred percent, to Philip Taylor, (formerly packer in Leadenhall street) [9] with whom I once lodged, or to his wife or heirs; reserving the residue for her sole use and disposal as she shall see fit—

Though I am not lyable by Law to pay any of my Partnership's debts as set forth in my foregoing will, yet there are several of my Partnership's Creditors who in equity are entitled to my remembrance, particularly those who used me with humanity and benevolence and who had a first claim,— in which number I include several of those who sued me as well as those who did not,—of this however I am not at present Complete judge, it being necessary to be acquainted both with their Circumstances and my own. Should providence see fit to spare me, I mean, when possible, to make proper inquiries to this purpose, but meantime must observe that it is on this account that I take no notice now of my Blood relations, for all of whom I have an affectionate regard, but with whose circumstances, however, in general I am likewise at present unacquainted.

With respect to the Iron Works under my charge, I cannot, as things are now situated, do the owners greater justice than by Committing them to my Dear Executor's care till they take the charge off her hands; Recommending her to call for the assistance of any person or persons of honour and skilled in Accounts she thinks proper to settle their affairs, pay their debts, and do justice to the best of her and their Judgment, she being fully acquainted with the integrity of my actions and

---

[8] The payments required to be made under Codicil "A."
[9] Refer to the first chapter of this biography.

intentions respecting the Owners and all concerned, and I being in every respect fully assured of her benevolence, honour and integrity.

Robt. Erskine

The above added to the original this day and date as above by Robt. Erskine.
Philadelphia, April 27th 1779
Acknowledged before us:

Robt. Aitken ⎫
John Thornson ⎬ witnesses [10]
Robert Smith ⎭

Erskine's will and its appendices provide numerous bits of prima-facie evidence as to the testator and his circumstances. That Negro slavery existed at Ringwood is undoubted: as yet this dusky corner in the family-closet of American sociology had not been vacuum-cleaned. It further appears that Erskine, despite all adverse circumstances, was finding his way out of the dark woods of financial distress; yet—instead of hoarding gold—was content to trust his hard-earned gains to the future of America, having freely accepted of the Continental currency. Finally, his qualified remembrance of those friends of other days (who had been lenient with him in his early misfortunes) indicates the full measure in which he would have squared his old accounts had he been permitted to round out the traditional span of life.

Just why Erskine journeyed all the way to Philadelphia to have the last codicil acknowledged is not apparent. Possibly he realized that it would require the traditional skill of a "Philadelphia lawyer" to unravel the tangled threads of his estate; maybe he had some verbal explanations to

[10] An abstract of the will and codicils is given in *New Jersey Archives,* First Series, Vol. XXXIV, pp. 167–68. H. S.

make. We do not know, of course, whether his will remained there until it was probated in 1780, or whether it was in Erskine's personal keeping at Ringwood. Appended to the document is the following affidavit, in evidence that it was filed for probate in November following his death:

Gloucester Co., N. J.
Robert Aitken and Robert Smith, two of the witnesses to the Will and Codicil, being duly sworn, saith that they saw Robert Erskine sign and seal the same, and that John Thornson was present at the same time.

Sworn at Gloucester,
21 Nov. 1780.

The records of the Secretary of State at Trenton, N. J., give no further information in the matter other than an entry attesting to the fact that Mrs. Erskine soon qualified for her appointed task as executrix, being "sworn" in Bergen County, December 6th, 1780.

Of this worthy lady, whom the departed Surveyor General had endowed with all he had to give, and who, as the "widow Erskine" now found herself foot-loose and the lonely mistress of a large household (with the added cares and complications incident to a great industrial enterprise), history has left us several glimpses, most interesting of which, perhaps, is the record of her re-marriage, for she did not long remain without protection. In September of 1781, she was again bound in holy wedlock; the man of her second choice being the Honorable Robert Lettis Hooper, Jr., [11] one of the owners of the Durham

---

[11] For a sketch of the life of Robert Lettis Hooper, Jr. (the middle name sometimes spelled "Lettice"), see the *Pennsylvania Magazine of History*, Vol. 36, pp. 60 et seq., wherein is printed a very comprehensive article by Charles Henry Hart. Hooper came of a distinguished Pennsylvania family; and was the third to bear that name.

Iron Works, and a Deputy Quartermaster General in the American army.

In the interval between the death of Erskine and this auspicious event, the Ringwood Manor House was frequently visited by the friends of the late Surveyor General and by those persons of gentility who happened to pass through this section of the country.

The Marquis François Jean de Chastellux, friend of Lafayette, stopped at Ringwood, December 19th, 1780, and of course called at the Manor House to pay his respects to Mrs. Erskine. He says, in his *American Travels*, (published after his return to France):

Ringwood is only a hamlet of seven or eight houses, formed by Mrs. *Erskine's* manor and the forges, which are profitable to her. I had been told that I should find there all sorts of conveniences, whether in point of lodgings, if I chose to stop, or in procuring every information I might stand in need of. As it was early in the day, and I had travelled but twelve miles, I alighted at Mrs. Erskine's, only to desire her to point out to me some inn where I might sleep, or to recommend me to some hospitable quarters. I entered a very handsome house when everybody was in mourning, Mr. Erskine being dead two months before. Mrs. Erskine, his widow, is about forty, and did not appear the less fresh or tranquil for her misfortune. She had with her one of her nephews, and Mr. *John Fell*, a member of Congress. They gave me all the necessary information, and after drinking a glass of Madeira, according to the custom of the country, which will not allow you to leave a house without tasting something, I got on horseback, and penetrated afresh into the woods . . .[12]

[12] Marquis de Chastellux, *Travels in North-America, in the Years 1780, 1781 and 1782* (London, 1787), Vol. I, pp. 346–47. Since no translation of Chastellux corresponds with Mr. Heusser's version, I have copied the account from the first English printing! H. S.

In January of 1781, the so-called "Mutiny" of the New Jersey troops stationed at Pompton caused the Commander-in-Chief to dispatch Major General Robert Howe, with five hundred New England troops of unquestioned loyalty, to the scene of disturbance. Howe soon succeeded in reducing the recalcitrant soldiers to routine discipline, after finding it necessary, much to his regret, to execute two of the ring-leaders in the uprising.

Due to this circumstance, Washington in person repaired to Ringwood (which is about ten miles north of Pompton) on the 26th of January, where he remained until the 28th, being entertained by Mrs. Erskine. Of Washington's correspondence during this brief visit to Ringwood, at least one specimen is in existence, that being a two-page letter dated at this place the 27th of January, in which the General refers to affairs of the Quartermaster's department.[13]

Dr. Thatcher, in his *Military Journal*, tells us that, on the evening of Jan. 26th, 1781, the officers of General Howe's command (who had arrived from West Point by forced marches) were regaled at Ringwood by Mrs. Erskine. He says:

> We were entertained with an elegant supper and excellent wine. Mrs. Erskine is a sensible and accomplished woman, who lives in a style of affluence and fashion; everything indicates wealth, taste and splendor, and she takes pleasure in entertaining the friends of her late husband with generous hospitality.

Because of her natural spirit of good-comradeship, Mrs. Erskine, being unavoidably thrown into contact with many gentlemen holding high place among the patriot

[13] Fitzpatrick, Vol. 21, pp. 145–49, reproduces four Washington letters written from Ringwood. All are dated January 27, and all are in the handwriting of Alexander Hamilton. H. S.

legion, could not, I suppose, be indifferent to their polite attentions. Nor should she be censured for accepting the hand of Colonel Hooper; although I admit a certain feeling of resentment toward that gentleman for presuming to take the place of Robert Erskine. Undoubtedly, Hooper had been one of Erskine's personal friends, for his services in the Quartermaster's Department, covering certain counties of Pennsylvania and New Jersey, must have thrown him repeatedly into contact with the proprietor of the Ringwood Iron Works. That he was known and favorably regarded by Washington is also a fact indisputable, for it was into his care and custody that many of the officers of the British general staff captured at Saratoga (among them Baron Riedesel and Gen. William Phillips) were entrusted on parole. Indeed, the man who wooed and won the heart of the gentle mistress of Ringwood within a twelve-month was no slouch. Nevertheless, I cannot bring myself to like Hooper, simply because he strove to win for himself the affections of her whom Erskine had adored. It has always seemed unbelievable that another could possibly supplant Erskine; and rather would I have recorded the fact that his sorrowing wife, refusing to be comforted, had gone to her grave wearing widow's weeds. But time, the healer of all things, is strange and mysterious in its workings, and without doubt Colonel Hooper did his best to turn the hands of the clock ahead.

There is a very interesting letter of Hooper's now preserved at Ringwood Manor, bearing date of September 7th, 1781, and written from the home of his fiancee to a very dear friend and business associate in Pennsylvania.[14]

---

[14] To Richard Backhouse, Esq.—(Both he and Robert L. Hooper, Jr., were interested in the Durham Iron Works, according to Mr. B. F. Fackenthal, Jr., of Riegelsville, Pa.)

Therein Hooper announces the forthcoming nuptials, setting down with evident complacence the fact that his betrothed is a lady of many charms and virtues, added to which she has a "plentiful fortune."

And so, in mild September, Mrs. Erskine and Colonel Hooper were married, and we have no reason to doubt that they "lived happily ever after." Together they contrived to keep the iron works in operation,—for a time at least,—being assisted by Ebenezer Erskine, the nephew of the Surveyor General, who continued to remain a member of the Ringwood household. Incidentally, Ebenezer was a bachelor, and probably endeavored to make himself as little of a nuisance as possible. The fact that Mrs. Erskine regarded him with favor is shown by the circumstance of her settling upon him a snug sum of money about the time of her remarriage.[15]

Until the end of the Revolution, Ringwood maintained its importance, not only because of the iron works, but as a halfway station between Morristown and the Hudson.[16] The fact that Col. Hooper had succeeded General Erskine as the Lord of the Manor does not seem to have caused any of its former noted guests to avoid its comforts nor to refuse its hospitality.

Washington himself again visited Ringwood on March 29th or 30th, 1782.[17] He was accompanied in this instance by Mrs. Washington. Together they had left Morristown on the morning of the 28th, en route to Newburgh, where the General was about to begin that long period of nearly

[15] See record of Ebenezer Erskine's will. This gentleman subsequently removed to Trenton, where he resided until his death.

[16] Numerous letters in the Washington correspondence show that supplies were kept in a "magazine" at Ringwood. H. S.

[17] Since he left Pompton on March 30 and arrived at Newburgh on the next day, his visit at Ringwood would have been during the day of March 30. See Fitzpatrick, Vol. 24, p. 94 n. H. S.

permanent residence which continued, with occasional brief absences, until the end of hostilities. Washington and his lady were escorted over the mountains on this occasion by two officers and a squad of twelve dragoons. The original order for this detail was long preserved at Ringwood Manor.

What was in all probability the most important occasion in the Revolutionary history of Ringwood Manorhouse, was the conference which was held here on Sunday morning, April the 20th, 1783, between General Washington and the Secretary-at-War, Major General Benjamin Lincoln, relative to arrangements for the release of British prisoners. Upon the previous day, notice of the proclaimed peace with England had been posted at Newburgh and there was joy and gladness on every hand. Washington's visit to Ringwood must have been made in great haste; for, having left Newburgh at noon on the 19th, he was back again at headquarters by the following evening.[18] In his book of Accounts with Congress we find this entry:

April 1783—To the Expences of a Trip to meet the Secretary-at-War at Ringwood for the purpose of making arrangements for liberating the Prisoners, etc.....£8.10.8

It is interesting to recollect that, but two or three weeks later, the establishment of American independence was a fact so well recognized by our late enemies that when Washington and Sir Guy Carleton met in conference at Dobbs Ferry on May 8th, the British ship of war in the Hudson thundered a salute of seventeen guns—the first official recognition of the new nation.

---

[18] See letter to Gov. George Clinton in Fitzpatrick, Vol. 26, pp. 342–43.

The good old-fashioned way of drawing a story to a conclusion was for the author to tell just what became of each of his characters. Now styles have changed, and "psychological endings" are in greater favor. But, as I am dealing with real old-fashioned people, and what I have told happened a long time ago, there is no excuse whatever for being "up-to-date" in this regard. I have but to record the fate of the Ringwood iron works and to detail the closing events in the lives of the Hoopers; then my tale will be told.

The final settlement of the American investments of the London capitalists (who had been led to play such heavy stakes upon the strength of Hasenclever's representations) was never accomplished. Erskine had dreamed of some such happy consummation of affairs, whereby each and every one interested in the New York and New Jersey Iron Works should receive dollar for dollar of his original investment, with interest added aplenty; but this ideal adjustment was never to be attained.

During his life-time, Erskine had wrought two achievements for the stock-holders. Prior to the war, he had succeeded in making the works pay for themselves: then, despite the severance of relations with Great Britain, he had been successful in preventing the official confiscation of their property.[19] All through the period of the Revolution the vast landed estates of these London Proprietors were preserved to them inviolate and intact, while around about and on every hand the property of other

---

[19] James Board, one of the old settlers in the Ringwood region, and a son of Cornelius Board, the pioneer, was a member of the Bergen County commission to arrange for such divestments of property. Neither among his records, nor in any other of the *Lists of Confiscated Lands in the County of Bergen* is mention made of Ringwood. The confiscatory sales, according to all available records, were held between June 10th, 1779, and March 8th, 1787.

Royalists was sold under the hammer for the benefit of the patriot cause.

Quite naturally, I suppose, Robert Lettis Hooper, Jr., felt no such sense of personal obligation as did Erskine. There is no reason for the belief that any of the *American* creditors of the iron works went "a begging" for their claims, being probably reimbursed from balances in the hands of Mrs. Erskine; but it is equally certain that the *English Proprietors* were entirely unremembered, simply because there were no means available. An examination of Erskine's books reveals the fact that his London employers were actually indebted to *him* for upward of £586, which he had paid out of his own pocket to satisfy claims against them. It is also noted by Ebenezer Erskine that, in 1781, Mrs. Erskine burned the evidence of these obligations, she apparently having no disposition to negotiate for a settlement.

The following official item of New Jersey legislation shows some disposition on the part of Hooper to bring things to a settlement:

An ACT *to vest* Robert-Lettis Hooper, *the Younger, and* Elizabeth *his Wife, and the Survivor of them, with Powers of Agency, to take Charge of and manage the Estate of the* American Company, *commonly so called, in the Counties of* Bergen *and* Morris, *and elsewhere in this State, for the Purposes mentioned therein.*

Passed June 20, 1782.—

Forasmuch as *Robert-Lettis Hooper,* the Younger, by Petition to the Legislature, hath set forth, That *Richard Atkinson,* and sundry other Persons residing in *Great-Britain,* usually stiling themselves *The American Company,* heretofore purchased certain Lands in the Counties of *Bergen* and *Morris,* and thereon erected extensive Works for the Manufacture of Iron; that

Robert Erskine, late of *Ringwood,* in the said County of *Bergen,* Esquire, deceased, was about twelve Years since appointed Manager and Agent for the said Company, in which Capacity he continued until his Death, from whom the Possession and Care of the said Estate devolved upon the Petitioner by his Intermarriage with *Elizabeth Erskine,* Relict, sole Executrix and Devisee of the said Agent; that the Property of the said Company is considerably indebted to the Estate of the said Deceased, and also to sundry Persons who are Inhabitants and Citizens of these States, for many of which Debts the said *Robert Erskine* was, and the Petitioner is become, responsible; that by the *Act* of twenty-ninth of *December,* One Thousand Seven Hundred and Eighty-one, *for taking Charge of and leasing the Real Estates of the Subjects of the King of* Great-Britain *lying within this State,* the respective Agents for the Counties in which the said Lands and Works are situated, have Power to take Possession of and lease the same, which the Petitioner alledges would tend to involve him in great Inconvenience and Distress, liable as he is, for the Debts aforesaid, and would be very prejudicial to the said Estate, inasmuch as the Proceeds in the present Condition thereof are scarcely adequate to pay the Taxes chargeable upon it, and Lessees may be tempted to impair the same to the Loss of all the future Use and Profits; that the Accounts of the Estate of the said Company are so blended and interwoven with the personal Concerns of the said Deceased, that the Books and Papers cannot be transferred to the Agents of the said Counties without subjecting the whole to much Derangement, and the Petitioner to much Risque and Detriment; and therefore praying, that an Act may pass to vest the said Petitioner and *Elizabeth* his Wife, and the Survivor of them, with Powers of Agency, for taking Charge of, and managing the Estate of the said Company, and closing the Affairs of the said late Agent *Robert Erskine,* under such Conditions, Limitations and Provisions as to the Legislature may seem meet; and forasmuch as the said Request appears reasonable,

Sect. 1. BE IT ENACTED *by the Council and General Assembly of this State, and it is hereby Enacted by the Authority of the same,* That the said *Robert-Lettis Hooper,* the Younger, and *Elizabeth* his Wife, and the Survivor of them, be, and they hereby are empowered to take Charge of the Estate of the said Company in the said Counties of *Bergen* and *Morris,* or elsewhere in this State, and the same or any Part thereof to let on Lease at publick Auction for any Term not exceeding three Years, under such Terms and Restrictions as may be most effectual and conducive to preserve the same in full Improvement and Value, to prosecute in their own Names, or in the Name of the Survivor of them, his or her Executors, any Action or Suit in Law or Equity, for the Recovery of any Debt, Demand, Possession or Right, due, owing or belonging to the said Estate and Company, and to receive, adjust and satisfy any lawful Demands against the same; and generally to order, direct, defend and administer all the Affairs and Concerns of the said Estate and Company, from the Commencement of the Management and Agency of the said *Robert Erskine,* deceased, to the present Time and henceforward.

2. AND BE IT FURTHER ENACTED *by the Authority aforesaid,* That the said *Robert-Lettis Hooper,* and *Elizabeth* his Wife, and the Survivor of them, shall yearly, or as often as thereunto required, lay the Accounts and Vouchers respecting the said Estate before the Auditor of Accounts, that the same may be examined and balanced, and that a Report and State thereof may be laid before the Legislature for such Order and Disposition as they may think proper to take or direct thereon.

3. AND BE IT FURTHER ENACTED *by the Authority aforesaid,* That on all Payments made into the Treasury of the State, if any be, the Agents hereby empowered are entitled to the like Allowance for their Expences and Troubles as the Agents in the respective Counties appointed by the Act of twenty-ninth *December,* One Thousand Seven Hundred and Eighty-one, above recited, are entitled to and may retain.

Things did not go well at Ringwood, however. Post-war conditions brought a decided business depression. The following advertisement, in the *New Jersey Journal* of April 23rd, 1783, tells a dismal story of an auction sale—which was to be the beginning of the end in so far as Ringwood was concerned:

To Be Sold

By way of publick vendue, on Wednesday the 30th of April, at Ringwood Iron-Works, in the state of New-Jersey and county of Bergen, the following articles, viz:

Milch cows, horses, mares, and colts; feather-beds, sheets, blankets, bed-quilts and counterpanes; plain and painted bedsteads, mahogany dining and tea tables, desks with drawers, fitted for counting houses; looking glasses of various sorts and sizes; a variety of kitchen furniture, china, glass and queen's-ware; two eight day clocks.

The following articles will be sold at private sale, if applied for any time before the day of sale, viz:

Refined bar-iron, forge and furnace plates; forge hammers and anvils, carts and wagon boxes, whip-saw plates; a quantity of old iron, suitable for nails, rods or smiths use; carpenters and joiners tools; scale beams of all sizes, cast metal weights from 1 pound to 112, several pair of furnace and forge bellows, in good order; a large assortment of furnace and forge tools, blacksmiths bellows, bickhorns, vises, hammers, &c.: several complete sets of nailers, and miner's tools, one pair of Eusophus grist mill stones.

All those who are indebted to the American Ringwood Company, by bond, note or otherwise, are requested to pay off their balances at Ringwood on the first day of May next, or they will be proceeded against as the law directs, and those who have any demands against said Company are desired to attend at that time to have them settled. Attendance will be given by the subscriber at Ringwood, from the 30th of April to May 3rd.

Robert L. Hooper, jun.

Trenton, March 19th, 1783.

Perhaps it was an evidence of wisdom on the part of Mr. and Mrs. Hooper thus to sell out and retire from the hopeless entanglements of Ringwood; but this melancholy ending to the expectations of twenty years of investment and effort on the part of the English proprietors and of Robert Erskine,—their final hope of salvation,—is enough to bring tears from the eyes of a sphinx. It were just as well, for Erskine's peace of mind, that he was "beyond the smiling and the weeping."

Shortly thereafter, the Hoopers moved from Ringwood to the neighborhood of Trenton, where together they resided at the beautiful estate called "Belleville" at the falls of the Delaware, about a mile above the city. Mrs. Hooper died in 1796; and her husband passed away on the 30th of July, 1797, being in his 67th year. He served as one of the Justices for Hunterdon County and as Judge of the Common Pleas for 1782, 1787 and 1792; succeeding John Cleves Symmes as Vice President of the Council of New Jersey in November, 1785. This office he continued to hold for three years, being chairman of the Joint Meeting of the Legislature in 1788, and during the absence of the Governor, acted in his place.[20]

There is a puzzling hiatus in the story of the Ringwood Estate. Concerning the dozen years and more immediately following the removal of the Hoopers, little or nothing has come to the knowledge of the writer.

On June 25th, 1795, Sir George Jackson and Robert

[20] See "The Penna. Mag. of Hist. & Biography"—Vol. XXXVI, No. 141, Jan. 1912, pp. 88, 89, 90.

Muir, "Trustees" of the American Iron Company, by Phineas Bond, their American agent and attorney-in-fact, made a contract with one James Old of Pool Forge, Lancaster County, Pa., for the sale of the Ringwood estate, "supposed to comprise about 12,000 acres in the County of Bergen, State of New Jersey." The stated consideration was £9000, to be paid in gold or silver, in four installments covering the years 1796 to 1799. In order to meet these obligations, Old endeavored to sell portions of the property to other Pennsylvania iron men, but the transactions seem to have miscarried; and on Jan. 1st, 1798, he shifted the burden to the shoulders of his son John Old.[21]

There is good reason for the supposition that neither of the Olds met the requisite payments, nor that either of them ever had a full and debt-free title to the vast tract of land at Ringwood. As an upshot to their affairs, and as a death-blow to whatever interest the poor proprietors may have had, High Sheriff Bell of Bergen County soon took matters in hand and disposed of the estate for accumulated and unpaid taxes, these delinquencies covering a period of many years.

In the *New York Herald* of November 5th, 1803, the Ringwood estate is again advertised for sale, it being stated that the property belonging to the Long Pond and Ringwood Iron-Works consists of two tracts totaling 12,800 acres, of which 600 were "cleared land" and 250 "good meadow land," and that the iron mines on the estate were "numerous and good."

Somewhere about 1807 Martin Ryerson acquired title to the "forges and manor of Ringwood." Until his death

---

[21] Heusser forgot to footnote this interesting but not very pertinent development. Several documents concerned with Ringwood during this period are in *The Manor and Forges of Ringwood*, I, 85–91. They seemingly only make the mystery a deeper one. H. S.

in 1839 he operated the iron mines and furnaces with great success, accumulating one of the largest fortunes hitherto amassed by any Jerseyman in that field of endeavor. Early in his regime he caused the old homestead where Erskine had dwelt (so graphically invested by historic fact and fiction) to be demolished; replacing it with a new mansion, portions of which are comprised in the Manor house of to-day. In 1815, in commemoration of the Treaty of Ghent (marking the close of the War of 1812) a row of thirteen trees was planted before the mansion. Many of these stately monuments of Nature remain to this day, dignifying the beauty of the well-kept grounds.

The sons of Martin Ryerson possessed neither the ability nor the adaptability of their father. After continuing the iron works for a dozen years with indifferent success, they succumbed to new business conditions. In 1853 William S. Hogencamp, Sheriff of Passaic County, was called in to readjust matters, and by deed of sale, dated Sept. 1st of that year, conveyed the property to Peter Cooper, the eminent inventor and philanthropist of New York City—and the founder of Cooper Union. Since that time the exploitation of the mineral wealth of the estate and its manufacture into pig-iron has given employment and been the means of prosperity for many hundreds of workmen.[22]

The Hon. Abram S. Hewitt, son-in-law of Peter Cooper, and for more than fifty years the controlling spirit in the industrial enterprises of Cooper, Hewitt & Co., was the first to interest himself in the career of Robert Erskine.

[22] The making of iron was transferred to Hewitt furnace, three miles from the Manor House, about 1850, and was continued there until 1885. Ore was mined from a number of shafts on the Ringwood property until 1931. In 1936 Ringwood Manor House was presented to the State of New Jersey by Erskine Hewitt. Ringwood Manor State Park today includes a portion of the old American Company holdings. H. S.

And it is by reason of the author's professional services for Mr. Hewitt's family—who have spared neither means nor energy in the effort to bring to light the documentary evidence requisite to establishing Erskine in his true position as one of America's great characters of the Revolutionary period—that the data presented in the foregoing pages have been made available.

Appendix

The following itemized summary of Erskine's Maps, is a copy of his own autograph index, preserved at the New-York Historical Society, together with the major portion of the maps themselves, and entitled:

A List of the—Rough Draughts of Surveys by Robert Erskine F. R. S. Geog^r A. U. S. and Assistants. begun A. D. 1778.

incorporated with which are a few more detailed listings of minor surveys mentioned in the account of General Sullivan's expedition against the Indians, published by the New York State Legislature in 1879; and referred to in the text.

Num^r	*Principal Places*
1	Road from Suffrans to Junes, Kings Ferry, Fort Montgomery &c, on the other side, Peeks kill, Tellers Point, Tarrytown &c. Sheets A. B. & C. D—Nichols hill N. R^r. Butter Hill &c. E—
2	Road from Ft. Montgomery to West Point &c.

3 —— from D⁰. to Forrest of Dean &c.
4 —— from Junes up the Clove.
5 —— Clove continued to Newborrough.[23]
6 Newborrough to Fishkill.
7 —— Fishkill to Peekskill & West Point.
8 Roads from Peekskill to White Plains, Mamaroneck &c. &c.
8 [24] White Plains.
9 Road from Whiteplains to Dobbs Ferry.
10 D⁰. from D⁰. to East Chester.
11 Tuckeho Road.
12 Road from Tarrytown to Crotton River.
13 Sawmill River Road, Valentines Hill, Post Road.
14 Road from Haman's to Gen'l. Gates, W. Plains.
15 —— from Artillery Park W. Plains to Dobb's Ferry Rᵈ. D⁰.
16 Cross Road above Dobb's Ferry and Post Rᵈ. to Saw Mill.
17 Road between Sawmill & Tuckeho, N. & S.
18 Young's Tavⁿ. to White Plains.
19 Cross Roads to East Chester & above.
20 Cross Roads between Mamaroneck, Rye &c.
21 D⁰. from White Plains to Kings Street, Wrights Mills.
22 From Andrew Purdees towards Davanport's, & from Carpenter's towards SingSing.
23 From Crotton Bridge towards N. River.
24 From Saw Pits to Stamford Bedford, Crotton.
24 [25] & from Stanwich to Kingsstreet.
25 A Contraction of Ditto joined to N⁰. 59
26 R. from 15 Mile Stone near Suffrans to Ft. Lee, Hackensack, Closter, Tappan, Clarkstown, Haverstraw, &c. by Capt. John W. Watkins, A. B.
27 Roads about Clarkstown &c.—by Dᵈ. Pye, Esqr.
28 from Bedford to Ridgefield, Danburry &c.

[23] Newburgh.
[24] The number is repeated.
[25] The number is repeated.

29   from Fishkill to Fredericksburg, Crotton Bridge Quaker Hill &c.

30   from Pines Bridge or Crotton towards Fredericksburg & Cross to Peekskill.

31   A contraction from Bedford to Danburry.

32   A Ditto. Peekskill to Pines Bridge—Join'd to No. 59.

33   Road from Stamford to Greenwich.

34   A contraction of D°.

35   A D°. from Fishkill to Danburry &c.

36   A D°. from Newborrough to Fort Lee.

37   General Contraction 2 miles to an Inch by R E.=3 pieces & 1 D°.

38   Road from Judge Jay's near Fishkill to Robertsons Mills &c.

39   Road from New Millford to Hartford & back to Bulls Iron Works, 11 sheets marked 39—A, B, C, D, E, F, G, H, I, K & L.

40   Course of Farmington R. the Bearings taken by Mr. Porter. 1765.

41   Road from Ringwood to Slotts, Maces &c.

42   from D°. . . . to Pompton Suffrans &c.

43   from Woodbury to Crumpond, 5 sheets A, B, C, D & E.

44   Contraction from Danbury to Crumpond.

45   D°. from Robertsons Mill to Peekskill.

46   Road from Pompton towards Morristown.

47   —— to Morristown.

48   —— from Rockaway Bridge to Horseneck to Totawa falls and up to Pompton, 3 P's.

49   Contraction from Quaker hill to Hartford 1 mile to an inch

50   Road through Peekskill hollow A. & B.

51   —— near New windsor through Chester to Maces.

52   from Albany to Schoharie & Contraction 4 pieces

53   Road from Ringwood to Longpond towards Warwick.

1779

54   General Contraction 4 miles to an Inch by R^t Erskine.

55   Road from Quibbletown to Amboy & places by bearings fr. Capt. Scull.

56   Road from Pompton Paramus great falls &c.—A & B Sheets.

57   Road from Bethlehem to Broad Ax and Chestnut hill Pennsylvania A, B, C, D & E.

58   Contraction of D⁰.

59   D⁰. about White Plains.

60   D⁰. D⁰. D⁰.

61   Plan Charlestown, S⁰ Carolina—by J. Watkins.

62   Draught of the Southern Cost of Lake Erie A, & B a contraction of D⁰.

63   Map of Niagara R. on the Straits between Erie & Ontario.

64   Map of the Ship Channel on Lake St Claire.

65   Part of the Susquehanna & Delaware—Ononough-quago &c.

66   Small Contraction 8 miles to an inch fr S. Dewitt.

67   Road from Forks Passaic to Scotch Plains A. B C & D.

68   From Chester to Easton, a Contraction of the follᵍ

69   from near Chester to Bethleham 10 sheets marked 1st, 2ᵈ & 3ᵈ &c.

70   Road from Duyckinks mill to Germantown.
  B. from Cross Roads through Pluckemin towards Morristown;
  C. Past Baskenridge and from Bebouts towʳ Quibbletown;
  D. from Mᵗ Bethel M. Hse. to near Quibbletown, and from Quibbletown to Brunswick.
  E. from Brunswick to Bound Brook.
  F. from Bound Brook to Duyckinks Mill.

71   Road from Duyckink's Mill to the South Branch Garison's, Somerset Bound Brook, from South Branch to Reddington Brokaws & from near headquarters to S⁰. Branch.

72   From Duyckinks Mill White House Potterstown, Germantown Lamatunck

73   From Skeepack Road cross Corriells ferry to Morristown

74   From Boundbrook, Quibbletown . . .[26] Elizabethtown, Wood Bridge, Amboy . . .[26] Piscataway, Brunswick, Somerset and Vanvoghton's Bridge—A, B, C, D, E, & F.

75   Morristown, Bottlehill, Chatham, Springfield, Elizabethtown, Raway, Westfield towards Short Hills A, B, & C.

76   Road from Headquarters to Middlebrook Pluckemin, &c.

77   Roads by Potterstown, Hickery Tavern, Muscanecunk Mountain, Reddingtown Johnstons Forge, Easton A, B, C, D, from letter B to the Road from Corriels to Morristown E from near Henry Camps on the road from Corriels to Morristown to Reddington.

78   From Short Hills Tav[n]. to Spankton & Craigs Tav[n].

79   From Elizabeth townpoint, Newark, Acquackanonck, Wesel, Totawa A B & C.

80   From near Garrisons Tav[n]. to past Gen Heards & from near Heards to Princetown, Somerset thru Kingston.

81   Rough Contraction in the Jerseys. 8 miles to an inch

82   Contraction from Elizabeth townpoint to Totawa 2 miles an Inch.

83   Contraction to Easton & Corriels Ferry 4 miles 1 inch.

84   Road from Widow Van ambrose to Forrest of Dean, & Cross roads from Smiths Clove A & B.

85   From Smiths Clove to Chester.

86   From Junes to Archer & Warwich.—A. B. & B[2].

87   Roads from near Somerset Court house by Pennytown to the Different Ferrys to Trenton, to Bristol Philadelphia, Coopers Ferry, Mount Holly, Allenstown, Cranburry & Brunswick A, B, C, D, E, F, G; & H from Chesnut Hill to Philad[a].

[26] Parts of original list missing.

88   The county of Albany by Mr. Vromer & a contraction of D⁰.

89   The River Schuylkill from Falls to Reading by Dᵈ. Rittenhouse; with the Depths, A, B; Do. D a Contraction of D⁰.

90   from near Warwick to Morristown, Booneton, & from Pompton by Charlotteburg Iron Works, Newfoundland to the Warwick Road A. B. C.

91   From Easton to Wioming, Northumberland to D⁰. Contraction 2 miles 1 inch.

92   From Easton to Wioming to Tioga A, B, C, D, E, F, G, H, 2 inches a mile; J, K, L, M, 1 inch a mile.

93   From Newborrough to Albany and from Albany to Fishkill; 20 Sheets A, B, C, D, E, F, G, H, J, L, M, N, O, P, Q, R, S, T, U, V.

94   Contraction of above from Albany to Newborrough & Fishkill 2 miles an inch.

95   From forks Susquehanna to Wioming A B, C, D, E, F, G, H, J, K.

96   Rout from Fort Sullivan to Chemung, & to Newton A, B, B²ᵈ, C, D, E, F, G, H, J, K.

97   From Seneca Lake to Chenissee A. B. C.

98   Contractions in the Jerseys 2 miles an inch A. B. C, Large Paper, by Capt. Scull.

99   Projections of Lat & Departure for Closing & . . . ? . . . the meeting of Surveys 2 miles to a inch A. B. C. D. Large paper by Capt. Scull.

100   Spherical Projections 2 miles to an inch by R. E. 4 sheets, large paper.

101   From Hartford, New haven, Norwalk, Bedford &c. A, B, C, D, & E.

102   Contraction of D⁰ 4 miles an inch by R. E.

1780

103   D⁰. of the Rout of the Western Army 2 miles an Inch A, A²ᵈ, B, C, & D., by Lᵗ Lodge.

104 Roads about Cam Morristown A, B, C, D, & E. From near Chatham to Horseneck.

105 Survey of Morristown by the Chain only by R[t]. Erskine.

106 Contractions in the Jerseys 1 mile an inch by S. De Witt A. B.

107 Roads between Chatham, Scotch plains, Turkey & Springfield.

108 —— from Col. Deys to the Ponds & from Wykoff to Bellgrove.

109 From Little falls to Acquacknunck.

110 from Dobbs Ferry to Paramus.

111 Contractions in the Jerseys 2 miles an inch Amboy, Brunswick, Pluckemin, Morristown, Newfoundland, Charlotteburg, Paramus by R. E.

112 Width of N. R.[27] at Closter A. B. at Dobbs Ferry. Measured with a Theodolite by R. E.

113 Roads between Suffrans, Tappan, Kakiate, Paramus, Dobbs Ferry, Clarkstown, &c.

114 Contraction of D[o]. & Sundry places Rectified.[28]

115 Country between Hudson & Delaware.

116 Between Passaic & Paramus, Hackensack & Zabriskies.

117 From M[t] Pleasant to New Germantown & from Pluckemin to Black River A. B. & C.

118 From Morristown towards Sussex C. H. by J. Armstrong A. B. & C.

119 From Sussex C. H. to Pittstown & Ringoes and back past the Union & from Hackettstown to N Germantown. A, B, C, D, E F.

120 from the Sawmill River road towards the Brunks to near Tho[s]. Thompsons.

[27] North River.

[28] Item No. 114 is the last entry in the handwriting of Erskine in this "index" at the New-York Historical Society. Nos. 115–116 have been entered in an autograph strikingly similar to that of Washington himself. The remainder of the charts are, with the exception of one or two, listed in De Witt's writing.

121   From where a road branches off to Middle Bush to Trenton. A. & B.

122   The Environs of Kingsbridge.

123   The Slote 4 ch. to an inch.

124   The route to York in Virginia.—A B C D E F G H J K L M N O P Q R S T U.

125   The route from Virginia. A, B, C, D, E, F, G, H, J, K, and a ½ sheet.

126   Camp at Verplancks Point.

127   The line between Pennsylvania & Maryland.

128   Roads from New Windsor to Goshen, Florada, Chester, &c.

129   Moores Land at W. Point.

NOTE.—Mr. A. J. Wall, the librarian of the New-York Historical Society, records the following numbers as "missing" from the collection of Erskine maps there preserved: Nos. 1 B, part of No. C, Nos. 2, 4, 8, 10, 14, 17, 25, 27, 28, 29, 30, 33, 34, 37, three pieces 39, 49,—62, 63, 64, 65, 76, 80, 83, 85, 88, 89, 94, 101, 109, 111, 112, 114, 115, 126, 129.

Index

Aberdeen, Scotland, 9
Acquackanonck, 29, 82, 200
"Address of Mr. Erskine to his and Erskine and Swinton's Creditors," 15n
Aitken, Robert, 229, 232, 233
Albany, New York, 192, 209
Albany County, New York, 192
Albany Institute, 25n
Alexander, William ("Earl of Stirling"), 40, 80, 81, 97; levy on Hibernia ore, 141–46; Ringwood road and, 197; New Jersey maps and, 210
Allicocke, Joseph, 124
Americana (periodical), *xi*
American colonies, 14, 25, 28, 66; journey to, 67–77, 78; Revolutionary sentiment in, 111–37. *See also* American Revolution; *and see specific colonies*
American Iron Company (London syndicate), 29, 42, 47n; Franklin Committee Report, 33–40; Erskine engagement by, 43–44, 67, 68–75, 83–84, 85, 86, 88, 94, 101, 165, 239; stockholders, 79, 109, 239–42; iron transport, 82–83;

Faesch withdrawal from, 90–94; debt collection, 99, 100, 126–37, 157, 240–44; Erskine on Hasenclever's relations with, 102–108, 112–13; Erskine will and, 227, 228, 230n, 231; Hooper and, 239, 240–42; Ringwood sale and, 243–45
American Revolution, 111–37, 182, 197; Erskine activity in, xii, 3, 119, 120, 138–59, 204–205, 247; battles of, 167, 171, 173, 176, 189, 195, 214, 236; Indian victims of, 184–86; New Jersey ironmasters and, 199–200; peace, 216–17, 238; property confiscations and, 239–40
American Travels (Chastellux), 234
American Union (Masonic) Lodge, Morristown, 206
Anderson, George, 201
Andover, Pennsylvania, 86
André, John, *maj.*, 214–15, 217, 218, 219
Annely, Edward, 139
Anthony's Nose, 175
"Apraxin, Count," 107
Armstrong, John, *capt.*, 206

Arnold, Benedict, 216, 219
Arnold, Jacob, *col.*, 206
Arnold's Tavern, Morristown, 206
Associate Brethren, 8
Atkinson, Richard, 45, 49, 55, 230, 240; surveys for, 59–60; Erskine voyage to America and, 68–69, 71; on Hasenclever records, 107; Curson and Seton and, 129, 130, 132, 133, 134
Attwood, Thos. Bridgen, 124
Austin, Peter Townsend, 180n

Babcock gang raid on Ringwood, 154–55, 191–92, 211
Backbarrow, England, 55, 58, 59
Backhouse, Richard, 236n
Bailey, John, 139
Baker, Luke, 152
Bakon, Anthony, 59
Banks, David, 198n, 199
Bartholf, Crynes, 201
Bartholf, John S., 201
Basking Ridge, New Jersey, 40n, 97
Beam, Anthony, 201
Beam, James, 201
Beam, John, 201
Bear Mountain, New York, 50n
Beckford, William, 24
Bedford, New Hampshire, 196
Belleville, New Jersey, 27, 40n, 244
Bellgrove store, 98n, 120n, 121, 122, 123; accounts, 124n; Washington at, 213
Bergen County, New Jersey, 26, 34, 36, 89, 121; Revolutionary sentiment in, 116, 119; British troops in, 152; British land holdings in, 240–42, 245. *See also specific placenames*
Bergen County Militia, 119, 120, 145, 152; provisioning, 138–39, 140; personnel, 200–201; Ladies' Aid, 216
Bernardsville ("Veal Town"), New Jersey, 156, 157
Bersham, England, 63
Bethlehem, Pennsylvania, 156, 157
Bilstone, England, 55–56, 57

Birmingham, England, 53, 54–55, 56
Bleecker, Jacobus, 123
Block-house Point, 214–15
Bloomfield, New Jersey, 27
Board family, 97
Board, Cornelius, 26–27, 200, 239n
Board, Cornelius D., 201
Board, James, 239n
Board, Joseph, *capt.*, 200
Bolton, Reginald Pelham, 150
Bond, Phineas, 245
Boonton, New Jersey, 90, 144
Border Wars of the American Revolution (Stone), 183
Boston, Massachusetts, 114–15, 116
Boston Port Bill, 115
Boulton, Matthew, 54–55
Brandywine, battle of, 167
Brant, Joseph, 182
Brecknock, Wales, 48, 51
Brewster's Forge, 180
Brinkerhoff family, 97
Brisbane, Arthur, cited, 12
Bristol, England, 47, 51
Britannia (vessel), 76
British Museum, 207
Brosely, England, 57
Brown, Anthony, 201
Bruce, Robert, king of Scotland, 5, 6
Bruce of Kennet, Lord, 19
Bruen, Jeremiah, *maj.*, 206
Bull's Ferry, 214
Burch, John, 124
Burgoyne, John, *gen.*, 160, 162, 171, 176
Burk, Thomas, 201
Burling, Thomas, 123
Burns, Robert, 5
Butler, John, *col.*, 182
Butler, William, *col.*, 182, 184, 185, 186

Cádiz, Spain, 25n
Campfield, Jabez, 206
Canada Bills, 115
Canmore, Malcolm, 6
Cardiff, Wales, 51
Carleton, Guy, 238

Carlisle, England, 60
Carlyle, Alexander, quoted 10
Carnegie, Andrew, 6
Carnegie Public Baths, Dunferm-line, 6
Carolinas, the, 14, 15n, 114, 152
Carron, Scotland, 61, 62–63
Cato (slave), 157, 158
Cayuga Lake, 186
Chalmers, Rev. Thomas, quoted, 6–7
Charlotte, queen of England, 33, 55
Charlotteburg ironworks, 26, 29, 70, 91, 92, 93, 121; Franklin Committee report, 33–37, 38; Erskine's first visit to, 80, 82, 86; Erskine's management, 99, 102, 108, 109, 123, 136; British attack, 153
Chastellux, François Jean, marquis de, 216; quoted, 234
Chemung (Elmira), New York, 183
Chepstow, Wales, 49
Cherry Valley, New York, 182
Chester, New Jersey, 192
Clark, William, 177
Clinton, George, *gen.*, 170, 173, 213, 283n; Hudson River chains and, 175, 177
Clinton, James, *gen.*, 183, 186n, 188
Closter, New Jersey, 215
Clyde River, 159
Cole, Henry, 177
Cole, William, 18, 23
Colebrook Dale, England, 57
Colford, Wales, 46
Colne (Colme) River, 21–22, 50, 58
Connecticut, 183, 187, 209, 216
Constitution Island, 179
Continental Army, 139–40; Geographer and Surveyor-General appointment, *xv*, 160–62, 163, 166–67, 168, 170–71, 173, 186n, 210–11; Quartermaster's Deparment, 179, 234, 236; Erskine summons to accompany, 189–93; troop quartering, 197; burials in Ringwood, 201–202; Surveying De-

partment salaries and, 208–12; Totowa encampment, 215n
Continental Congress, 115, 116, 118, 175–76, 189; debt to Erskine, 155–56, 157–58, 168–69; Surveyor-Generalship and, 160–62, 163, 174n, 186n, 207–12; Verplanck's Point-on-Hudson and, 193; Washington accounts with, 238
Continental Loan Office, 230
Cooper, Peter, 246
Cooper, Hewitt & Company, 181, 246
Cornwall, New York, 151
Cortlandt furnace, 82, 83, 121, 123
Cortlandt ironworks, 81–82, 109
Coryell's Ferry (Lambertville), New Jersey, 156, 157, 162–63
Coutts, William A., cited, 8n
"Cow Chase, The" (André), 214
Coxe, MacGrance, 180
Crown Point, 31
Crugers, New York, 82
Cumberland County, England, 59
Cunahunta (Indian village), American destruction of, 185
Cupar, Scotland, 6
Curson, Richard, 128, 130, 135
Curson and Seton, 109–10, 119, 126–33
Curtis, Coleman, 177

Daughters of the American Revolution, 202
Dayton, Elias, *col.*, 206
Deane, Silas, 171
Declaration of Independence, 146
Dee River, 5
DeGraw, Walter, 201
Delaware County, New York, 182
Delaware River, 163, 182, 184, 185
Devonport, Robert, 177
Dewar, Elizabeth (Ayton), 7
Dewar, John, 7
Dewitt, Andrew, 173
De Witt, Richard Varick, *xvi*, 224n
Dewitt, Simeon, 173–74, 186–87, 209, 220; Surveyor General appointment, *xvi*, 224

Dey, Theunis, *col.*, 40, 215, 216, 223
Dey, Mrs. Theunis, 216
Dietz (Titts), John, 98
"Dissertation on Rivers and Tides, A" (Erskine), 207
Dobbs Ferry, 238
Doland, Elizabeth, 154, 155; quoted, 120, 153
Donaldson, Robert, 19
Doylestown, Pennsylvania, 173*n*
Dryburgh Abbey, 3, 5, 6
Dunblain, Scotland, 221
Dundass, Laurence, 19
Dunfermline, Scotland, 4, 5–8, 61
Dunfermline Grammar School, 8
Dunken Pond, 35
Durham Iron Works, 233–34, 236*n*

Eagle Valley Road, 198
"Early History of Morris County, New Jersey, The" (Tuttle), 13*n*, 140*n*
"Early Settlements and Settlers of Pompton, Pequannoc and Pompton Plains" (Schenck), 27*n*
East Indies, 19
Easton, Pennsylvania, 186, 209
Edinburgh, Scotland, 4, 6, 61
Edinburgh, University of, 8–9, 10–11, 65
Edward I, king of England, 6
Elizabeth, New Jersey, 142
Elmira (Chemung), New York, 183
Emlen, George, 167
England, 28, 74–75; imports, 30, 32, 100–101, 105; iron mines of, 45–64, 70; American Revolutionary sentiment and, 114–15, 116–19, 146; American troop action, 147, 151, 152–53, 160, 162, 167, 171, 173, 176, 194, 207; peace treaty, 216, 238; American land holdings, 239–40
Erie Railroad, 121–22
Erskine, Anne, 7
Erskine, Ebenezer, 7, 219, 221, 237, 240; quoted, 187–88, 217–18
Erskine, Elizabeth (Mrs. Robert),

see Hooper, Elizabeth Erskine (Mrs. Robert Lettis)
Erskine, Henry, 7
Erskine, Mrs. Henry, 68
Erskine, James, 7
Erskine, John, 7
Erskine, Margaret, 7
Erskine, Margaret (Dewar), 7
Erskine, Margaret (Simson), 7; quoted, 12–13
Erskine, Ralph, 3, 6–8, 112*n*, 205, 220, 226
Erskine, Robert: maps by, *xii*, 50*n*, 73, 86, 156, 161, 163–65, 172, 180, 182, 184, 186–87, 191, 192–93, 195, 196–97, 200, 206–207, 209–10, 212, 213–14, 224–25; death of, *xiii*, *xiv*, 100, 186*n*, 217–22, 223–24, 241; early life, 4–16; inventions, 14, 16–24, 64–65, 70, 86, 146, 147–51, 158, 170, 229; marriage, 20–21; Hasenclever and, 41, 102–108; London Syndicate engagement of, 43–44, 67, 68–75, 83–84, 85, 86, 88, 94, 101, 165, 239; tour of British iron mines (1770), 45–64, 70; luggage list for American voyage, 76–77; Ringwood management, 96–110, 112–13, 118–19, 120, 122–37; magistrate appointment, 99–100; Revolutionary involvement of, 119, 120, 138–59, 204–205; 247; "Waste Book" of, 123, 139; captaincy, 138, 139, 140; meeting with Washington, 160–61; as Surveyor-General, 160–74, 186–87, 210–11; summoned to attend Washington, 189–93; freemasonry of, 205–206; book by, 207
Erskine, Sarah, 20–21
Erskine & Swinton, 14, 227*n*, 229
Erwin family, 97
Essex County, England, 22
Ewing, Walter, 112, 113

Fackenthal, B. F., Jr., 236*n*
Faesch, John Jacob, 42, 43, 83, 97, 100, 108, 120, 194; Erskine

quoted on, 69–70, 79, 80, 81, 84–85, 86, 90–94; biographical sketch, 88–90
Fairfield, Connecticut, 196
Farmington, Connecticut, 187
Federal Hill, New Jersey, 33
Fell, John, 140, 234
Field Book of the Revolution (Lossing), 171
Fifeshire, Scotland, 61
Fisher, Isaac, 201
Fisher, Rev. James, 112, 113; quoted, 68
Fisher, Ralph, quoted, 19
Fishery Bill, 117
Fishkill, New York, 158, 209
Fitzpatrick, John C., *see Writings of George Washington, The* (Fitzpatrick, ed.)
Flemington, New Jersey, 162
Ford family, 97
Ford, Jacob, Jr., *col.*, 143, 144, 202
Fordyce: Erskine reports to, 47, 48, 50, 53–54, 55; ore samples for, 81, 86
Forest of Dean mine, 47, 48, 50, 52
Fort Clinton, 176
Fort Constitution, 170
Fort Defiance, 184
Forth, Firth of, 5, 6
Fort Lee, New Jersey, 146, 152, 158, 175
Fort Montgomery: construction, 170; Hudson River Chains and, 175, 176–77, 179, 181
Fort Schuyler, 183
Fort Sidman, 202
Fort Washington, 146, 150, 152, 158, 175
France, 170, 171, 202, 216, 234
Frank, Conrod, 94
Franklin, Benjamin, 65–66, 171
Franklin, William, 33, 34, 102
Franklin Committee, report on Hasenclever enterprise, 33, 34–39
Fraser, Rev. Donald, cited, 20*n*, 24*n*, 68*n*, 188*n*, 218*n*
Frederick the Great, 33*n*
Fredericksburg, New York, 183
Furman, Moore, quoted, 197–98

Gage, Thomas, *gen.*, 31, 114–15, 116
Gage, Mrs. Thomas, 128
Galloway's, 197
Gascoigne, 61
Gates, Horatio, *gen.*, 162
Genesee River, 183
George II, king of England, 53, 55
George III, king of England, 66
German Flats, New York, 31
Germantown, Pennsylvania, 156, 158, 167
Germany, 23*n*, 25*n*; workmen from, 26, 29–30, 88, 89, 93, 104, 108, 120
Ghent, Treaty of, 246
Gibraltar, 176
Girard, Stephen, 41
Glamorganshire, Wales, 59
Glasgow, Scotland, 5, 19, 20, 23, 45, 68
Glasgow, University of, 12, 13
Gloucester County, New Jersey, 233
Gloucester, England, 46
Goelet, Peter, 123
Goldsmith, Richard, Jr., 177
Good Hope mine, 37, 38
Goshen, New York, 154
"Gospel Sonnets" (Ralph Erskine), 226
Gouvernour, Nicholas, 27*n*, 29
Gouvernour, Samuel, 27*n*, 29
Graham, William, 75
Gray, William, *capt.*, 182, 183; quoted, 184–86
Green, John, 201
Greene, Nathanael, *maj. gen.*, 26
Greene, Norvin Hewitt, *xv*
Greenwood Lake, New Jersey, 33, 38
Grey, James, 40
Guillam, Michael, 201

Hackensack, New Jersey, 82
Hackensack River, 27, 121
Hale, Nathan, 187
Halifax, Nova Scotia, 147
Hall, Rev. Archibald, quoted, 23–24

Halle University, 33*n*, 41
Hamilton, Alexander, 162, 235*n*
Hammersmith (London), 16
Hand, Edward, *gen.*, 213
Harrison, Robert Hanson, 162*n*
Harrison, William, 200
Hart, Charles Henry, 233*n*
Hartford, Connecticut, 196, 209
Hasenclever, Adolf, cited, 33*n*, 41
Hasenclever, Peter, 25–26, 120;
    Ringwood purchase, 29–30; min-
    ing enterprises, 31–42, 43, 81–
    82, 86, 100–101, 102–108, 112–
    13, 239; Fraesch and, 88, 90, 97,
    194
Hasenclever, Seton and Crofts, 25–
    26. *See also* American Iron Com-
    pany (London syndicate)
Hasenclever Iron Mines, 31
Hasenclever Mountains, 31
Hasenclever Patent, 31
Haverstraw, New York, 82, 147,
    172
Hereford, England, 53
Herkimer County, New York, 31
Hesse-Cassel, 88
Heusser, Albert, *x-xvi;* style of, *xii-
    xiv. See also Manor and Forges
    of Ringwood, The* (Heusser)
Hewitt family, 96, 194; Heusser
    and, *xi*, 246–47
Hewitt, Abram S., *xv*, 181, 182,
    219*n*, 246
Hewitt, Erskine, *xi*, *xv*, 201, 246*n*
Hewitt, Mrs. Erskine, 225
Hewitt, New Jersey, 33
Hibernia Ironworks, 26, 141
Hibernia Mines, 40*n*, 80, 81, 97,
    199; Sterling levy on ore, 141–46
Hillburn, New York, 201, 202
History of Dunfermline (Chal-
    mers), 6
*History of Morris County, N. J.,
    The* (W. W. Munsell & Co.),
    100*n*
Hoff family, 97
Hoff, Charles, Jr., 143, 144, 146,
    199–200
Hoff, Joseph, 141–46
Hogencamp, William S., 246

Homes, Henry A., cited, 25*n*
Hooper, Robert Lettis, Jr., 233–34,
    236–37; American Iron Com-
    pany and, 239, 240–44
Hooper, Elizabeth Erskine (Mrs.
    Robert Lettis), 20–21, 24, 74, 86,
    220; at Ringwood, 96, 97, 155,
    169, 211–12, 217–18; war work
    of, 216; Erskine bequests, 226,
    228–29, 230, 231; remarriage,
    233–34, 236–37; Chastellux visit,
    234; Washington visit, 235;
    American Iron Company profits
    and, 240, 241, 242; death, 244
Hope, New Jersey, 157
Hopewell, New Jersey, 173*n*
Hopper, Andrew, 122
Hopper, John J., 201
Howe, Robert, *gen.*, 162, 235
Hubbart's Mill, Essex, 21–22
Hudson Highlands, 150, 160, 171,
    172, 180, 196, 217
Hudson River, 50*n*, 82, 121, 172,
    183; "chevaux-de-frise" on, 146–
    51, 156, 158, 175; Chains, 175–
    88; surveys, 192, 213
Hughes, Hugh, 179
Humfray (Homfray, Humphries),
    Jeston, 41–42, 105–106, 120
Hunter, Andrew, *chaplain*, 206
Hunterdon County, New Jersey,
    244
Hutton, Laurence, quoted, 9–10

In the Footsteps of Washington
    (Heusser), *xi*, 154
Ireland, 59
Iroquois (Six Nations), American
    massacre of, 183, 184–86
Irving, Washington, 215–16
Ithaca, New York, 186*n*

Jackson family, 97
Jackson, George, 26, 244–45
Jacobus', 156
Jamaica, 19
Jeffrey's Hook, 150
Jersey City (Paulus Hook), New
    Jersey, 147, 151, 195
Johnson, Sir William, 31, 32, 192

Johnson Hall, 32
Johnson Manuscripts, 31*n*
Journal of the Continental Congress, 161*n*

Kakiate, New York, 194
Kendal, England, 58
Kilsyth, Scotland, 61
Kingsbridge, 150
Kinney, Thomas, *capt.,* 206
Knox, Henry, *gen.,* 216; Hudson River chains and, 177

Lafayette, Marie Joseph Paul, marquis de, 216, 234
Lake Champlain, 31, 107, 176
Lambertville (Coryell's Ferry), New Jersey, 156, 157, 162–63
Lancashire, England, iron ore, 50–51, 58, 61, 62
Lancaster, England, 58
Lancaster County, Pennsylvania, 245
Landeshut, Silesia, 33*n*
Lassodie, Scotland, 7
Laurens, Henry, 189*n*
Laurens, John, 189*n*
Lawrence, Daniel, 176
Lee, Henry ("Light Horse Harry"), *gen.,* 210, 214, 215*n*
Letters of Moore Furman, 199*n*
Levy, Hayman, *xiv,* 123–24
Lewis, 135
Lewis & Son, Francis, 139
Life and Diary of Rev. Ralph Erskine (Fraser), 20*n*, 24*n*, 68*n*, 188*n*, 218*n*
Life of Washington (Irving), 216
Lime Kilns, Scotland, 61
Lincoln, Benjamin, *maj.,* 238
Lists of Confiscated Lands in the County of Bergen, 239*n*
Litchfield, Earl of, 22
Literary Landmarks of the Scottish Universities (Hutton), 9
Little Falls, New Jersey, 27, 40*n*, 215*n*
"Lochaber" (Ramsay), 159
Lodge, Benjamin, *lieut.,* 186, 209
London, England, 30, 61, 66, 103–

104, 105; Erskine in, 11–13, 15, 18–24, 43, 45, 49, 68, 75, 205
London Chronicle (newspaper), 24
London Company, *see* American Iron Company (London Syndicate)
Long Pond, *see* Greenwood Lake, New Jersey
Long Pond Ironworks, 26, 29, 121, 152, 245; Franklin Committee report, 33, 37, 38; Erskine first visit to, 80, 82, 86; Erskine management of, 99, 102, 109, 123, 136
Lossing, B. J., cited, 171
Loudon, Samuel, 124
Louis XVI, king of France, 202
Lower Preakness, New Jersey, 40*n*, 215, 216, 223
Lyon, Samuel, 201

McCormack, Daniel, 139
McDonald, Alexander, 201
McDougald, Patrick, slave of, 177
McGregor, David, 205, 206–207
Machin, Thomas, 151, 177, 178, 179
Maclaren, Ian (John Watson), 5
McReady, Dennis, 124
Magazine of American History, 215
Mahwah, New Jersey, 122
Makapin Pond, 35
Mandevile, John, 178
Mandeville, Henry, 100
Manor and Forges of Ringwood, The (Heusser), 12*n*, 21*n*, 45*n*, 65, 71*n*, 87*n*, 94*n*, 110*n*, 133*n*, 155*n*, 174*n*, 218*n*, 245*n*; Tuttle and, *xiv, xv,* 111*n*, 140*n*; Washington correspondence in, *xiv,* 162*n*, 166*n*, 167*n*, 170*n*, 172*n*, 190*n*, 191*n*, 193*n*, 196*n*, 197*n*, 203*n*; on *chevaux-de-frise,* 150; on Pittstown, 199*n*
Marcelles, Edo, 201
Margaret, queen of Scotland, 6
Marsh, 198
Masonic Order, 6–7, 205–206
Maxwell, William, *gen.,* 206

Index

Meade, Yelas, 140
Mercer, Robert, 229
Middlebrook, New Jersey, 189, 190, 193n, 194
Mifflin, Thomas, *gen.*, 157, 168–69, 170, 179
Military Journal (Thatcher), 194n, 235
Minisink, battle of, 182
Mohawk River, 30, 31, 192
Mohawk Valley, New York, 31
Monmouth, England, 45, 46–51
Monmouth, battle of, 173, 189
Monteath, Robert, 221, 229
Montgomery, Richard, *gen.*, 118
Montressor, John, 193
Moodna Creek, 180
Moore, Henry, 31
"Moore's House," West Point, 196
Morgan Library, J. P., 225
Morris County, New Jersey, *xv*, 26, 34, 81, 85, 89, 90, 100; Stirling and, 141; British land holdings in, 240–42. *See also specific placenames*
Morristown, New Jersey, 90, 97, 137, 170; Washington's Headquarters at, 141, 143n, 200n, 202, 204–207, 237; roads, 197, 198
Morristown Road, 196
Mt. Hope Ironworks, 89, 90, 91
Muir, Robert, 230, 244–45
Mure Son & Atkinson, 64
Murray, Sanson & Co., 142, 145, 146

Neath, Wales, 47
Newark, New Jersey, 28, 29; Josiah Ogden in, 27n, 198n
Newark Daily Advertiser (newspaper), 120n, 153
New Bridge, New Jersey, 215
Newburgh, New York, 151, 177, 178, 237, 238
New England, 114, 141. *See also specific placenames*
New Haven, Connecticut, 196
New Jersey, 30, 209, 210; New York border, 27, 121. *See also specific placenames*

New Jersey Gazette (newspaper), 216, 223
New Jersey General Assembly, 27n, 89
New Jersey Historical Society, 12, 14, 27n, 45n, 112, 188, 200n; Erskine account books in, *xiv*, 122, 169
New Jersey Journal (newspaper), 89, 243
New Jersey Legislature, 138, 240, 244
New Jersey Militia, 200; Mutiny of 1781, 235. *See also* Bergen County Militia
New Jersey Provincial Congress, 140
New Jersey Secretary of State, 226, 233
New Jersey State Constitution, 99
New Jersey Supreme Court, 191
New Petersburg, New York, 31
Newton (Sussex Court House), New Jersey, 157
New Windsor, New York, 151, 170, 171, 180, 197, 209; Erskine survey, 172, 210; Washington at, 194, 195
New York City, New York: Hasenclever in, 26, 32, 104, 106; American Iron Company agency in, 74, 85, 97–98, 123; Erskine in, 78, 79, 112, 114, 116; Curson & Seton of, 109, 119, British troops in, 147, 150, 151–52, 153, 171, 214, 226
New York Gazette (newspaper), 94, 101–108, 121
New York Gazette and Weekly Mercury (newspaper), 98n, 99
New York Herald (newspaper), 80n, 245
New-York Historical Society, *xv*, 187, 196, 214, 224, 225
New York Journal (newspaper), 12
New York Mercury (newspaper), 28–29, 41
New York Public Library, 25n, 225

New York State, 27, 30, 121, 183, 209; Hudson River defense, 147, 176; Surveyor-General of, 173, 186n; "Secret Committee," 176
New York State Library, Albany, 25n, 31n, 180n
Nicoll, John, *capt.*, 177, 178
Noble family, 97
Noble, Isaac, 121n
Noble, Townsend and Company, 179
North River, 82, 83, 151, 170, 171; Erskine map, 209
Norwalk, Connecticut, 196

Oakland, New Jersey, 122, 198
Obstructions to the Navigation of the Hudson River (Ruttenber), 158n, 175n
Odel, Garret, 201
Ogden, David, Jr., 27n, 29
Ogden, David, Sr., 27n, 29
Ogden, John, Jr., 27n
Ogden, Josiah, *col.*, 27n, 198n
Ogden, Samuel, *col.*, 141, 143, 144, 145
Ogden, Uzal, 27n
Old, James, 245
Old, John, 245
Ononaughquaga, American destruction of, 184–85
Orange County, New York, 50n, 180
Oscawanna, New York, 82
Oswego, New York, 192
Otsego County, New York, 182
Oxford Hospital, 22

Pagan, Will, 229
Pagan & Company, Lewther, 123, 124
Passaic County, New Jersey, 246
Passaic Falls, 40n, 215n
Passaic River, 27, 40n, 82, 215n
Paterson, William, 140
Paterson, New Jersey, 140n, 215; Heusser in, x, xi
Paulus Hook (Jersey City), New Jersey, 147, 151, 195
Peekskill, New York, 179

Pennsylvania, 182, 183, 184; Erskine maps of, 209, 210. *See also specific placenames*
Pennsylvania Historical Society, 196
Pennsylvania Magazine of History, 233n, 244n
Pentlands, Scotland, 4
Pequannock River, 33, 34, 36
Peter the Great, czar of Russia, 156, 158
Peters mine, 37, 38
Philadelphia, Pennsylvania, 104, 117, 196, 208, 209; Erskine trips to, 155–58, 168–69, 232; Washington journey to, 162–63, 167; British troops in, 171, 173, 199n; Centennial, 181
Phillips, William, *gen.*, 192, 236
Phllips farm, 215
Phillips Pond, 82
Piatt, William, *lieut.*, 206
Pittstown, New Jersey, 199
Polopels Island, 151, 158
Pompton, New Jersey, 153, 160, 161, 163, 170, 193, 237; Supreme Court at, 191; roads, 198; mutiny of 1781, 235
Pompton Mountains, 27
Pompton Plains, New Jersey, 100
Pool Forge, Pennsylvania, 245
Post, Adrian, 201
Potts' House, Valley Forge, 172
Poughkeepsie, New York, 176
"Practical Works" (Ralph Erskine), 112n
Preston, J., 15
Princeton College, 205
Princess Mary (vessel), 21
Pringle, John, 65, 66
Proceedings of the New Jersey Historical Society, xiv, 13n, 27n, 88n, 111n, 140n; on Ringwood looting, 154, 155n

Quakers, 117
Quebec, 118
Queen Anne Street United Presbyterian Church, Dunfermline, 6

Radière, Col. La, 170, 171
Ramapo, New York, 121, 213
Ramapo Mountains, 152, 153, 160
Ramapo River, 37
Ramapo Valley, 198
Ramsay, Allan, 157, 159
Rappard, Bert'd, quoted, 18
Reade and Yates, New York, 94, 97–98, 101–102
Red Brook, Wales, 46, 48, 50
"Remarkable Case of Peter Hasenclever, The" (Hasenclever), 25n; Erskine on, 102–108
Remscheid, Germany, 25n
Revolutionary Fragments, Morris County, New Jersey (Tuttle), 120n, 153n
Rhinelander, Frederick, 123
Richard's Coffee House, Temple Bar, London, 19
Ringwood, New Jersey, 27, 201; French bivouac at, 202
Ringwood Company, 26–29, 144n
Ringwood Iron Works, 26–29, 30, 31, 70, 73, 88, 89, 121; Erskine papers at, *xiv, xv, xvi;* Franklin Committee report (1768), 33, 35–38; Erskine first visit to, 79–80, 82; Faesch departure from, 90–94; Erskine management, 96–110, 112–13, 118–19, 120, 122–37, 165, 239–40; Bergen County Militia at, 120, 138, 140, 152–53; South Carolina trade, 152; raid on, 154–55, 191–92, 211; Hudson River Chains and, 175, 177–78, 179, 180, 181–82; entertainment of British officer at, 192–93; Washington visits, 193–94, 195, 218–19, 235, 237–38; manor houses, 194–95, 220–21, 234, 246; road, 197–98; supply base at, 198–99, 213, 237n; Erskine tomb in, 217, 219–21; New Jersey Act (1782) on management of, 240–42; auction proposal (1783), 243–44; Ryerson purchase, 245–46
Ringwood Manor State Park, 246n

Ringwood River, 27, 33, 36, 37, 38; aqueducts, 86; dam, 87
River Edge, New Jersey, 82
Rivington's Gazette (newspaper), 214
Rochester, New York, 173
Rockaway, New Jersey, 90, 97
Rockland County, New York, 26, 31. *See laso specific placenames*
Roman History (Rollin), 125
Royal Gazette (newspaper), 194
Royal Society of London, Erskine fellowship, 64–66, 67
Runels, James, 178
Ruttenber, E. M., 158n, 175
Ryerson family, 45n, 96, 194, 246
Ryerson, George, 201
Ryerson, Martin, 12n, 245–46
Ryerson, Martin G., 201
Ryerson, Peter, 181
Ryerson, Peter M., 12n
Ryerson, Ryor, 201

St. Andrews, Scotland, 9
Saint John's Day (1779), 206–207
St. Leger, Barry, 183
Sandy Hook, 209
Sanford, John, 206
Schenck, Rev. Garret E., cited, 27n
Saratoga, New York, 171, 176
Saratoga, battle of, 236
Schenectady, New York, 183
Schoharie, New York, 182, 183, 184, 209
Schoharie County, New York, 182
Schuyler family, 27
Schuyler, Arent, 160
Schuyler, John, *col.,* 40
Schuyler, Philip, 31, 207
Schuylkill River, 173
Scotland, 3–5, 59, 60–61, 68, 112, 187, 220, 221. *See also specific placenames*
Scott, John Morin, *gen.,* 146, 150
Scott, Walter, 3
Sermons (Walker), 169
Seton, Andrew, 32, 104
Seton, William, 130, 132, 133–37
Severn River, 45
Shearer, Andrew, cited, 8n

Shrewsbury, England, 55, 61
Simson, Daniel, 7
Sisco, Nathaniel, 201
Sisco, Peter, 201
Sisco, Peter J., 201
Six Nations (Iroquois), American massacre of, 183–86
Sloat family, 97
Small, William, 55
Smith, Claudius, 154
Smith, Platt, 147–48
Smith, Robert, 229, 232, 233
Smith's Clove, 160, 194, 198
Smith's Tavern, 194
Soho Engineering Works, Birmingham, 54–55
Somerville, New Jersey, 156
Sons of the Revolution, Paterson chapter, *xi*
Sorel River, 176
South Carolina, 152
Springfield, battle of, 207, 213
Springfield, New York, 183
Stamford, Connecticut, 196
Staten Island, New York, 147, 180*n*
Stephens, Thomas, 16
Sterling Iron Works, 26, 179, 180
Sterling Lake, 27, 180
Sterling Pond, 27
Steuben, Friedrich Wilhelm, Baron von, 195
Stirling, Earl of, *see* Alexander, William ("Earl of Stirling")
Stirling, Scotland, 19, 61
Stone, William L., cited, 183
Stony Point, New York, 180*n*
Stony Point, battle of, 195, 214
Storms, John, 201
Stuart, Charles Edward ("Bonnie Prince Charlie"), 5
Sturbridge, England, 57
Suffern, New York, 122, 198, 202
Suffern's Tavern, 161
Sullivan, John, *gen.*, 182, 183, 209
Sunbury, Pennsylvania, 186
Susquehanna River, 184, 186
Sussex Court House (Newton), New Jersey, 157
Sussex Road, 196
Sutherland, David, 178

Sweden, 53
Swinton, 14, 15*n*, 228*n*
Symmes, John Clever, 244

Tappan, New York, 217, 218, 219
Tappan Bay, New York, 147
Taylor, John 201
Taylor, Philip, 14–15, 231
Taylor, William Graham, 230
Temple Sowerby, England, 59–60
Thames River, 24, 75–76
Thatcher, James, 194*n*; quoted, 235
Thornson, John, 229, 232, 233
Thurlow, Edward, 1st Baron, Lord Chancellor, 40–41
Ticonderoga, 176
Tilghman, Tench, 167, 190; quoted, 202–203
Tintern Abbey, furnace near, 49, 50
Tioga Point, Pennsylvania, 183
Titts (Dietz), John, 98
Totowa, New Jersey, 215*n*
Totten, Robert, 151, 152
Towle, F. A., 65
Townsend family, 97
Travels in North America, in the Years 1780, 1781 and 1782 (Chastellux), 234*n*
Trenton, New Jersey, 140, 226, 233, 237*n*; Hooper residence, 244
Trinity Episcopal Church, Newark, 27*n*
Trossachs, Scotland, 5
Turse (Tice), Jacob, 201
Turse (Tice), John, 201
Tuttle, Joseph F., *xiv–xv*; cited, 13*n*, 88*n*, 111–12, 119, 120*n*, 140*n*, 153; on Ringwood raid, 155
Tuxedo Lake (Toxito Pond), 37, 86–87, 197
Tweed River, 9

Ulster County, New York, 173
Ulverstone, England, 58
Unadilla (Unendilla), 184, 185
United States of America, *see* American colonies; Continental Army; Continental Congress, *and see specific states*

DUE

PRINTED IN U.S.A.